BORDERLINE

BORDERLINE

A psychological study of paranoia
and delusional thinking

Peter K. Chadwick

London and New York

First published in 1992
by Routledge
11 New Fetter Lane, London EC4P 4EE

Simultaneously published in the USA and Canada
by Routledge
a division of Routledge, Chapman and Hall Inc.
29 West 35th Street, New York, NY 10001

Typeset in Times by Selectmove Ltd, London
Printed and bound in Great Britain by
Biddles Ltd, Guildford and King's Lynn

British Library Cataloguing in Publication Data
Chadwick, Peter K.
Borderline: a psychological study of paranoia and
delusional thinking.
I. Title
616.897

Library of Congress Cataloging in Publication Data also available

ISBN 0–415–07151–8

(Ancient Chinese Fable)

Buying a pair of shoes

A man in the state of Cheng decided to buy some new shoes. He measured his feet but left the measure on his seat, and went to the market without it. There he found a shoemaker.

'Why, I forgot to bring the measurement!' he cried. He hurried home to fetch it.

By the time he got back to the market, the fair was over, so he failed to buy his shoes.

'Why didn't you try the shoes on?' asked one of his neighbours.

'I trust the ruler more' was his reply.

Hon Fei Tzu
(*circa* 250 B.C.)

This book is dedicated to
Carl Jung and Wolfgang Pauli
who probed and probed to glimpse The Borderline.

CONTENTS

FIGURES AND TABLES

FIGURES

TABLES

PREFACE

In their attempts to understand schizophrenia, psychiatrists and clinical psychologists are rather like impotent men writing about the joys of sexual intercourse using verbal reports and physiological recordings as their data. Distanced from the phenomenon, their reports often seem contrived and alien. The research presented in this book differs from this state of affairs because I personally have experienced borderline psychotic, and at times even outright psychotic, functioning but returned to tell the tale. It is possible, given my highly relevant research interests at the time, that I unconsciously engineered my own crisis (described in Chapter 4) so as to be able to write about it later – as Strindberg apparently used to do (Storr 1972: 209–10; Sprinchorn 1968); however if I did this (which I very much doubt) I in no way found what I expected. The edges of sanity and the territory beyond it turned out to be of a character quite beyond my wildest dreams or nightmares.

This research has, therefore, been very much a therapeutic exercise for me. I have used an approach also advocated by Frankl (1959, 1963) to the management of and recovery from extreme crises: I have tried to see meaning in it and tried to relate it to my spiritual life. This book is partly the result of that effort.

To begin: I shall preface the body of this work by comments first on its form and then on its content.

The book is perhaps rather strange. This is because I am, in the spirit of Stack–Sullivanian participant observation and observant participation, exploring a strange realm: the mystical and psychotic mind. I seek to claim epistemological validity for mystical, and for islands of the psychotic experience, to show their parallels and interrelationships and to suggest how these states are achieved or suffered. In doing so I am not only writing *about* them, in a scientific spirit, but am relating experiences within them, including my own. Hence we have not only knowledge by description of these domains but knowledge by acquaintance.

I shall adopt a 'funnel approach' in the presentation of this research. At the beginning the very broad molar speculations which led to the investigation are reported, and the style is very general and light. As the text continues the inferences and predictions gradually become more detailed and fine-grained and the text more intense; therefore, Chapters 1 to 9 deal with the hunches derived largely from case studies and my previous research while, in the experimental study (Chapters 10 and 11), very specific issues are focused upon experimentally as the impressions presented earlier are gradually hewn into an experimentally testable shape. There are, however, differences between the two parts: in Chapters 1 to 9 I am largely dealing with the 'why' of delusional thinking; in Chapters 10 and 11 with the 'how'.

Throughout the book I shall attempt to relate real life behaviours to experimental and psychometric measures to bring the psychotic's identity alive. The essence and character of the psychotic subject is so easily lost or obscured in the, usually, rather dry pages of the experimental psychopathology literature – a fact which cannot help researchers and practitioners in this field to relate their conceptual knowledge to the flesh-and-blood people they deal with daily. In this book I hope the discrepancy between the representation of the subject in the literature and the reality of the actual person in everyday life will be reduced.

The book is perhaps more personally and 'warmly' written than would traditionally be expected in an academic work, because I have deliberately shunned the 'author's formula' of presenting research in a very terse, obscure and cold manner – a manner often used as a means of enhancing its apparent scientific respectability. Although I have sometimes written in this manner prior to about 1980 – as the readers will see from my 1979 diary quotes in Chapter 4 – I eventually decided: no more. There is, I feel, too much 'alienation from self' (Federn), 'lack of actuality' (Husserl) and 'loss of the sense of the real' (Pierre Janet) in social science writing and this can surely be of no real value to the endeavour. This book is therefore designed for easy reading. I hope the readers approve of this and that it enhances their enjoyment and understanding.

As a final comment on the form of this work (although it has content relevance), it is necessary to emphasize that I have tried to keep my inferences as close to the empirical evidence as is reasonable, given the nature of the phenomena under study. These remarks are very relevant if the readers wish to understand the general tone or flavour of my attitude to much (if not all) psychoanalytic thinking in this book. In my own on-going self-analysis, which began in 1967/68, I often used psychoanalytic concepts and methods (despite the fact that in my official psychological research my approach was experimental and cognitive). Over the last twenty years of experience with the psychodynamic approach I became sensitive to what I now call, rather jaundicedly, 'the psychoanalytic con'. This is the implicit communication to the effect that if one does not accept or seek seemingly deep and far-fetched interpretations one is vulnerable to a charge of shallowness and superficiality, perhaps even timidity, in one's thinking.

This many intelligent thinking men and women cannot bear, and thus they accept and revere ostensibly more 'profound' interpretations to avoid the charge. In my research for this book I therefore have deliberately tempted my potential accusers. Having indulged in psychodynamic acrobatics and convolutions to a considerable extent over the years I eventually became disillusioned with the parochialism, the low predictive validity and the massive imbalance that usually obtained when interpretations were weighed against actual evidence. Therefore, in the case study reports my interpretations are well constrained and deliberately do not reach to 'depths' which, although easy to reach, would go far beyond the information given.

The content of the book is heavily influenced by the ideas of Hermann Lenz (on mysticism, 'supersanity' and delusion), Hans Eysenck (on arousal and psychoticism), Gordon Claridge (on arousal, psychosis and creativity), Wolfgang Pauli (on physics and psychology) and Colin Martindale (on arousal and creativity), all of whose work provided the foundations on which I tried to build. Apart from acknowledging the importance of genetic influences and physiological and neurochemical processes in schizophrenia I also present an understanding at the cognitive and social psychological level. I raise, for example, a social psychological perspective on delusional thinking in the form of 'social class programming' (Chapter 2). This enables us to see the context within which the personality and the form of the crisis of a paranoid schizophrenic developed. It also reveals an additional approach to the understanding of personality, so necessary according to Brody (1972), to that provided by Eysenckian arousal levels (Eysenck 1967) or Grayian reward–punishment sensitivities (Gray 1970, 1972, 1973) which attach personality dimensions to a biological substrate but which are less productive of predictions of social behaviours.

The endeavour to relate the mystical and the psychotic is, of course, not entirely original. Previous writers (Laing 1969; Lenz 1979) have emphasized that psychotics are not denied the transcendent experiences, during their crises, that are also experienced by normal people. In this respect, the most original material on this issue here is in Chapter 9 where I describe in some detail the parallels and the differences between mystical and psychotic thought. The theme is also more dominant and is developed to a greater degree in this book than in previous research.

It is well known that low social class and schizophrenia are linked and that life changes can precipitate psychotic states, but there is no consensus on just how (Davison and Neale 1986). Chapter 5, therefore, contains a reasonably fine-grained description of one special case: the specific stresses one encounters when moving from a middle-class intellectual environment to a working-class non-intellectual one and the kinds of confusions and invalidations to which this can lead.

Contrary to much previous research, I attempt to present the psychotic in as positive a light as I think fair and reasonable. Although this long seemed to me a possibility, I was struck by a particular incident in 1980 which made me feel that it was all the more important. I was talking to a previously psychotic black man of little education about my own battles with my previous research. In this I had become disillusioned to the point of distraction with the possibility of creating real practical suggestions to facilitate observation and theory building in science. My disillusionment was due to me using analytical experimental methods which only revealed biases and illusions on a very small scale and in tasks which were totally out of context. Far from this leaving him speechless, he immediately retorted with brilliant analogies: 'You're trying to climb rain Peter, or sweep sun off the pavement.' My previous predicament could not have been better put – and this was from a man who once firmly believed that he had been communicating with 'the water people', by whom he meant people who lived under the sea.

In addition to emphasizing and assessing the talents and limitations of the psychotic I shall present the psychotic experience not only as an experience which reveals an inner self or an inner realm thus to be assimilated and 'worked through' in the interests of personal growth, but a partly external realm beyond the personal and private which the mind in the psychotic state may have accessed.

In seeking the positive side of the psychotic and the psychotic experience I am, however, sometimes seeking a rather weak signal buried in noise. In order to achieve this aim I have had to adopt a risky criterion in signal detection terms with the consequent risk of making false alarms. Time and future research will, I predict, sift this material yet reveal genuine nuggets of lasting value.

It has not been my purpose in writing this book to present a preliminary textbook on paranoia and delusional thinking. My approach and the content of this work is therefore not as systematic or as descriptive as such an enterprise would require. My emphasis is on ideas and processes rather than on description and diagnostic categories. I am also examining delusional thinking, in the first instance, as a Unity rather than as subclassified into so-called 'primary' or 'out of the blue' delusions and 'secondary' delusions which traditionally (but, except in the very simple cases of partial deafness, I think wrongly) are taken to be post hoc explanations by the patient of prior perceptual or attentional disturbances. I believe the label 'primary' to be a confession of ignorance as to the patient's prior history and state at the time of delusion crystallization. Students of psychiatry are well versed in examples repeated ad nauseam in standard texts where, after salt cellars or biscuits are whizzed across café tables, so-called 'primary delusions' of spectacular form suddenly 'appear' in the person's mind 'explaining' his or her whole life and/or future mission or fate. I very much doubt that these oft-repeated examples really accurately describe what actually was going on in these cases in all its richness; delusional thinking is just not like that. The fact that the mathematician Poincaré may have had a brilliant idea while putting his foot on the steps of on omnibus in no way justifies our calling this a 'primary creative act' as if it were somehow qualitatively different from all other creative acts. The distinction between primary and secondary delusions is, I believe, of no theoretical or practical relevance and will not be discussed further.

The paranoid/non-paranoid distinction, however, is (at least judging from previous research) much more significant and serious and in the experimental phase of the enquiry will be used to try to uncover genuine causal differences. Alas, there were far too few volunteers for the case studies for me to delve into this distinction in any detail or with any degree of confidence there – although, of course, it was ever present in my mind.

In summary: in Chapters 1 to 9 I examine the history, phenomenology, kinematics and dynamics of delusional thinking using a case study approach, while in Chapter 10 I use experimental and psychometric methods to try to prise out some of the mechanisms and processes that might predispose a person to develop delusional thoughts. The earlier material – as well as striving for a coherent picture, in its own terms, of delusional thinking – also is the soil out of which the hypotheses for the experimental enquiry grew. It uses a family-resemblance-seeking and top-down approach. In Chapters 10 and 11 the hypotheses are tested, the results evaluated and generalizations are sought within a basically bottom-up approach.

I should like, finally, to express my appreciation to Dr John Wilding for his advice and encouragement and also for his patience during this long study (which began as a second doctorate thesis) and to Professor Brian Foss for his faith at the outset that the angle at which I was coming at this topic was likely to be a profitable one. I have also benefited immensely from the reactions of the many students whom I have taught personality and abnormal psychology, at various levels, over the last eight years. I am grateful for valuable conversations on this topic with Dr Gordon Claridge, Professor Norman Dixon, Rev. Richard Harries, Rev. John Johnson, Professor Roger Drake, Dr Mary Pickersgill, Rosalind Phillips, Dr Robert West, Dennis Shutte and my wife, Jill Chadwick. Professor Hermann Lenz of the University of Vienna kindly read Chapters 1 to 9 and Professor Brian Josephson FRS of the Cavendish Laboratory, Cambridge, also read large tracts. Both made many valuable suggestions for which I am indebted.

I shall also be eternally grateful to Sylvia Greenwood for typing this work and for many discussions on its contents.

The research was helped by financial assistance from a British Medical Association Exhibition and a post-doctoral award from British Gas.

P. K. Chadwick
London

1

INTRODUCTION

Thinking in science, sex and madness

FROM ROCKS TO PSYCHOTICS

Psychology is my second career, but my interest in it has – via a long and winding path – in part developed from my first. When I tell the readers that my previous research area was in structural geology and rock mechanics (e.g. Chadwick 1971, 1976a), while this research is, of course, on paranoia and delusional thinking, they will no doubt be astonished that there could be any connection at all between the two. To explicate the full history of how my previous research identity metamorphosed into my present one would take too long but some brief comments may be useful as they highlight the early hunches on which this investigation was partly based.

My work on rock deformation was not only of a theoretical and experimental nature but was also observational. During my field research I realized that there were many biases and illusions in perception and thought that could distort a geologist's reports and lead to false inferences and interpretations. This insight led me to develop a research domain, which I referred to as 'geological psychology' – the psychological study of geological work. After early investigations on judgement and attentional biases (Chadwick 1971, 1972, 1975a, b), and on visual illusions in geology and related disciplines (Chadwick 1976b, 1977a, b, 1981, 1982), I began work on the interrelationships between memory and aesthetic judgement (Chadwick and Hughes 1980), the education of interpretation and thinking (Chadwick 1978a, b) and then, critically, on distortional influences on thought itself. One early road from this research connected with mainstream geology (Chadwick 1976a, 1977c) and one, eventually, to perception psychology (Chadwick 1983) but the work on thought was the road that led me into the territory of my current research. One particular problem in cognitive psychology captivated me: 'confirmation bias' (Wason 1960; Wason and Johnson-Laird 1968; Mynatt *et al.* 1977; Tweney *et al.* 1981). This is the bias to select and accept data that *confirm* one's ideas and hypotheses at the expense of data that refute them, obviously a very common and pervasive phenomenon! It seemed to me that confirmation bias and high creativity

1

often went together. Eysenck (1981: 2) even suggests that in the early stages of the development of a paradigm we not only do but *should* preferentially seek confirmation – an idea I had often played with. Only in this way, I thought, can we elaborate something from the quivering vulnerable status of a hunch to that of an edifice to be challenged and metamorphosed into something more mature and of more general explanatory power. I speculated that even good ideas would die young if our cognitive processes were designed so as to be dominated by refutation bias.

The popularity of Popperian falsification ideas (Popper 1959, 1963) in the 1970s therefore greatly troubled me. I battled with the literature on the philosophy of science and concluded that confirmation bias is a double-sided coin. The positive side attracted me at the time. On this side is persistence, steadiness of feeling and judgement, courage to stick with an idea to see how far it will go, faith and confidence in one's own decisions and a moral sense that one should stand by one's convictions. With hindsight we may see that we were wrong, but in the foresight situation our amount of information is less, and limited. On the starting grid, it seemed to me, the successful and the unsuccessful scientist might not be so very different. This attitude was never completely submerged and, as we shall see, very nearly led to my own destruction.

Between 1972 and 1981 my interest in geological matters was gradually eclipsed by those of a psychological nature; I moved away from geological psychology into the field of personality and abnormal psychology. As a counsellor, between 1978 and 1981, I became impressed also by the negative side of the coin of confirmation bias: its role in psychological disorders. As is well known, paranoid individuals hold onto ideas very tenaciously, resist argument against them and select and distort input so as to confirm their paranoid ideation. They are also, and thus, very creative in the sphere of elaborating their delusional constructs. These people seemed to me to be almost personifications of confirmation bias and bore out the ideas of Bennett (1964) and Toulmin (1972) that rationality and irrationality should not only be assessed on the content of a belief but on the manner in which the belief is held. It therefore seemed worthwhile to investigate this phenomenon so as to give continuity to my research and, perhaps, to make a small contribution to the understanding of the puzzling phenomenon of delusional thinking.

As the readers will have noticed, in the mid-1970s I worked on visual illusions in perception, mainly in the context of scientific research. Just as the phenomenon of confirmation bias might, I thought, be relevant to the understanding of paranoia, so it seemed that some of the principles I had obtained from my study of illusions might equally be relevant to the understanding of *delusions*. Illusions represent the results of processes which, with certain stimulus configurations or in impoverished viewing conditions, can lead us astray, but usually these processes give us a good anchoring in the world at a certain level of description. Delusions, so I speculated, might also represent the results of processes which usually enable us to make sense out of the world and to predict accurately. They might even lead to valuable creative insights, but under certain conditions, such as impoverished external input, they might lead us into self-defeating, chaotic or confused behaviour. This seemed a useful angle to pursue.

In my counselling work I met a wide range of people but they happened to fall mostly into two main categories: those with sexual or gender identity problems (homosexuals, fetishists, transvestites, transsexuals and masochists) and recovering psychotic clients. Apart from the oft-encountered confirmation bias it also seemed to me that there were other connections and similarities in the mentation of these two very broad classes of people. Of course, Freud (1911) had previously suggested a connection between paranoia and unconscious homosexuality, but this now seems to have been largely misguided (see, for example, Hastings 1941; Rosenfeld 1949; Klein and Horwitz 1949; Thornton 1948). One very unfortunate masochist, for example, said to me that he had eventually reached the stage where he wanted his 'madame' to control everything he did, the clothes he wore, the records he listened to, the cereals he ate. This total control is a *sexual* experience for the submissive, yet such a longed-for situation is what some paranoids actually do believe is happening to them – via the medium of computers or hypnotic suggestion at-a-distance. The possibility thus presented itself that the whole of the paranoid psychotic episode may well be suffused through with a non-overt sexual masochism or involve disinhibition of masochistic tendencies. Such disinhibition has actually been suggested by Arieti (1974).

Some of the delusional systems which my clients articulated to me were also of great interest in their own right. If only they had written them out as a story for publication they would in some instances have made good novels or films. Alas they lived them, believed them totally and in some cases were very nearly destroyed by them. Nevertheless, there was clear evidence of talent in these people, perhaps displaced and unappreciated, but there. Having come from research in the psychology of scientists I was therefore more impressed by the similarities than the differences between scientists and deluded psychotics in their creativity and style of thinking. Table 1.1 explicates this comparison between the two groups. My first impression was that scientists were creative people who were judged as 'right'; the psychotics I dealt with were creative people who were judged as 'wrong'. The label 'psychotic' was perhaps socially referenced rather than brain referenced.

The readers will by now be getting some idea of 'where we are coming from'. My academic training at university level was in psychology, geology, physics/mechanics, physiology and mathematics; my applied work was, as

Table 1.1 Similarities and differences between thinking in delusion and in science

Delusional thinking	*Scientific thinking*
Thought is often distressing.	Thought not usually distressing but certainly can be if conflicts greatly with orthodoxy, e.g. Darwin, Galileo, Jung.
Style of thinking tends to distance person from all others.	Style of thinking does tend to distance scientist from family and friends, but not colleagues.
Preoccupation with coincidences.	Preoccupation with causality.
Evidence on which thought is based *seems* slender.	Evidence on which thought is based seems quite substantial.
Thought often (but not always) held with complete certainty, a sense of utter and complete conviction.	Thought often (but not always) held with complete certainty, a sense of utter and complete conviction.
Thought very preoccupying.	Thought very preoccupying.
Thought characterized by hasty speculation followed by tenaciously hanging onto hypothesis.	Thought characterized by hasty speculation followed by tenaciously hanging onto hypothesis.
Thought associated with quite basic emotions such as high anger, high fear and/or eroticism.	Thought associated with more subtle emotions such as wonder at the harmony of nature, but attitude to research is usually high on aggression.
Thought often, but not always, seems implausible and unlikely.	Thought usually seems plausible and even when unusual, colleagues feel person 'may have a point'.
Person cannot usually (but sometimes can) be argued out of belief.	Person can hardly ever be argued out of belief but can be affected by new data.
Feelings of grandiosity sometimes to often accompany thought.	Feelings of grandiosity occasionally to sometimes accompany thought.
Delusions give order to person's life.	Person's theory gives order to his or her data and sometimes also to his or her life.
Person's delusions attach him or her to the world.	Person's theory attaches that individual to the world.
Person has little capacity to be objective about his or her thoughts.	Person has considerable capacity to be objective about his or her theory.
Person often not willing to talk about thought.	Person usually (but not always) willing to talk about thought.
Talking about thought often causes considerable emotion to be expressed.	Talking about thought often causes considerable emotion to be expressed.

Person gets angry with people who do not accept the validity of his or her thought/system.	Person gets angry with people who do not accept the validity of his or her thought/system.
Thinking sometimes sounds like that of a mystic.	Thinking sometimes sounds like that of a mystic.
The delusion promotes a vigilant search for evidence and ideas that confirm it.	The hypothesis promotes a vigilant search for evidence and ideas that confirm it.
Person tends to regard disconfirmatory evidence as invalid, e.g. 'You're lying to me' or 'You don't understand me'.	Person sometimes regards disconfirmatory evidence as invalid, e.g. 'Your experiment was badly controlled/conceived', 'Just an isolated instance' or 'You don't understand my theory'.
Evidential basis can collapse yet the conceptual structure of the belief may remain in place.	If evidential basis collapses the theory, at least eventually, also collapses.

we have seen, in helping people with sexual variations, gender identity disorders and psychoses. Clearly my background is very different to that of most researchers in personality, psychiatry and abnormal psychology and this book will reflect that. When I tell the readers also that I was at first destined at school to be a historian, they will see that the present approach will attack the phenomenon of paranoia and delusional thinking in a multi-dimensional, multi-faceted and rather different way to those previously articulated.

THE CONTEXTUAL APPROACH

Before we attack our problem area head on it is necessary to outline the general 'philosophy' I have adopted in this investigation and the reasons for it.

The first issue we must address is that of *complexity*. A field area of rocks of, say, thirty square miles and a person are more comparable in complexity than are a billiards ball and a human being. Field areas, like people, and unlike billiards balls, cannot be isolated; cannot be understood out of context; cannot be taken apart and put back together again. Whenever one analyses a rock one always keeps in mind its field context and the broader context of the area on a global scale. Every rock sample is like an intersection point in a vast intertwining network of relations. Thus to see a rock is to see beyond it.

Rather than taking the methods of classical Newtonian physics – which deals very well with the movements of billiards balls – as our model of how to approach the study of people, which is what usually is done, we shall therefore borrow from the methods of geology and modern physics. There will be no testing of 'subjects' in soundproofed cubicles by an experimenter with a cold 1930s style 'objective' mentality intent on isolating one small aspect of the person for detailed analysis. We shall 'get in close' and funnel down from broad social, even spiritual, levels of understanding to narrow molecular brain processes and back up again – always keeping the context and the distorting role of the investigator (me) in view.

No geologist can map an area with a 'distanced off' attitude of mind. Good field mapping means engrossing oneself in the rocks such that when one's interpretation of an area has gelled, there is a sense of unity between oneself and it. Every outcrop 'means' something, everything is part of a pattern; one does not 'observe' the rocks, one 'reads' them as if gripped by a good story. Movement and perception are fluent, there is a sense of harmony between inner and outer realms; the model and the reality, the psychological and the physical are one. Only when one has achieved this state is one confident enough to go into print. So I think it should be in psychology. Rather than adopting a solely analytical approach, my approach will be largely contextual. My training and research in perception showed me that we never perceive an object, only a pattern of relations in a context. To concentrate on parts or minutiae alone can never be worthwhile science.

In this book we shall adopt the view that reality inclusive of people is an interconnected whole. Related to this we shall seek correspondence between different levels of analysis within a contextual frame, but argue that no level of understanding or language of investigation is primary.

As in geology, a rock sample *can* be taken into the laboratory and squeezed, crushed, chemically analysed, dated, etc. Analysis has its place. But the dates and/or chemical analyses mean nothing out of a field context and may even be questioned on contextual evidence as unreliable or invalid. No one has the last word; everything is negotiated via shifting up and down the phenomenal scale.

Hence, to return, at last, to psychology, we shall not rest content with our questionnaire scores, our physiological recordings or our experimental results. Everything must be embedded in a whole and seen in the light of wider issues. We shall be holistic, looking at how more global higher processes affect lower ones (top-down); within-level, thereby looking at the development of a person's processes and products over time; and reductionistic, seeing how processes at brain or intrapsychic level may structure their interaction with, and in, the world (bottom-up). We shall only put down our pen when we have a coherent story, a feeling of unity, a feeling of at-oneness with the phenomenon.

INTRODUCTION
THE POSITIVE VIEW

One of the unfortunate consequences of the analytical reductionist view in psychoanalysis, behaviourism and cognitive psychology has been a certain negativism, a certain coldness.

Freud's penchant for explaining 'downwards' went hand in hand with an assumption that the negative underlay the positive. Hate was older than love; selfishness behind altruism. It has created in many people an attitude whereby anything negative in someone else is accepted for what it is but anything positive has to be reduced to neutral or malign language. (I was indeed brought up in such an atmosphere.)

Similarly, reductionism and the 'objective' mentality has created cynicism throughout the western world for religion, mysticism and spirituality. Neuroscientists in this tradition have related religiosity (Bear and Fedio 1977) and mysticism (Geschwind 1978) to right hemisphere temporal lobe pathology. The implication has been that such experiences exist 'only in the person's mind', are totally subjective and have no objective reference. We shall find in this book reports that bring such an implication very much into question and raise the possibility that the psychotic state may involve 'access' to domains, nonetheless real, denied to those who are too insensitive to experience them.

One can see the effects of the negative bias very clearly in recent research in schizophrenia which is dominated by investigations in search of 'the schizophrenic deficit'. There is little search for the 'schizophrenic credit'. Exceptions here include the papers by La Russo (1978) on paranoid schizophrenics' high sensitivity to non-verbal cues, and by Keefe and Magaro (1980) on the high creativity of non-paranoid schizophrenics compared to normal controls. Kar (1967) also found a non-predicted superiority in the schizophrenic group in veridicality of perception of the Muller–Lyer illusion.

The mechanistic reductionist view, thanks partly to Julien Offray de la Mettrie (1709–51) through his book *L'Homme Machine*, has also fostered an ideal of independence, selfishness and hedonism. Economic calculations are still done on the assumption that people are out to 'maximize profit margins'. Mechanism and objective psychology induces the belief that Man is an island. This is an inevitable consequence of an isolationist rather than a contextualist *Weltanschauung*.

A contextual view, however, which stresses interdependence and holism leads in quite a different direction. Rather than locking us up in our own mental processes it puts us into the world of relations. We punch through the membrane surrounding us through a Freudian idealistic intrapsychically dominated psychology into the total flux of reality. In this book, therefore, we shall dare to look at the positive side of the psychotic, at macroconsciousness – sometimes loosely referred to as the 'superconscious' (in ratio with the attitude of the artist Malevich) – as well as at the unconscious, and at the spiritual nature of experience as well as at CNS pathways.

MURDER

It is commonly the case, at least in fiction, that the detective in search of a killer has three things in mind: motive, opportunity and weapon. Although we shall look at the positive side of the psychotic, paranoia and paranoid schizophrenia are nonetheless killers or at least sometimes can be. We are therefore also in the hunt for how they strike or suffuse themselves through a person's mind.

It is my belief that for a person to suffer from such debilitating experiences that cause them to be diagnosed as 'deluded' or 'paranoid', there has to be: motive, precipitating event (opportunity) and capacity (weapon). It is useless to study or search for the qualitative aspects of a precipitating event using experimental methods. Our method of attack must suit the target. One does not dig for coal with a computer. The experimental method *is*, however, relevant to understanding capacity and, related to this, the quantitative side of motive, and we shall use it to that end. For the nature of the motive and the precipitating event we shall use case study methods. These will also give us some insight into capacity and will form the context within which certain experimentally derived results can be assessed.

The case studies, to which we now turn, will emphasize to the readers both the uniqueness of every person who suffers from delusional thinking as well as certain family resemblances between them.

2

AN INTRODUCTION TO THE CASE STUDIES AND THE CASE OF DAVID B

'Erratica and Erotica'

Traditional therapists and counsellors usually obtain their information from their so-called 'patients' or 'clients' in an isolated laboratory kind of situation. Personal Construct Psychologists even refer to the therapy session as taking place in a 'protected laboratory'. In psychoanalytic therapy this approach is taken to the extreme. Clients lie on the couch for session after session for a carefully predetermined length of time and cannot even see the therapist while they are recounting their thoughts. All this I think, stems from the classical psychologists' great love of somehow standardizing their methods and perhaps from a wish not to get in too close lest they become lost in the phenomena they are studying. A 1930s style philosophy of science still reigns supreme even in the most modern and 'liberated' of these people. Distance has to be put between observer/therapist/experimenter and the 'subject' of their study.

Some experimental psychopathologists, so the grapevine has it, never even meet the people whose scores and data make up the roughage of their published papers. This is rather like geologists doing geology by sitting in their rooms and having field workers deliver hand specimens with little comment on where they came from – unless perhaps they are markedly unusual. They would certainly find patterns in their data, even very regular ones – after all, most rocks are made up silicate minerals and can be distinguished from other rocks such as carbonates – but clearly the approach is nonsense and would tell us only the very broadest and most general characteristics of the earth's crust, which would be of very little theoretical or practical relevance. The science of geology would never have progressed to its present status if this had been its method.

Our case study approach will therefore be very different. In trying to understand and help the people I have known who have suffered from paranoia and delusional thinking, my 'method' has been to mingle my life with theirs. There have been no set times and no set places for interaction between us. They are not 'patients' or 'clients' or 'subjects'; they are friends. In this study we are blurring the boundaries between befriending and counselling. The number of people involved in the case study approach

9

has therefore had to be small – seven in fact (inclusive of my own report), although the material on Simon T is very brief. These people also took part in the experimental study. This gives us a golden opportunity to see their experimental data in the context of their total selves and total life situations. It will give us some very interesting insights into the validity and meaning of these data. Most experimental psychologists bemoan that most of the really interesting sources of variance are relegated to the error term in the statistical analysis. In this book I hope that this will not be so.

A qualifying note, however, needs to be sounded. I found in my counselling work that I was unable to handle or establish rapport with extremely talkative or manic clients; those who were very low in self-disclosure and/or those (very few) of puritanical bent. The single case study volunteers were tacitly accepted on the basis that they were not disposed in those ways.

The volunteers nonetheless cover a demographically wide spectrum. Although they are all young (under 35 years of age) they range from the very non-academic, working-class David B to the middle-class educated Alison; from scientist and economist Shafiq to artists Chris and Alana J. David B, Chris and Shafiq had both parents living, Alison and Simon T neither, and Alana J one. Three were working (Alana J, Simon T and Alison) and three were unemployed (David B, Shafiq and Chris). In addition, David B and Shafiq were extraverts, Alana J, Alison and Simon T ambiverts and Chris an introvert. All had one thing in common: for them their delusions *were* their 'illness'.

To obtain accounts of the suffering that these people have experienced has been very difficult. At various times they have all said that they will write about their 'episodes', and provide me with accounts of them (in the spirit of Harré *et al*. (1985)), but none has ever actually done so. The experience is too painful and to write it down requires one to relive it. No one can ask them to do this. The memories and style of thinking must not be brought back in full fluency lest they reactivate the psychotic state. Hence the accounts I have collected are the products of fragments told to me at different times, sometimes years apart. I have known most of the people concerned here for up to ten even years. This has been a long project. The number of hours I have spent talking with each of them is incalculable; it must run into thousands. To help to understand David B, for example, who is the first case study, I once lived with him for a week and often discussed things while we were walking around South London. Discussions with Shafiq, case two, with whom I lived for a year, would sometimes start at 9 p.m. and go on, if necessary, until 4 a.m., walking around a kitchen table, heads (alas) down, consuming tea in great quantity, digging, generalizing, joking, up and down, left and right in 'mind space'.

Time and time again I have asked these people, 'What did your psychiatrist at the hospital say when you told them that?', and back would come the reply, 'Oh, God, I haven't told them *that*!', or words to that effect. Really the traditional helping agencies know very little about these people. Traditional helpers – through shortage of time and resources – are put in the situation of geologists who map by helicopter rather than geologists who pour over the area on foot for years. This very much restricts the data they are able to collect.

Traditional case studies of psychotic patients and their families are usually very negatively toned. Sometimes this can be extreme (e.g. Arthur and Schumann 1970). They are rather like von Krafft-Ebbing's descriptions of 'sexual psychopathy' (1886), emphasizing weakness, pathology and degeneration in sexual variants. Havelock Ellis (1936, 1942) changed this in the realm of sex, describing the people he studied in more positive terms, e.g. 'a manual worker . . . mentally bright, though not highly educated, a keen sportsman, and in general a good example of an all-around healthy Englishman'; 'B.O., English, aged thirty-five, missionary abroad . . . has never had any definite homosexual relationships although he has always been devoted to boys'; 'S.W., aged sixty-four, English, musical journalist', etc. As Celia Haddon (1982) points out, this, in its day, was very courageous. We shall, in a somewhat diluted form, use Ellis's approach here and try to see beyond the slime of conflict and illness. Rather than finding that such an exercise is contrived and alien we shall see that to present a positive view of the psychotic is, in fact, easy and refreshing.

DAVID B

I first met David B in November 1979 when he was 23. He was recovering from his second episode at the time (the first one was in 1975) and was rather troubled. I have often been told that I look like a policeman because of my boyish face and love of blue shirts. David B also commented on this and said he found it disturbing. Persecution by the police was a central feature of his delusions.

David looked tall (6' 3"), tough and hard. Were it not for very bad acne he would have been a handsome young man. He had a very attractive smile and when he did smile, which was often, he bore a marked resemblance to David Bowie, hence his pseudonym.

I saw him as intelligent. In a rather Burtian fashion I once guessed his IQ to be about 120. He was lively and amusing and all of us who knew him agreed that deep down he had 'a very nice nature', and that at his best he was 'a good laugh'.

Like all of the people in these studies he was a person of many opposites. His conversation was very sexually oriented. At first I took this to be in part because of my great interest in the subject; however, when he was with his closest friend, who we shall call Ash, it became even more so. His language was often sexist in the extreme. He would occasionally refer to women as

11

'meat', for example. In stark contrast to this, however, he would often go through periods when he read the Bible every night with an attitude of great devotion. He would mix spiritual sensitivity with tough mindedness in such phrases as: 'He's a bastard The Devil, I hate him!' Although he smoked heavily, at least forty a day, he would not do so while Bible reading.

When he was in hospital after his third episode he visited the chapel regularly and once read The Lesson. During this time he said he felt close to God, even at one with Him, and that for a moment he actually *was* Jesus. (He interpreted this [well, I thought] as a means of explaining all the good feelings he had towards people.) There was no doubt that David's religion was a great source of strength to him; it helped to prevent relapse and promoted recovery.

I found it generally difficult to probe deeply in conversations with him. His (usually light) statements made on different occasions would often contradict one another. Added to this he would often deny that he had said certain things, especially deeper things, or that he had 'really meant' them. For years this man's conversational 'slipperiness' and his inconsistencies left me and everyone who knew him totally bewildered. Psychiatrists just asked him how he was feeling and plied him with drugs and ECT. Many people said of him that his conversation was 'just silly', 'meaningless', etc. Although he looked like a tough man, the process of understanding him was rather like chasing a butterfly. Nonetheless, I loved him and perhaps because of this he once said I had a magical effect on him, to the good. (Paradoxically he accused me, in the same breath, of being The Devil because of this.)

David had a younger sister who was also diagnosed as schizophrenic, but an elder sister who was quite 'normal' (a teacher, married, with children) and a twin sister, also 'normal', married, with three children. Their mother was a lovely warm and caring woman who rather spoilt them all. David's father had been absent for several years during his childhood. He had walked out on his wife. David found him rather irritating: 'He's driving me crazy Peter!' he would often say. I could not, however, see any really punitive intent on his father's part. The father's attitude to the younger sister was also very protective; he was not a generally cold or dominating man. David's main complaint seemed to be about his father's incessant chatter; he would never leave him in peace and would continually try to jog him into doing things that he didn't feel well enough to do. But these were innocuous and quite reasonable things like trying to get a job, getting up at a reasonable hour and helping with the washing up. None of the father's behaviours seemed to be particularly malign. David was never 'shown up' by him and all his father's 'hostility' towards him was very much on the surface. Both parents, despite their perfectly human limitations, were consistent and caring. David was not dominated or caught in double binds or Catch 22 situations. Although it could be said that he was punished and criticized, yet overprotected at the same time, this was no more so than millions of other young people living at home all over the country.

David also did not lack self-assertiveness. He was not under his mother's thumb. Indeed, once when we were talking at his home he said to her, 'Right, leave us now Mother', whereupon she dutifully and rather apologetically walked out of the room. In fact David's biggest problems at home were those brought about by his own laziness (not once did he wash up) and those stemming from his difficulties in hiding his store of soft pornographic magazines from his father: 'He'd go *mad* if he found them!' David's attitude to his father seemed to me to be out of all proportion to the man's actual portentousness. To be able to write a story about an individual's personality one has to see that person in many different contexts. I had seen David with many people, and he was undoubtedly most troubled in the company of much older men. He had played truant at school and had been put on probation. Teachers and the police unnerved him. He also showed much rebelliousness to older male psychiatrists and was regarded as an uncooperative patient when in hospital. This aggressiveness to men was coupled with an expectation of, and fear of, punishment from them. He feared violence because of his complete awareness of his own hostility. However, although David looked tough and did not lack self-assertiveness he was not a physical fighter. He had been a follower of Chelsea for many years but when his friends had taken to beating people up for fun he had broken off with them. While to a moderate but not extreme extent he liked the show of hardness, he was afraid of overt violence and was genuinely repulsed by it.

He was most fluent when talking about sex, popular music and his dreams. He often said that his problems would be completely solved if he could live on a desert island. Once while in hospital he escaped by taxi in his pyjamas to an airport to 'get away' with this in mind. He had the dream of one day being a pop idol but had no clear idea of how he was going to achieve this. It would be easy to look for pathology in all this; there must, however, be thousands of young people in this country with similar dreams.

David craved mental pleasure. He described his life as boring; he wanted excitement. This he got through his music, which he would play for hours on end, through pretty girls in magazines, through visits to Soho with Ash and through the stimulation of cigarettes and an endless stream of colourful fantasies. David essentially tried to keep himself simmering. He always needed thrills *now*; to get a job to obtain the money to get more thrills later was too much.

His conversation was bright and colourful although tangential; at times crude, at other times odd. Always there was this self-stimulation. He confessed to me on a walk that he was bisexual and would gladly go to bed with David Bowie. He felt guilty about masturbating – surely the neighbours would hear him. Although there was a shallow side to him he could write quaint poetry and listen with an attentive ear to other people's problems. (He was also capable at times of walking and sprinting at remarkable speed – something I found out to my cost!)

David's personality cannot be understood fully through the use of questionnaires. Basically he saw himself as a 'good working-class lad'. His perception of himself as working class structured his behaviour and thoughts far more than did cortical or limbic arousal levels. Because of this he followed certain implicit working-class 'instructions' or 'rules' such as 'play snooker', 'know a lot about football', 'don't use long words', 'don't be intellectual', 'be practical not academic', 'don't do women's work', 'don't be squeamish', 'say "Fuck" a lot', 'value women for their looks/bodies', 'read *The Sun* or *The Mirror*', 'don't go to the opera, ballet or theatre', 'be a "good lad"', and so on. When I discussed this interpretation of him with him he wholeheartedly agreed: 'That's right Peter! Good! Good!' He added that there were *more* rules that both he and his friends of old had always followed, such as 'Look and don't look away'.

David was very much a product of this class and was good at following its rules. He used to be a very talented snooker player before his episode intervened. He was a devoted football fan; never did 'women's work' (hence his oft-mentioned washing-up problem); and talked rough, tough and crude – much to the disgust of Alison, whom we shall describe later. His high *P* (psychoticism) score of 10 on the Eysenck Personality Questionnaire (EPQ) (Eysenck and Eysenck 1975) also reflected his tough-minded mentality.

David therefore has to be seen as embedded in a fairly average caring family within a working-class network of rules and guidelines. In the experimental and psychometric study his quite high scores of 16 on Extraversion (out of 21), 16 on Impulsiveness (out of 24) and 11 on Venturesomeness (out of 17) also have to be seen in this context. The working-class favour the cheerful, assertive, extravert, the spontaneous and the warm and friendly. David was all of these things. This being the case, what went wrong?

After trying, unsuccessfully, to fit several extant theories to his case, a promising insight occurred to me. If a thought emerged in my mind, nowadays, to the effect that the police were monitoring and persecuting me I would immediately counter it with three propositions:

1 I don't deserve it.
2 I'm not that important.
3 People wouldn't go to all that trouble on account of me.

To understand psychotic mentation we must invert the reasoning. Then it becomes:

1 I *do* deserve it.
2 I *am* that important.
3 People *would* go to all that trouble on account of me.

Statement 1 implies guilt; statement 2, arrogance and/or selfishness; statement 3, perhaps that one has, in lay language, been 'spoilt'. Let us look at these interpretations in turn with reference to David, bearing in mind that they obviously are not entirely independent.

Guilt

It would probably occur to the man in the street that anyone who thinks he is being persecuted probably has a guilty conscience. The guilty man feels that he deserves to be betrayed. Yet apart from Freud's concentration on the effects of the guilt surrounding homosexual impulses, it does not figure very prominently in current theories of paranoia. (See, for example, the reviews by Arthur (1964) and Winters and Neale (1983).)

There was no doubt that David had a heavy conscience. At times it felt that one could almost 'see' it in his face as a higher order property of his facial expression. When I decided to live with him for a week it was because I felt he needed support as he seemed to be developing incipient hallucinations[1] (see Figure 2.1) involving occasional voices of people in the house next door. (He was living alone at the time in a council flat.) He was concerned that they were following and commenting on his actions. By the end of the week this had passed but during that week I saw a frightened man preoccupied with self-monitoring.

His crudity, obsessiveness with sex and guilt about masturbation he would regularly purge with his Bible reading – although it would be wrong, and cheap, to imply that this was his sole motive. Nonetheless, it gave him some peace, some forgiveness. His working-class guidelines brought out in him extraversion and warmth, but the thin end of the wedge was that they made him see the world as a tough place where everybody's business was everybody else's business. David felt that he both deserved and expected to be betrayed.

Arrogance

'I'm the champ!', 'I'm the greatest' he would often say with a beaming grin. Yet this superiority feeling clearly concealed some deep worries about his own adequacy. I have said that I had estimated his IQ to be 120. How wrong I was. The Mill Hill vocabulary test revealed to me what hours of talk had not. When David took this test in June 1983 as part of the experimental and psychometric study he scored a mere 3 out of 33 on the Definitions part of the test and 7 out of 33 on the slightly easier Synonyms. He did

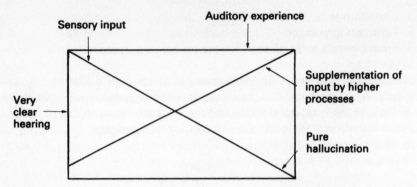

Figure 2.1 Auditory experience ranging from very clear hearing (largely sensory input) at left to outright hallucinations (input from higher dynamically organized processes) at right – the two exist on a continuum

not even know the meaning of such words as 'provide', 'formidable' or 'anonymous'. I started to see why his conversation involved so many sudden changes of topic and why it was so tangential. Previously I had naively put this down to being a symptom of mild thought disorder. It was nothing of the kind. David would ignore what one said to him and would change topic brusquely because he simply could not understand some of the words he was being presented with. By superb cunning he had kept his ignorance concealed from me for three years! By keeping my sentences very simple and checking with him that he understood even mildly uncommon words, such as 'adjusted', it was possible to keep him 'on track' quite easily. It became clear that he was fluent on sex and popular music because his factual knowledge and vocabulary were adequate to the topics. David's 'thought disorder' had evaporated.

His only two jobs had been working in a garage for a few weeks and a job as a messenger, again short-lived. I subsequently discovered that he could neither compose nor write a decent, legible letter, even when quite strongly motivated (it was to an attractive girl). His arithmetic was abysmal yet he aspired to be an office worker. David completely lacked confidence in anything that seemed to require academic skill. My experimental work, as he knew, involved thinking tests and it took him a year to summon up the courage to participate. (Even then I had to pay him £5 to coax him.) In this light it is clear that his reported stress score of zero at the beginning of the experiment (on the MacKay *et al.* (1978) inventory) is nonsense.

He must have known that in the world of work he was inadequate. In his relationships with girls, other than prostitutes, he was also unsuccessful. To compensate for all this he was, as he put it, the Champ. He would be 'Number One in the Top Forty in three years!' Beautiful girls would beseech him to go to bed with them. He would be a millionaire. He would retire on a desert island. As Anthony Storr has said (1970: 130), and as Stekel also often used to assert (much to Freud's chagrin), anyone who is at the centre of a persecutory plot must at least be a person of consequence.[2]

David's arrogance also reflected itself in the confidence he had in his beliefs and ideas. One could easily imagine him holding a delusional system with utter conviction. This was manifested in the experimental work in his subjective confidence levels in his judgements of out-of-focus slides. (The Slide Viewing Task we shall discuss later.) Indeed, to compute his B Index (McNicol 1972: 123–9) on this task, which is a measure of a bias to risk or caution, I had to extrapolate his data far beyond the range of confidence level categories available! He was clearly a very risky thinker.

Spoilt?

We already have said that David's mother was probably no more spoiling than millions of others. She certainly had a tendency to dote and indulge. David would be able to lie in bed until 4 p.m.; he would pay no rent out of his sickness benefit; he could nearly always borrow money from his parents for cigarettes and records; all his meals were provided; he could come and go as he pleased. Nothing very much was asked of him and certainly not by his mother. Now although this level of freedom was offered, most children would probably not utilize it to the full. They would try to get a job, if only part time, help a little around the house, pay something towards the rent. David did none of these things. As we have seen in his behaviour with his mother, he selfishly behaved as if he was the king of the house who deserved to be waited on hand and foot despite the fact that he was, when at home, totally dependent on his parents and the state for his entire existence. He even borrowed money from his younger sister. Just as he expected that people at home would go to endless trouble for him (and they did), so he expected, in his delusions, that people in the world would go to endless trouble because of him. And in psychosis they did.

The onset of psychosis

David's delusions were seeded, I think, on veridically perceived events. This is something we shall meet many times. His first trouble apparently began when he overheard some people in the room above him plotting a burglary. Not all flats are well insulated in the Fulham area and it is impossible to obtain insurance cover against burglary in this part of London from some companies. (My wife and I have been the victims of one successful and two attempted burglaries in ten years.) Hence, although the average overworked psychiatrist would probably just lazily say that David was 'obviously hallucinating', I am not so sure. His delusional system was elaborated from this singular event. The potential burglars were then out to 'shut him up'. The police thought that 'he was in on it'. The delusion did not

17

grow largely intrapsychically as Freud would have us believe. It expanded using innumerable events in the external world – particularly comments from people in buses and shops – which pushed it in directions that were quite unpredictable on an intrapsychic theory. Always David found comments and events which 'fitted' his persecutory system. If he saw one person twice in the same day they were tailing, or monitoring, or plotting against him. His worse fear was that they were going to kill or shoot him. He kept feeling, perhaps through enhanced similarity perception, that he was seeing the same people in vastly different places. People in a football crowd or a bus would somehow be 'connected'. He saw people in public places as 'all in with each other' and, to his distaste, liking to be that way. Via being connected they would, at worst, be plotting against him. As well as perceiving the social world as a unity he also suffered disturbances in his sense of time. Time itself would somehow be 'going too fast' and then 'too slow'.

David's personality structure may have been influenced by the absence of his father during most of his childhood. It made him like to be, and expect to be, at the focus. His non-verbal behaviour in the company of older men seemed almost to *scream* the message, 'Shut up! I want to be the centre of attention!' It made him expect people to go to great trouble on his account and it structured an expectation, almost a *need*, for punishment. What he feared he also longed for (Freud) and what he longed for (certainty) he also feared (rather like Lord Arthur Savile in Oscar Wilde's short story). As we have previously emphasized, his delusional system itself was not something that grew entirely in his mind while he sat in a room staring at a blank wall. Soon after 'the overhearing' he feared that the people concerned might know that he was aware of their intentions. Coincidentally, he then noticed when someone in the street gave him a long stare or had a slightly threatening expression when they looked at him. Eventually his own expression became somewhat apprehensive and attracted stares and comments, which further fed his proto-delusion. It seems that via small increments like this, in the early days of his episode, a state of vigilance and escalating self-consciousness was set up which sustained and fed his evolving delusional system in a positive feedback manner.

In the middle of his third psychotic episode I had the opportunity to see his facial expression. It broadcasted intense fear and hostility. To say he looked haunted would be a massive understatement. Indeed, his face was of such a form that it could not have failed to attract the attention of anyone within thirty or forty yards.

To speculate: it could have been that his agitated state may have funnelled down his attention only to data relevant to this central delusional preoccupation. As Broadbent (1971: 432–3) and Eysenck (1982) have argued, high arousal promotes search of and retrieval from dominant sources of information. In this sense David's confirmation bias promoted enhanced agitation which further magnified the confirmation bias itself.

These cognitive processes, however, have to be seen in the context of the part they had to play in David's psychic economy. There was, I think, a denied need for punishment, a kind of disinhibition of masochism. David scanned the world and built what he found into a massive instrument for his own punishment while consciously rebelling and trying to evade every psychic blow. His own personality structure was, as we have seen, a rich soil in which a delusion could grow. He had motive and precipitating event. He also had capacity. To entertain the idea of a city-wide 'pseudocommunity', as Cameron (1943a,b, 1951) would call it, intent only on one's persecution, has the flavour of mania. David B always had a tendency, even when between psychotic episodes, for larger-than-life fantasies. Like all the people on whom we shall report who suffered from delusions, he singularly lacked the ability to 'modulate'. He was either preoccupied with the stimulating and fantastic or he was depressed, apathetic and lethargic. He would build his father up into an ogre or dismiss him as a trivial irritation. He would occasionally want to 'paint the town', but at other times to curl up in seclusion. Like many a creative writer there was a definite lack of cultivation in the middle ground. However, to be able to entertain his intense brightly coloured level of fantasy suggests a certain special capacity denied to more mundane people (but perhaps not to those who pen science fiction stories).

He was also very creative in the 'fluency' sense of the term, being a reasonable amateur poet and an entertaining, if at times rather bewildering, conversationalist. I can well imagine his thoughts racing and leaping at every passer-by's glance or at the hooting of the horn of every passing car or bus. In this respect his rather low scores on the fluency tests in the experimental part of the investigation are, I think, highly suspect. David was at his best when given the full run of the field. If he could go almost anywhere he would go there fast. Any slight constraints – as were given in this part of the experiment – clearly impeded him greatly. Hence his true retrieval speed was vastly underestimated.[3]

We have briefly looked at a number of aspects of David B, from his spiritual side to social-class effects, family background and cognitive processes. All these fit into a story which is the best I can construct regarding this exceedingly evasive man. David, like Shafiq, with whom we deal next, presents us with few clear glimpses. To understand him is rather like interpreting a field area in which there is only a hundred clean outcrops rather than a thousand. Psychoanalysts, in their wisdom, will easily be able to read between the lines above and see areas that provoke further, much further, thought. Although it would be possible for a geologist to infer, from a hundred outcrops, a wealth of complex structures, refolding and metamorphic episodes, faults and igneous intrusions in the rocks beneath, it would be appalling geology. My approach has been to construct the simplest interpretation possible given the data. To complexify it would take us into the realm of pure unconstrained speculation.

I broke off with David B in 1985. I felt he was eventually going around in circles in his life, making no move to improve his lot. His arrogance was becoming tiresome, his conversation repetitive and his aggressiveness was becoming irritating. It seemed to me that he needed both a sharp jolt to his life and to realize the consequences of his behaviour. Nonetheless, I retain a deep affection for him. Despite his sexist jokes and language, his often threatening behaviour and his manic fantasies I somehow feel he was being most true to his real self when he was sitting on his bed reading the Good Book.

3

SHAFIQ

'The greatest man in the world?'

In attempting to interpret Shafiq we face a mammoth task. Here we have a young man with a remarkably active mind who showed resistance to all forms of help from conventional agents and who was determined to take his own path in life wherever that might lead.

I knew Shafiq for five years from early in 1980, when he was 23, to 1985. He was a person of exceptional ability, gaining 'A' levels in Mathematics, Physics and Chemistry (a 'B' and two 'C's) after only six months of private study. He had been to university to study engineering but dropped out at the end of the first year when he started to have paranoid thoughts. His father had finally had him admitted to hospital when, after a period of disturbed and aggressive behaviour at home (he had hit his father), he had asked one of his sisters to strip.

To his social workers Shafiq presented an evasive, jocular and superficial front, parrying and laughing off criticisms, deflecting conversation and continually raising seeming irrelevancies. In groups he would apparently take off in obscure directions and react with great glee when challenged by irate or confused participants. He presented a classic picture of 'lack of insight' and 'tangential thinking'.

He once agreed to go for psychotherapy but walked out in disgust in the middle of the second session. Shafiq was particularly sensitive to having theories imposed upon him and said to me of psychiatrists and psychotherapists: 'They don't listen!'

For some reason I was able to strike up close rapport with Shafiq, possibly because we both shared a strong academic orientation and we seemed to give each other ideas about life, science, philosophy, etc.

DELUSIONS

His central delusion in 1980 was rather strange and not often encountered. He believed that a so-called 'scandal sheet' had been compiled about him. This was a piece of paper or leaflet retailing details about his personal life. It had, he thought, been devised by The National Front and carried his

21

photograph. The delusion was seeded by his overhearing, while travelling on a bus, a woman say to a friend that she'd seen a photograph of him. The sheet described him in very negative terms and printed copies of it had, so he believed, been distributed widely in London.[1] Because of this he continually thought he was 'being recognized', and repeatedly overheard people saying 'That's him'. Clearly this is a highly damaging delusion which provoked intense suffering.

On crystallizing this thought Shafiq became a haunted man. If he got on a bus he ran the risk of overhearing someone say the dreaded 'That's him'; similarly in shops. Nowhere was safe. Almost anything anybody said while walking past him in the street, such as 'Isn't that the bloke who . . .?', 'I'm sure I've seen him . . .', 'I remember . . .', 'Have you heard about . . .?' or 'Have you seen . . .?' was taken to be a reference to him and/or the scandal sheet. Not surprisingly Shafiq walked around the streets with his head down and suffered a degree of agoraphobia which was secondary to the delusional preoccupation.

In contrast, however, he also overheard some people, talking with an American accent, say, while walking past his house, that he was 'the greatest man in the world'. He heard people saying this more than once, and for this reason he thought that he was secretly being followed and filmed by an American television crew while he walked around Fulham. While believing that he was being monitored he also believed that people thought he was monitoring them. The National Front were also following him about; they kept talking about him and suggesting that he also should be a member of the National Front. He believed that, in addition to all this, he was being spied on by people in 'the paramilitary' – by which he meant an unofficial army.

It is fairly clear by this brief account that from the moment Shafiq stepped into the street – an act which at times took tremendous courage – he immediately walked into a drama beyond even the realms of a James Bond film.

Even in his bedroom he did not feel totally safe. For a few weeks he had the idea that women were coming into his room while he was asleep and having intercourse with him while his penis was erect during REM (rapid eye movement) sleep. He inferred this on the basis of the fact that his body felt bruised and painful when he awoke. He was often sure that girls were fancying him (which some told me they did), but he was not sure why. He admitted to me that he had indulged in mutual masturbation with a man while in hospital, but a few weeks later (interestingly) denied that he had said this, subsequently claiming, with a laugh, that he 'wasn't homosexual at all'.

Apart from the support I gave him he accepted only anti-psychotic medication. However, he would repeatedly stop taking this, become hypomanic for a week or two and then relapse into fantastic delusions.

At one time he thought that Milton Friedman was stealing his ideas. This he inferred on the basis of the great, almost uncanny, similarity in their thinking. I asked him how this could possibly be and he replied that 'people' had secretly implanted a microphone in his throat which transmitted his subvocal speech to receiving devices in the United States. When I said that this was absurd and ridiculous he replied, in a quiet voice, 'Come off it Peter, I'm a major thinker'.

LOVE

Shafiq was troubled by love. A mutual friend, Arthur, once told him that I had said that I loved them both. Shafiq was somewhat shaken by this and said to me that he couldn't 'handle' being loved. His family, who were deeply concerned about him and who cared for him greatly, were, it seems, similarly frozen out. Shafiq was very much an independent man and took the slightest restraint or sign of mutual dependence as threatening to his integrity.

SEX

We have had some glimpses to the effect that Shafiq entertained variant sexual impulses. At one time I therefore considered his sexual life to be critical to an understanding of him. However, through many discussions over the years it became clear to me that he took the subject quite lightly and as genuinely rather trivial. There were no long pauses, tense expressions or evasive comments regarding it, with the exception of the one noted earlier about his 'homosexuality'. His occasional escapades into unusual sexuality had the same flavour as his repeated escapades into unusual thoughts generally and I could not, in all honesty, find evidence to the effect that the former were in some way a generatrix of the latter, existing psychically at a deeper level.

VIOLENCE

He was, like David B, particularly unnerved, however, by physical violence. He was fully aware of his own hostility although, apart from brief episodes of shadow boxing, it showed itself largely in the ruthless but brave quality of his jokes and opinions. Once a very violent man, who shared a room with him briefly in a hostel, punched him hard on the arm and inflicted an extremely unsightly bruise. He was in an agitated state for weeks following this, even though he immediately moved out of the hostel and away from the source.

By now the reader is probably as amazed and bewildered by this man, as was everyone else who knew him. One social worker described him to me as 'a very deteriorated case' and many of his friends and acquaintances regarded him as 'just barmy'.

THE POSITIVE SIDE

What we have seen so far is the outright 'pathology'. But getting to know Shafiq, although difficult, disclosed quite a different side to him. First, this man was extremely intelligent. In the many long discussions I had with him he imposed as much cognitive strain on me as have colleagues in university departments. Once he came round to my flat in West London while I was marking an Open University physics assignment. The answer was extremely involved and the student had arrived at a totally nonsensical solution which was orders of magnitude out. I had battled for several minutes to see where, amidst all the trivial mistakes, the student had focally gone wrong but without success. I explained the problem to Shafiq and handed him the script. He detected the crucial error in seconds.

Shafiq was also an astoundingly accurate judge of people (surprising for someone regarded as thought disordered). I once had a friend who seemed to me to want to make our relationship closer still, and I was uncertain. I asked Shafiq for a one sentence overview of this man and he replied, 'home grown'. It was perfect. Similarly, a number of my friends were talking in a generally positive way about a mutual acquaintance when Shafiq piped up: 'He's a creep; all he talks is general knowledge!' It was a poignantly valid angle. These are fairly typical examples of a capacity that Shafiq deployed many times.

For someone whose thinking sounds so disturbed he had a remarkable ability to cut through 'the trees' to see 'the wood'. He could at times do this with a sweep that at first seemed quite brutal. When an acquaintance of his committed suicide after about a dozen previous unsuccessful attempts Shafiq said quietly: 'Another inadequate personality bites the dust.'

His thinking ranged widely over science, sociology, politics and economics. He read deeply and intensely. In one discussion I had with him I said, at 2 a.m., after a long pause, that I had better go to bed. He became quite angry at this and accused me of shallowness. He pointed out that we had reached quite a critical point in the dialogue and in the argument where the only thing we could do was to plunge deeper. This really shook me. He was right. I stayed up until 4 a.m.

Shafiq was very tough minded and obviously paranoid. On the P scale of Eysenck and Eysenck's EPQ (1975), which tends to reflect this, he scored 10 on one occasion and 14 a few years later. These are extraordinarily high scores. He had little respect for psychiatrists and their associated personnel and deliberately talked rubbish to them to show 'what fools they all were'. Then he would delight in their confusion. These 'fools', however, were quite right to argue that Shafiq lacked insight of a psychological nature. He was adept at discussing external realities such as physical science and the social and political plights of Indian and Pakistani people in this country – hence his obsession with The National Front – but he was still, even with me, evasive about the internal side of himself. It was a great shame that someone who suffered so much should not be at all psychologically minded.

Shafiq, being very much a polymath, lacked validation. As I am of similar bent I provided that. His father said to me: 'As long as you're around he'll be OK.' And, indeed, when we didn't see each other for several weeks he did have a tendency to relapse. He had no one to talk to. By projection he thought that I was a genius because I alone could appreciate his genius.

Thus, we have a picture of a highly able though arrogant man with a considerable capacity for abstract and profound thought, which strangely issued forth also in spectacular and disturbing delusions. The scenario is of brilliance wasted on self-aggrandising fantasies. Had he deployed his talent with persistence and patience I feel sure he could have made an original contribution to human knowledge.

EXPERIMENTAL MEASURES IN CONTEXT

In the experimental enquiry, Shafiq and David B, who both had very harassing delusions, were at the very extreme end of the whole sample (psychotics and non-psychotics) in two measures: subjective confidence levels in *incorrect* hypotheses and verbal confirmation bias (both scoring very high on each). To the extent that Shafiq ever lost any of his paranoid thoughts he did not so much conquer them as get tired of them. Although contrary to popular belief it *is* occasionally possible to argue people out of delusional thoughts (Rudden *et al.* 1982), this was not so with either of these men. (As an aside, their behaviour leads me to speculate that such disturbances partly involve a parallel disturbance in the biochemical and physiological processes that underpin the subjective sense of certainty.)

The limitation of the experimental method is that it only gives us a snapshot of a person's behaviour at a particular spot in time. Hence Shafiq and David B seem more similar from such measures than they really were. David's delusions tended to centre chronically around the police, 'neighbours', etc., whereas Shafiq's were more fragile and mutable. As also emphasized by Philippa Garety (1985), delusions can wax and wane rather than be chronically 'rigid' beliefs. By 1984 he had ceased to worry about the scandal sheet which was so central in 1978–80 and no longer believed in it. (He said that he had suffered the phrase 'that's him' so many times that it ceased to have any effect on him.) He also no longer believed in the idea of reference to the effect that he was 'the greatest man in the world' or various other fragmentary thoughts such as one about computer control, not so far mentioned, or the thought that he was considered by people to be monitoring them.

These and other spectacular ideas seemed to rise, float and then sink in his mind.

Shafiq had the arrogance and spoiling at home that we have seen with David B. He also had a similarly active, creative mind although capable of a far greater degree of abstraction. Any notion to the effect that psychotics are concrete thinkers (e.g. Goldstein and Scheerer 1941) founders in the context of Shafiq. He was probably as capable of abstract thought as the investigators who thought up the theory. Cameron (1944) also argued that abstract thinking can be evoked if rapport is established with such people.

In this light his poor performance on my own test of abstract thinking is a source of disappointment to me regarding its validity. He scored more concrete responses than abstract despite operating in conversation almost always at an abstract level. As Heisenberg has warned physicists, we also cannot test or observe a person without changing them. Under the beacon light of being 'tested' or being 'experimented on' my general impression was that he clammed up. His stress and anxiety scores were extremely high and he took over twice as long as most other people to respond on personality, vocabulary and thinking tests. It was largely on measures such as those dealt with earlier, which were not transparent, that he provided data that were more congruent with my expectations regarding him.

On the personality tests he emerged as a neurotic slightly extraverted man who was very low on venturesomeness. Indeed he did, like most of the psychotic sample, tend to live in a world of ideas and fantasies rather than in a concrete pragmatic world of everyday events. He was daring ideationally but not physically. His extraversion score of 14 (in 1982) was comparable to that of David B but was obtained by answering quite different keyed items. They were very different people. Two years later it had dropped to 9 and the change was observable.

Despite his remarkable judgemental efficiency with such complex gestalts as people (interestingly, engineers have been shown to be exceptional judges of people (Taft 1955)), his judgement on a more analytic task – guessing the identity of ambiguous out-of-focus slides – was the poorest in the whole sample of both psychotics and non-psychotics. An holistic thinker, Shafiq was much more at ease with *big* problems, the analytical methods of experimental psychology did not capture his essence at all. He would complete a difficult complex task very quickly but one that was more particularistic – such as defining or finding a word – only very slowly indeed.

So chronically intellectually active was Shafiq that I was particularly interested in the duration of his spiral after-effect. In that this after-effect must involve the activation of movement detection channels in neocortical areas 17/18 it seemed likely that it could be an indicator of cortical arousal. Shafiq's imagery was also, he reported, multimodal – suggesting recruitment of wide cortical areas, including the occiput, during his private mentations. On the Eysenckian arousal/activation based model of personality (Eysenck 1967), long after-effects would be expected in low impulsives (high cortical arousal). This has actually been found by Levy and Lang (1966), although anxiety and neuroticism also contribute (Levy and Lang 1966; Knowles and Krasner 1965). Shafiq was low on impulsivity.

In July 1982 his after-effect was 31.625s averaged over four determinations. This is extremely long. However, I tested him again in February 1984 and his duration at that time turned out to be a mere 8.8s, despite his being just as intellectually active. This makes one seriously question whether this measure is really reliably indicative of anything. It has been determined that major tranquillizers reduce the movement after-effect (Lehmann and Csank 1957; Janke and Debus 1972; Harris et al. 1983). However, he had been receiving modecate injections for five years prior to the first determination and, hence, it is unlikely that this massive reduction is entirely a drug effect. Shafiq's data clearly show that the spiral after-effect is a complex phenomenon involving the operation of many variables (Knowles and Krasner 1965). We therefore can expect difficulties in relating it to cortical arousal, cortical inhibition (Eysenck 1957) or to the activity level of an arousal-modulating system (Claridge 1967).

COINCIDENCES

In a sense Shafiq toyed with his own beliefs just as he toyed with social workers and therapists. There was always this intense mental activity. He would boost his concentration by chain-smoking sixty cigarettes a day. He was never at rest. It is in this context that he could process, digest and incorporate into some ongoing idea almost anything that happened around him. This is where, as with David B, we have to consider the role of coincidences. We would talk about this often. Shafiq would say, 'I just can't believe some of the things that are happening to me!' At one time, I think it was in 1981, he was concerned that 'something was going on in Fulham'. I went with a number of friends, including Shafiq, to a pub and while I was ordering drinks a stranger apparently had leant around the enclosure where he was sitting, noticed Shafiq and said to his friend in a loud voice, 'It's him!' Everybody else had heard this. We have previously mentioned that the persecuted are at least persons of consequence and it is interesting in this respect that Shafiq's face lit up and his conversation was very animated for tens of minutes after this event. This validation of Shafiq's belief as to his own fame was confirmed to me many times around this period in the 'knowing looks' which I noticed he had provoked from shop keepers and passers-by in the area where he lived. There was no doubt that Shafiq was 'known'. Alas we cannot say whether this was a cause of his behaviour or the result of it. He was small and had a slightly unusual walk and sullen expression. He may well have been known for unusual behaviours he had not told me of. However, it was easy to see how a proto-delusion seeded on accidental events could have mushroomed, with a mind at his level of activity, into his gargantuan beliefs in a London-wide persecutory and monitoring network. There was plenty happening around him for him to process once the flywheel of his delusional system had started, slowly at first, to rotate.

We must now round off our discussion of Shafiq, partial and fragmentary though it has had to be. He did not, of course, have the working-class programming that so characterized David B, but he was similar in having a critical stressor.

Whereas David B's central vulnerable spot was his total inability to relate to older men, Shafiq's was his 'felt' vulnerability because of his skin colour. Whereas David's chief persecutors were older men in positions of power, such as police sergeants and inspectors, Shafiq's was The National Front. A point of serious vulnerability in a person with a very high opinion of their own importance and/or considerable guilt about their own shortcomings presents a personality system that may crumble at any moment if a precipitating event of the slightest relevance occurs. The system is like an inverted triangle that may topple at the mildest imbalance of forces. Shafiq is adamant that the woman he overheard on the bus was talking about him, and perhaps her total behaviour including its non-verbal aspects would have given anyone that impression. David B is similarly adamant about the burglary plot. Feed such data into a self-preoccupied creative mind and the result is liable to be bizarre.

Both Shafiq and David B wanted to have 'the field' to themselves. Constraints, demands, compromises interrupted their flow – caused them a kind of psychic pain – and, as with David, these were really the main causes of disagreement between Shafiq and the other members of his family when he was living at home. Both of them wanted to 'do their own thing' and chase their thoughts and feelings wherever they led them to an extreme degree. This is very much the cognitive and personality style which lends itself to extreme confirmation bias and *is* in a sense the behavioural problem associated with a great predilection for this particular type of bias. We shall have more to say on this later.

I terminated my relationship with Shafiq because he was becoming too dependent upon me – visiting three, sometimes four, times a day. He had found great solace in his religion; he was a Muslim and visited the mosque in Regents Park regularly. It seemed to me that I had helped him as much as I could – no new developments were taking place – and that in this faith he had a much stronger support than anything I could provide.

4

MYSTICISM, DELUSION AND THE PARANORMAL

I suppose we have all unknowingly taken a well-trodden route believing that we were breaking new ground. It's easy to do. In 1979 I took the general direction of the poet-mystic Rimbaud (Zaehner 1957). I tried to storm Heaven from its least well-guarded entrance, the entrance from Hell itself.

The landscape for Rimbaud, the poet, was obviously different from that experienced by Chadwick, the psychologist, although the compass bearings were the same, so we shall not entirely be going over old pastures. I think it's therefore worthwhile to report my own experience to the readers – an experience which disturbingly straddles the borderline between sanity and madness. It will take us through largely different territory from that traversed in the other case studies and is in some ways quite unique. At times, however, it is unsettling; indeed I fear that many people have taken the knowledge contained in this chapter with them under the wheels of trains and tube trains, into the waters of the Thames and into the oblivion of drug-induced suicide. Fortunately I survived with a tale that must be told. It is a tale of what is to be found at The Borderline, where a dream world becomes a world dream, fantasy is reality, fears become certainties, and fate is a trap from which one cannot escape no matter how one struggles. This is existence at the razor edge between sanity and insanity, between Heaven and Hell; this is life at 'The Brink'. Not surprisingly this is at times an oppressive chapter – it is a chapter of danger and violence, but one, finally, of surrender.

Glasgow was not for me. I resigned from a full-time university lecturing post in psychology at the University of Strathclyde in August 1978. As an epicurean Oscar Wilde devotee, I was always sensitive to the unconscious of my sector and to the delicate undulations of the atmosphere about me. Calvinist puritanical 'decency' and its disavowed brothers – macho, chauvinist masculinity, violence and drunkenness – coexisted in such a way as to rob the ambience of all tenderness and freedom. I could not create.

My personality could never have fitted into such a city. To my friends and colleagues I was 'a maverick', 'very human', 'a divergent thinker', 'a screwball', 'a pioneer', 'a man who lives as if he's got a monkey on his back', 'an intellectual'. It all suggests an unstable but reasonably able and colourful personality whose passion had a driven quality to it and who lived at the periphery of life, of thought and of respectability.

Not unpredictably, in 1972, when I was still a geologist, John Ramsay had said of me: 'If Pete Chadwick's got a weakness as a structural geologist it's that he has *too many* ideas.' It never occurred to me that what was high creative fluency in 1972 was destined to be transformed gradually into something rather different seven years later.

When I went to London in October 1978 ('spirit freed') my psychological research had been, until then, entirely mechanistic and analytical. I had read neither Pauli nor Progoff and had only smatterings of Heidegger and Husserl. My knowledge of Jung was largely restricted to realizing that he had introduced the terms 'Extravert' and 'Introvert' into the psychological literature, had done some interesting reaction-time experiments and had noticed that psychasthenic neurotics (what we now call 'dysthymics') tended to be introverted, hysterics more extraverted. All else, so I thought, was 'Jungian mumbo jumbo'. Being still a philistine I had also read nothing of mysticism, not even William James's important views on it (James 1936; Knight 1954: 206–14), and if anyone had asked me what the *I Ching* was I probably would have guessed that it was a Chinese restaurant off the Earls Court Road.[1]

I did, however, have Christian religious beliefs and in a sense my research on the psychology of geological observation, in fusing the social and earth sciences, was in part a religious mission to humanize science and to induce scientists to look for value in the person as well as in their techniques and instruments. Other than this religiosity, however, I was quite raw and naive in the face of what I was to encounter.

It was difficult to get a counselling practice started and I had to take a number of other temporary jobs at the same time to make ends meet. The purpose of the move, however, had also been because I wanted to extend my interests into the fields of personality and abnormal psychology. It seemed to me that to do good work in these areas it was necessary to go beyond the confines of a university environment, where one mixed largely with other professional psychologists and with undergraduate students in psychology, and 'see a bit of life', meet a wide range of people and, in general, indwell in the world. So this was generally congruent with my intentions.

I was determined however to use my counselling work – and my own, always ongoing, self-analysis – as an arena in which to develop and use my ideas about biases in human thought itself. My intellectual adventure was in part in search of a way to bootstrap myself past my own thinking biases. I felt that to 'see' mind I had, without drugs, to somehow get outside myself and 'look back'. By jolting myself out of my habitual ways of living into a quite different style of life, I thought I might see the chains that previously had bound my thinking and limited my vision.

By May or June 1979, insights about biases in thought began to coalesce. I started, in a staccato fashion at first, to write and think myself into what to me was a 'new attitude of mind'. Central to this attitude was a notion about what a truly liberated person would be. I called this person-of-the-future a 'Borderline Normal' for want of any better phrase. The most easily communicable feature of Borderliners was ambiguity. They were both good and bad, masculine and feminine, strong and weak, active and passive, etc. In a sense they lived between the opposites and transcended them. They had no one specific personality (or in artificial intelligence (AI) terms, 'subroutine'); their identity lay at the level of process (in AI terms at the level of the 'computational system'). The Borderliner had dispensed with ego, was not oriented towards the world in a focused competitive or analytical way or in terms of a role or an identity. The Borderliner just 'was'. The Borderline state was a floating state of being with all that is. Having dispensed with ego, content jettisoned; *process* all important, the Borderliner was 'personified process'.[2]

While regarding the Borderliner as an ideal, I tried to identify with it, reach to it, realize it in action. Always the emphasis was on process and ambiguity and the transcendence of it. Quoting from now on from my journal of the day, the latter emphasis was reflected in statements such as:

> The Borderliner both happens to be and chooses to be . . . is subject and object . . . is a coherent pattern of eventuated opposites . . . is the basic generalized person.

The emphasis on process was reflected in my belief that the Borderliner could only be evaluated in terms of the 'how' or 'in what manner' they did (and in particular *loved*), not in terms of 'what'.

> The Borderliner is process integrated or process useful, process practised. The integration is *that* the machinery is working well and ticking over. The integration is the tuning of the parts to do the job, the Borderliner's personality is well tuned, the integration is not *in* the job that the parts do, it is not in the whatness of the parts . . . Hence the integration of the Borderline person is analogous to the process play of science in action over time.

> The Normal sees the world through adjective and noun coloured spectacles, summing people up with nouns as integers, adjectives as fractions and conjunctions as addition signs . . . The Borderliner is probably most accurately perceived with infinitives and adverbs, hence the Normal's bewilderment – his apparatus just cannot handle the job.

In my view the structure of language had strangled our thinking. (I wrote that 'The Borderliner does not belong, not even to language'.) Rational man thought in terms of Subject (Self or *res cogitans*) operating on the world (Object or *res extensa*) with all reality characterized as atomized into dimensions with positive and negative poles such as More–Less, Good–Bad, Strong–Weak, and so on. The basic code of the mind was:

$$\begin{array}{cc} + & \\ S & O \\ - & \end{array}$$

The Borderliner however lived, as I have said, in the middle ground between opposites and yet transcended them:

> The Borderline thinker sees the reality which the contrasts we usually deal with are merely differentiates of. Hence the Borderliner is the fluid reality between the concrete dogmatic reality of appearances.

In my own (very) abstruse way I was viewing the Borderliner as in touch with the ground, the ground or 'All' which lay behind the naively accepted reality of everyday life. This is, although I did not realize it at the time, clearly analogous to the Buddhist concept of the Tao.

The Borderliner was not just a meditator or a reflector, however, he was very much in action in the world, living as I put it at 'the point of potential to kinetic conversion', accessing the ground but effective and efficient in everyday life.

> The Borderliner's resting state is at the potential to kinetic conversion – the sparking point, the contact point, between the inertia of the ground and the blinkered unreflective state of figure.

In this context the Eriksonian concept of an identity (Erikson 1950) obviously was a naive capitulation. Identity was a restriction, a narrowing down from the truly rich array of infinite potentialities available to person. Ego, content, identity and language were all snares; the human person in all his or her perfection was behind all these:

> The Borderliner attempts to be himself. The Normal role plays a pattern which weaves together all the positive poles of word-opposites that language has crystallized out for us and which trap us. The Normal then re-presents a 'good' image of himself to himself – he shuttles the bad away, inside or out into others. The Borderliner holds back from falling victim to language, he lives tersely in the opposites, accepting himself as himself.

My 'point of potential to kinetic conversion' is clearly identical with Jung's 'psychoid state' where psychological events are incompletely differentiated out from what he called 'the continuum' – there the psychic and the physical are no longer differentiated from one another. For Jung, 'psychoid' is 'touching the undifferentiated state of nature' (Progoff 1973: 157). This was my 'All' or 'Ground'.

Thinking and feeling in this way I experienced the whole of rational thought as an illusion. The division of subject 'directed' to finding out about Objects or other Subjects usually construed in bipolar dimensions was a mistake. The Truth that I felt I had 'discovered' was that these were the structuring rules of rational mind, it was how rational mind *had* to think in order to have any purchase on the world in the first instance. And yet this was a bias, the true 'reality' behind all this was undifferentiated. In many ways my thinking was similar to that articulated by David Bohm (1985) who speaks of the 'implicate' and 'explicate order', the former being the ground which contains all forms in a kind of holographic potential.

The state of mind I experienced when reaching to these insights for the first time was one of vulnerability, yet of power. A feeling of passivity yet of activity. The insights had a quality of certainty, of absolute validity, which was beyond all question. My mind felt perfectly clear, as if psychically I could see to infinity. Rather than insanity, it was a superlative form of sanity. Unknowingly I had, of course, accessed a transcendent mystical state.

In this state there was a great sense of the unity of all things, time had no meaning; in the ground all opposites disappeared, all contrasts faded away, all difference and particularity was a consequence of being or actuality – in Bohm's terms they were characteristic of his explicate order.

As the full force of these insights impressed themselves upon me words became increasingly difficult to find to describe the experience. Indeed, in the act of verbalizing the state would be transiently lost. I wrote of 'throwing thoughts sling-like into the domain' but never being able to sit in it. As Laotzû said: 'He who knows does not speak; he who speaks does not know.' The Tao as expressed or represented is not the Tao.

As my thinking became less verbal, journal entries decreased. Having used words as ladders into the Borderline domain I essentially and eventually merged amoeba-like with it. It is interesting that when attempting to write or verbally think myself into the state where the essence of Borderlining would be captured, I experienced a strange alternation between feelings of great clarity of my body boundary and an irrational fear that if I ever did fully capture the essence in language, indeed any language, I would, the moment I moved beyond the last word or equation, actually *disappear* (!). I therefore gave up language. I moved without explicitly knowing how or why I was moving.

In this psychic zone 'at the point of potential to kinetic conversion' I was in touch, so I felt, with an all-embracing, awe-inspiring force. The keyboard of my mind was immense and stretched out before me. I knew that if I could play it I could do or be anything (the Borderliner 'severalizes the self'). Great 'energy' surged through me. I oscillated between a state of exaltation to the greatest heights and a state of condemnation to awesome depths. A great truth had been revealed to me. I felt 'not of this world'. There was a sense of unearthly joy. I would walk miles in exhilaration, head-on driving rain undeterred me. When I tried as best I could to explain how I was feeling to a friend, he said, 'You're like a cylinder open at both ends'. Indeed this was so, feelings of saintliness and union with the cosmos alternated with feelings of possession by demonic forces and of being a *channel*, for both good and evil to come into the world. With the loss of ego and identity my feeling was that of being a vehicle. There was, to me, no doubt that what was happening was in some sense real and important.

I felt most at peace and 'together' when lying on my back in the park at night gazing up at a star-spangled sky with which I was at one. Yet unlike a Zen meditator who may have similar experiences in a state of tranquillity and low arousal I had accessed this domain in great agitation. As Albertus Magnus emphasized, a state of mental excess, in my case due to intense abstract thinking and extreme sensuality, may help open the door to magical and mystical experiences, and it did.

Despite realizing how inadequate words were I longed to communicate my discovery. Eventually a kind of synthesis emerged in the form of an article entitled: 'Half man, half boat, the mind of the Borderline Normal' (Chadwick 1979). This effort was useless. Within a day or so I realized that between the lines was the implicit communication: 'The Borderliner is good.' I had not been able to hold the transcendent middle ground state while writing about my experience. The realization of this error came as a terrible blow. I sat in the park, with my head down, bitterly disappointed, even ashamed of myself. I had betrayed my lower, earthly, sensual nature. The article had been motivated by a wish for self-defence and self-justification. Even though I knew that the desire for self-justification can inspire much creative thought, I felt that I had been cowardly and pathetic. After this I ceased writing altogether. But my mental state had changed. And not only had it changed, I was soon to realize that it would never be the same again.

Following the failure of this attempt at self-definition my validity as a person, so I felt, lay in ruins. Well over a stone underweight, and at a time when I was smoking, I had come to look a sharp, hungry, hypervigilant beast. I was surrounded at the time by people to whom I could not relate; was regarded as an 'odd ball' by all who knew me (more of this later), was heavily overdrawn, had no secure job, was living only as a guest in a run-down boarding house and had no clear future. My best friend was my dog. Two other friends, Jay and Ron, were basically extraverted thinkers fluent on motor bikes and money, pubs and politics. Amidst all this I was busy climbing up inside my own head to ever more rarified levels of abstraction and nebulousness.

Having miserably failed to mesh with the world, I had tried not only to research biases in thought but to validate myself via the construction of some intrapsychically evolved system. For some reason I felt that it had been a race against time. It should have been obvious to me that I was stretching every sinew of my intellect to keep madness at bay. I had penned no less than ten totally unpublishable manuscripts in the first five months of 1979, my mind fevered by tobacco and lack of food, to somehow defend and acquit a wretched psyche which I felt was otherwise destined for the gallows.

In 'Half man, half boat . . .' I soared like a hawk to transcend and detach myself from all 'the evidence'. For a few days I climbed above all, and reached complete blissful purity of spirit. The particulars of my worthless, abject existence – from smelly feet to the murder I had done in my mind of my long dead mother – were all temporarily forgotten. I had achieved innocence and absolution.

But the whole defensive operation could only be a success if the elaborately constructed system was *perfect*. As I say, I quickly found the flaw, the dam was *cracked* . . . immediately I was in deep, serious trouble.

To speak of 'The Good' beyond 'good' and 'bad', as does Humphreys (1986), was to me not good enough. The problem could not be solved by changing the size of the letters. If 'The Answer', the characterization of the transcendent realm, lies beyond good and bad then one is far distanced from it if the bad has never even been faced fairly and squarely.

With the sincere facing of 'the bad', the council for the prosecution was allowed to speak. Even as he drew breath I knew I was faced with the infernal.

At this point most dynamically oriented readers will expect that I was 'flooded with the unconscious'. That would seem to be a likely consequence. Defences were breached, the dam cracked; surely I would just be over-whelmed by the previously repressed. Alas it didn't work out quite like that.

The reason for this is that I simply would not give in. This anguished resistance produced a strange genuinely borderline form of quasi-psychotic experience which was positively uncanny. An experience in which madness coexisted with sanity, within with without and fact with fiction in a strange twilight world seemingly far beyond the reach of rational thought.

I found myself noticing colours, how intense, iridescent and significant they seemed to be. (This is a fairly common psychotic symptom.) I rushed up to my room, irrationally convinced that there would be a discussion on the radio which involved at least something on the hermeneutics of colour. There was. I sat in the park probing the evidence within for my own damnation. I dug deeper and deeper. My dog even began to dig, something she rarely did. Disturbed by this 'coincidence' I stood up and walked to another bench at the side of a main path. I wondered if there might actually be something in the mediaeval idea of possession and whether it might apply to me. A little girl walked past me with her mother, and after a brief glance my way she said to her, 'Mummy, is *that* man possessed by The Devil?' Her mother also looked at me and replied, 'Yes dear'. Yet as far as I was concerned, all I looked was thoughtful. If it is possible to plunge a knife through a mind, those words did so.

I went back to my room and turned on the radio. My thoughts turned to my former girlfriends. In contrast to the lofty statements in my flawed article I had long been deeply troubled by my total failure to find love – a failure which, after over forty affairs in sixteen years, had led me to secretly conclude that I was basically *incapable* of real love. I remembered sitting in a railway carriage at Highbridge station in 1975 with my then current girlfriend Denise. Denise was low at the time and we were talking morbidly about suicide techniques. How on earth we got onto this topic I cannot remember. She said that if she ever 'did it' she would hang herself. Instead of saying, 'Oh my God don't *ever* consider killing yourself!' I replied to her comment, with my characteristic shallowness, 'Oh, don't do it *that way*!' She had looked at me suddenly, aghast. I felt my soul perceptibly darken, the sense of wretchedness was unutterable. I had looked the other way and caught my breath.

I was thinking of this appalling incident when talk came on the radio about a man treating a girl badly. I homed in on what was being said and the narrative continued with:

'You know you told her not to do it *that way*?!'
'Yes'.
'Well she did!!!'

All the rest was a blur as I reeled on the bed in utter torment, my stomach feeling as if it were writhing and contorting within me, my breath hard to get. Another knife had been 'plunged in'.

These were fairly typical incidents from my life in June, July and August 1979. In an attempt to cleanse my tarnished self-percept I gave up smoking for about the fifteenth time, but the psychological relief was minimal. I saw my life as basically embroiled in self-indulgence, sensuality, sugar and sweetness. Although I had developed the capacity to approach what I feared, I could never resist what attracted me. Like Oscar, the only thing I could not resist was temptation. I decided, therefore, to live a stoic spartan existence of early to bed and early to rise. Smoking was already behind me, sugar came next. I took sugar as somehow symbolic of my sybaritic life. Needless to say, when I turned on my television set while thinking about this I was met with an image of someone scraping a large block of sugar with pincers followed by an image of a ball-bearing being dropped through a hole in the bottom of a pan. Although it was merely a cookery programme, to me it looked like my soul being dropped into Hell. Then as I sat on my bed daring to entertain an image of a scantily clad blonde, Pete Murray, on the radio, piped up to the effect that he was sitting where he was in stockings and suspenders, etc. I didn't laugh.

Experiences of this kind – some very striking, some less so and thus probably explainable by my rapidly increasing associative looseness – were pounding at me twenty to thirty times a day. I was not mindful of the Jungian concept of synchronicity (Jung and Pauli 1955); I called it, crudely, 'clockworking'. This was a bungled attempt to express my feeling of my thoughts being somehow entrapped in a harmonious flow of events. Indeed there was no 'synchronization' of outer reality and inner thought, 'it' all happened as if in one great clock-like machine, wheels within wheels, inner and outer reality fused and transcended. I was at one with the world, with space-time itself, and it was at one with me.

This period, however, was absolute agony and work was impossible during it. I had neither the intelligence nor the conceptual apparatus nor the spiritual development to handle the experience that was now going out of control.

It is ironic that many people seek the development of paranormal powers (if what I experienced was evidence of the paranormal) and Progoff (1973: 167) even wonders if there might be *value* in seeking and encouraging synchronistic experiences. Once noticed they tend to increase in frequency – what thinkers sympathetic to Jung refer to as 'the synchronicity of synchronicity' (Vaughn 1979). Having experienced this amplification of the uncanny I can assert that this is the most stupid and dangerous idea Progoff has ever had.

As the 'clockworking' continued I frantically and largely unsuccessfully tried to weave theories to account for it.[3] I thought of myself experiencing the 'dovetailing of contexts' and of being 'at the intersection of meaning planes'. I was attentive to the events but I never 'forced' them. If I adopted an attitude of deliberate focused attention and calculated planning they would not occur. Always they would – like all the features of the Borderliner and the Borderline state – have the character of being both between opposites and transcending them. They would in a sense be suffered *and* engineered, both caused *and* allowed. When my mental state was between activity and passivity, between listening and hearing, watching and seeing, they would occur. Hence they jolted, jogged and surprised me, yet in a sense I expected them.

The only peace I knew was when talking to vicars (other than those of Roman Catholic persuasion, who made me feel worse) and when reading Tennyson's poetry. But, sadly, these strategies eased me only temporarily. I knew I was on a roller-coaster ride; I somehow had to know where it would lead. There was no getting off, even if it led right into the jaws of Hell itself.

In late August, early September I was forced by financial circumstances to get back into work. I was offered a mundane temporary job that I thought I could easily handle – an accounts assistant. I worked at Argus Press, off Finsbury Circus, a company that, in part, distributed children's comics and magazines. (I was quick to notice, in horror, that 'Argus' was an anagram of 'sugar'.) Synchronistic events bore down on me relentlessly. I was not sure whether they were 'engineered' by some 'organization' out to trouble and destroy me, whether they were manifestations of the paranormal or of some extradimensional aspect to reality or whether they were spiritually engineered. The coincidences were so numerous that I *was* sure that there was a pattern there; my difficulty was in weaving theories to explain it.

I was using about a tenth of my 'capacity' to do the job I had taken (which I wasn't doing very well), the rest I was using to process the kaleidoscopic events going on around me as I either thought things that people then said or heard things that were perfectly reasonable 'answers' to what I had just thought. (This again is also quite common in madness.) I felt like glass and as readable as a book. Eventually, and not surprisingly, I decided that suicide was the only solution to this diabolical state and situation. I even thought that perhaps in some way it was 'required' of me either by God, the Devil, 'the organization' or by 'Fate'. I wondered what would be a fair, appropriate and somehow 'right' way to do it. With the typical smoothness to which I had almost become accustomed, the manager in the office where I worked said loudly over the telephone to someone 'Bus Fayre!' (the name of a children's publication). This fairly weakly 'fitting' remark did shake me somewhat although not *very* strongly. However, I was much later questioning the 'meaning' of the remark when, again typically, one of the manager's assistants shouted out 'What? He's got to do it by bus!?' (exactly what was on my mind) and the reply came back, 'Yes!' Even ruminating about my own doom did not shake off the coincidences which, unabated, now continued on quite mercilessly, making me walk around the large office like a zombie.

'This is torture, chaos, agony', I thought. 'How could this come about? Who could do such a thing to someone over and over again?'

'That's Nick again!', shouted the manager down the 'phone ('Nick', of course, being a common name for the Devil).

'Why is this happening?', I asked myself for the thousandth time, whereupon a sequence of mind-scorching coincidences related to my narcissistic past seared through my conscience like hot irons for about an hour. I came out of a sub-office shaking like jelly and wondering, as I had been for some time, *when* I should 'do it' when an expected phone call came for me concerning a delivery just as I was (typically) blaming it all on my long dead mother.

'I am sending the magazine (slightest pause) "*now*" (slightest pause) to Paddington. It should arrive at 4.50.' The voice was soft yet almost menacing. I passed on the message and its details (probably incorrectly) to the manager and then, without a word, walked out into the street. I had blamed my mother for 'everything' just once too often.

Still I fought and ducked 'the inevitable'. The early strong feeling of being a kind of tunnel or channel for good as well as evil to come into the world, a kind of channel in 'mind space', gave me some small hope. I remembered having visited St Botolph's church in Aldgate earlier in the summer and had promised them then that I would go back. This seemed a good time to fulfil that promise. Rather than throw myself under the wheels of one of the innumerable buses encircling Finsbury Circus (which I could not bring myself to do) I walked to the church. On the way I tried to 'rescue' a dead leaf from being crushed under people's feet. That dead, dried up leaf was how I felt, only a late good deed could save me. I picked it up. It wasn't a leaf after all, it was a kind of moth and it was alive. As it fluttered aside it almost seemed to 'say' to me 'Fooled you!'.

A man who said he was a Samaritan crossed the road and offered me help. He said he thought I looked distressed. I thanked him and said I would be 'OK'. This event somehow made me think that I was 'on the right track' to unravelling this knot in my life.

When I reached the church I gave the money I had left to three down-and-outs who were sitting outside (much to their delight) and went in, saying that I was in the grip of the Devil, that I was a channel for evil to come into the world and that I wanted to give my life to God. A deacon inside recognized that I 'needed a priest' and directed me to the Reverend Richard Harries of Fulham. This, I felt, was a real, constructive, positive move.

When I saw Reverend Harries on the evening of Wednesday 12 September 1979 at about 10.30 p.m. I was in such a dreadful state that he would, understandably, only speak to me outside in his driveway. He gave me many words of comfort and the whole conversation was uncannily free of 'synchronistics'. I made an appointment to see him again at 10 a.m. the following morning. As we started to part I really felt that the coincidences could be beaten and that I was to be 'reprieved'. On parting he said to me, 'What was your name again?'

'Peter Chadwick', I said. It was a *slightly* windy night and we were about six or seven feet apart. He didn't quite catch what I said.

'Peter Channel?' he replied.

There was no escape. My life had caught up with me. I went back to the house into which I had just moved. I shredded some manuscripts which I had written to praise the path of Dionysus. Like a hero who had lost his nerve I thought now was the time not for pleasure and rapture but for punishment and/or repentance. A minute flake of paper fluttered to the floor having escaped the shredder. I picked it up and turned it over. The fragments of writing left made sense. It read:

39

During the rest of the evening my 'house-mate' was echoing my own actual ongoing thoughts so much in his monologues that I asked him, realizing at the time how crazy it sounded: 'Can you hear my thoughts?' He replied in the negative, smirking as he did so.

On the morning of Thursday 13 September 1979 at about 9.05 a.m. I threw myself under the wheels of a double decker bus on New Kings Road in Fulham when it was travelling at full speed between stops. 'New King's Road' was to be the road where the 'old king', Satan, was to be cast out and the 'new king', Jesus, was to come into the world to reign. I intended the wheels of the bus to go over my head, thus forcing Satan out of my mind and into oblivion and, perhaps, saving my soul.

Obviously I survived. Through brilliant driving the bus driver 'arced' the left nearside wheels over me so that only my right hand, which was down by my side at the level of my chest, was crushed by them. The wheels 'squeezed' my right shoulder and grazed my right temple, rotating my whole body as they went past. I was taken to Charing Cross Hospital by ambulance. The two ambulancemen were called Peter and Paul. Four fingers of my right hand had been squashed like sausages under a sledge hammer. (I at first took this to be my 'punishment' and initially refused to have the hand operated on.)

I was taken to a side ward, Ward J, of the orthopaedic department on the seventh floor of the hospital. But if I thought my horror was over, or would be eased, I was quite wrong.

Lying in bed in Ward J I was not even certain that the whole operation of taking me to hospital was not some kind of 'trick'. I trusted no one, felt safe nowhere. During this hot 'summer madness' in the mad hot summer of 1979 I had rewritten my entire past, seeing it as one great con trick leading up to *this*. My work in geological psychology, in which I had warned geologists not to miss synforms (Chadwick 1975a, b) – particular structures in rocks which by virtue of their trough shape are easy to disregard – became 'don't miss the sin-forms'. I had advised them to beware of illusory halo patterns (Chadwick 1977a), and this became 'beware of *my* false halo'. I had been tricked by the Devil, tricked by people, betrayed by everyone, and hated by all. I was totally alone in the universe, kicked around like Judy in a Punch and Judy show. My writing hand, the right hand, was in ribbons, punishment I thought for every Devil-inspired word I had ever penned.

The Chaplain at Charing Cross visited me regularly as I fought to retain some semblance of sanity. Intermittently I would blither out gibberish about 'the Devil' and 'the organization', that both were out to induce me to kill myself.

Then the Arch Fiend seemingly put the icing on the cake of my torment and anguish. I noticed that taps and clicks, coming from various parts of the room, were synchronized with the termination of every thought that *I feared was true*. I quickly discovered by 'talking to them' subvocally, that one tap meant 'Yes', two taps 'No'. They were always synchronized in such a way that the thought sequences they 'guided' me through always led to:

'So I must kill myself?'

'Tap.'

'Can I be reprieved?'

'Tap, tap.'

'I must do it *now*?!'

'Tap.'

'Right *now*?!!'

'Tap.'

I tried to break the windows of the side ward to cast myself down from the seventh floor. The windows would neither break nor open. The nurses hurried me into bed. Later they tried to put my right arm, bent at the elbow, into a suspended sling. As the sling swung around towards my face the linen moulded itself into the unmistakeable form of the Madonna. My blood-oozing right fist and forearm were right up inside Her. I screamed like I have never screamed before or since. They removed the sling.

The following day, after yet another tap and click reinforced sequence, I raced downstairs to throw myself under a lorry. The door at the foot of the stairs opening on to the outside wouldn't open.

But now 'the drive to suicide' was upon me. I was undeterred. I tried to plunge down the stairwell. It was too small and narrow – the architects had obviously anticipated such acts. There was nothing for it but to plunge headlong down a flight of stairs. Which I did. 'Alas' my body somersaulted in mid-air, I landed on my buttocks, slightly scratched my right toe, and bounced down the last few steps on my rear, otherwise unharmed. After this I 'knew' that suicide attempts were useless. Somehow I wasn't 'meant' to die.

As the taps and clicks continued reinforcing such thoughts as 'This is Hell. I am in torment for ever' I eventually broke down screaming. The nurses and doctors rushed into my room, realized of course that this could not go on, and I was injected with anti-psychotic drugs.

The rest is a blur, but when I regained almost full consciousness my right hand had been operated on (brilliantly) – making it in fact better eventually for writing than it had been before (!) – and my crisis and delusions had completely *vanished*. I was as sane as I had ever been and wanted to go home immediately.

Through excellent physiotherapeutic advice, plenty of exercise and through being a very fast healer I regained about 90 per cent of the function of my right hand in a few weeks and after the medication had been administered was rational, cooperative and reasonable for the whole period although conceptual thought at first was impossible. Steven Hirsch and Malcolm Weller realized that this was not a schizophrenic episode and that any conventional label to be put on it would have to carry the adjective 'atypical'. One psychiatry student to whom I 'opened up' rather more enthusiastically than to anyone else thought that my crisis would be best understood in a Jungian rather than a medical framework but begged me not to tell anyone that he had said this. (I reveal his insight now since it is highly unlikely that his identity could be traced.)

When my hand had healed and was functional I was discharged, and after discharge I eventually resolved, against all medical advice, to stop medication or to take only minute occasional doses, as, deep down, I wanted to face the world and any similar crisis again and beat the latter without pills.

As is fairly obvious from the foregoing details there is no way, I think, that I could have regained a clear and conventionally rational state of mind in 1979 without anti-psychotic drugs. The effectiveness of these drugs I found positively incredible. Personally I do not think, given the data that I was confronted with and experienced day in, day out for several months (far more than is reported here), that it was totally unreasonable to conclude at the time that some paranormal or spiritual 'force' was operating and/or using my mind/brain to manifest itself. As my friend and colleague Ivor Pleydell-Pearce said to me, 'If we'd have been in the same situation as you Pete, we might have done exactly the same thing.' I myself have also often thought of this dreadful period: 'What was I expected to think given the evidence?' It would therefore seem that whatever brain mechanism facilitates such strange manifestations (if indeed my interpretation at the time was veridical) anti-psychotic drugs block it. There may thus be only a fine line between the hallucinator and the audio-clairvoyant and, given the contribution of overactivity in dopamine pathways to schizophrenic symptomatology, it may be worth looking also at dopamine receptor densities in the brains of people who have precognitive, psychokinetic mediumistic and clairvoyant gifts. I would predict that there will be very little difference, if any.

The value of anti-psychotic drugs therefore cannot, I believe, be underestimated. They clearly operate on brain processes which are critical for the realization of unusual and, in some cases, heinous states of mind, giving calm, peace and conventional socially shareable rational thought. I would personally confirm that, whatever mavericks may say, they should be the foundation of treatment.

After discharge I was, as I say, rather rebellious nonetheless about taking tablets, and even to this day I only rely on minute doses of haloperidol.

But the price of my rebelliousness was that early in 1980 the taps and clicks returned. Other people could hear them. There was no question of their being hallucinations.[4] Once, when I was lying in bed with a girlfriend, they were rampant as my thoughts at the time were kaleidoscopic. She suddenly said, 'God! What's all those clicks?!' I replied lazily that they were 'just my clicks' to which she said that I must be 'sending out vibrations'.

The auditory code, one tap or click for 'Yes' and two for 'No', I quickly discovered was not that of an 'all-knowing' source of infinite wisdom because on one occasion the rappings tapped 'Yes' to two logically contradictory thoughts that were separated by a period of about three to four minutes. Importantly: I did not consciously engineer this 'test', I only realized the contradiction after hearing the second, single, tap. I concluded that they were paranormal psycho-acoustic or psychokinetic phenomena which correlated with *my own* unconscious belief as to whether the current thought was true or false – rather than Ouija board style 'evil spirits'. As with the (other) synchronistic experiences, they would only occur when not 'forced'. If I strongly listened out for them nothing would happen. I had to have a kind of floating attentive borderline state somewhere between hearing and listening. However, and disturbingly, one was noticeably louder – that which followed the spontaneous thought: 'I must not tell anybody about this.'

In late August 1981 the taps, clicks and other synchronistic events occurred yet again for a period of several weeks. I tried, vainly and rather stupidly, to counter them at first by deliberate thought blocking and through indulgence in various distractions. These machinations did not work. Eventually I accepted that only by opening up again to forces beyond myself would this 'wound in mind space', as I picturesquely thought of it, be healed or blocked. I put aside my scientific knowledge and with an optimistic attitude of faith, hope and reverence I sat down and began reading not the *British Journal of Psychology*, but the New Testament. Immediately the taps and clicks, although present, began as if to 'misfire'; it was as if a machine had started to malfunction. As I started to read, some of them ceased to be synchronized properly with thought termination. By the time I had read about three pages any occasional taps I heard were quite random. Essentially they had gone. The 'episode' was over.

5

THE ROUTE TO HELL
AND BACK

In the previous chapter I presented the phenomenology of mystico-delusional thinking using my own case as an example. The purpose of this chapter is to dig a little deeper than that and outline the causes and predisposing and situational factors that could have brought about such a horrific episode. The reader may well be rather bewildered and shocked by Chapter 4 and is probably asking 'How could this possibly have happened?' Here I shall attempt to go some way towards answering this question.

Although it was difficult to convey this in one chapter, the horror of my experience made watching 'The Exorcist' feel like viewing an early afternoon children's programme. 'The Exorcist', although based on fact, was fictional. My story is true. The reader merely has to read the résumé, I actually had to *live through it*. The overriding qualities in my experience were guilt, fear and the experience of being *hated* to an ineffable degree.

Psychoanalysts may lazily put this down to a form of intrapsychic projective 'trick', viz.: 'It is not I who hate, I am innocent, you hate me.' What such thinkers simply do not understand is that the inception of madness cannot be explained by a mistake of thought; it is based on real events out there in the world. These help to shift control from within to without.

From my experiential account it may seem that this crisis ensued because of the stress of developing, and then seeing the collapse of, a research programme. This is not really so. This crisis was always possible because within myself was a feeling, not so much of self-hatred, but of being a kind of symbolic vortex for the hatred of the world. Far from my research driving me mad, my research was one of the things that always kept me sane. Creative work was for me an experience of enchantment from a life of anguish.

Without wishing to bore the reader with too much detail I can say briefly that my mother was very loving for the first five years of my life and then turned on me and everyone else like a viper when she discovered that my father was having an affair with another woman. He died soon after the affair ended, at 52, and she took her revenge out on my brother and me, the children of this unfaithful man – a man of whom she never said a kind word in twenty-five years. She would call us 'bloody Chadwicks', 'no goods', 'no good rats' and such like, once asserting herself against me by kicking me between the legs. ('I wanted to make you hard.') Outside in the street she would convey the image of being a completely 'devoted Mum' (which in many ways she was) but inside the locked front door she was, alas, a woman who was *totally incapable of loving anyone for what they were*. One had always to be better, to strive, to improve, to 'get on'. This did terrible damage. By the time I was 22 I felt totally hated for myself alone. My whole psychological survival depended on continually 'improving'. And when I 'achieved' I always felt that she would somehow take the credit. ('I should never have *sent* you to university', etc.)

Added to the effects of this dreadfully unhappy, bitter, complaining, Victorian woman, who, to give her credit, would from time to time turn into a radiant loving angel to ease our wounds, was the general despite from masculine 'real men' of the First XV rugby team variety, particularly in Manchester, the West Country and Glasgow, for the soft empathic 'feminine' personality that I continually presented to the world. In these bastions of masculine purity and 'pansie-bashing' a gentle, tender man was like a butterfly among bulls. My good qualities were bad and my strengths were weaknesses. Like Alan Turing, the freedom and challenge of science and the beauty and ecstacy of sex were my validating obsessions and soporifics. Creative work and loving girls kept me stable and sane, allowed me to express myself, and allowed me to feel accepted for what I was.

However, by 1978 and 1979 I felt most at ease only when I was with other 'battered butterflies', homosexual and bisexual men. Although I am no more homosexual than the average man I only really felt safe away from the gender-role stereotyped and the spartan, stoic, self-deniers, yet always knew that they were the models of conventional Judaeo-Christian virtue. In my delusion about 'the organization' its members were all white Caucasian, staid and stolid, conventionally gender-roled, tough-minded heterosexuals, steeped in gossip, with not a trace of dirty laundry and who slept between cotton (not satin) sheets. Far from this 'organization' being a projection of myself it was a fair replica of the people who *really had* caused me most trouble in my development.

I had been fighting an Old Testament 'thou-shalt-not' version of Judaeo-Christian puritanism all my life. With the collapse of the Borderline manuscript I let the right-minded decent people of Manchester, the West Country and Glasgow have their prosecutionary say. The result was a total imploding of the little self-esteem I then had. God would triumph and the Devil would take the hindmost. In the end I had only one chance left to save my despised sensual and epicurean soul: I had to present my head to the wheels of a double decker bus – packed with gender-role stereotyped puritans all with smirks on their faces and seated as if in church listening to a sermon about the evils of the silken way. Such are the fruits of hatred, criticism, violence and negative thinking.

MAGIC AND MADNESS

The developmental aspect to my own crisis makes any suggestion that psychosis can be totally explained at a biochemical level quite ridiculous. It is also evident that there is method and sanity in madness. Real events often act as a trigger, not fantasies. Remarkable things really do happen. What are we to make of these strange coincidences? Perhaps there *is* 'ESP leakage' in madness as suggested by Toronto parapsychologist George Owen (Brian Josephson, personal communication, 7 September 1989). The striking coincidences act as the real sharp evil gems which destroy one, but between their scratches and cuts are an entire host of much weaker 'coincidences' which are more the yield of genuinely psychotic thought but which act as kindlers or as a kind of high-pitched scream which is the music to the ongoing stream of slashes and lacerations.

Of course two events, close together in space and time, are almost irresistibly connected in a causal way even by normal people. This is the 'false connection' of Koffka (1935) and of Nisbett and Ross (1980), and the 'magical thinking' of Johnson-Laird and Wason (1977).[1] Paranoid people, for example, when sitting in a pub, often assume that if they say something and a group of people sitting across the room happen to burst out laughing, then the two separate events are causally connected.

A one-off event of this kind is easily 'laughed off' but when events of this kind occur continually one begins to afford them a special reality status of their own, as I did, and catastrophically, this seems to make them even more frequent. It is impossible to assess statistically whether or not such trains of re-occurrence are beyond chance probability. In my own experience I intuitively thought that they were (and in objective tests my own intuitive statistical judgement turns out to be really quite good), but of course this can never be proved. In my Borderline crisis I was continuously sifting intuitively 'remarkable' from 'mundane' coincidences and clear from poor overhearings, and attempting to act only on the most 'striking' data. But whether this crisis was a 'paranormal attack' or a product of my own vastly enlivened cognitive processing I shall never be one hundred per cent sure. One point, however, needs to be made: when I tried to relive the crisis in the summer of 1989, as a control experiment, I could pick up only one to three striking coincidences, at most, each day.

The 'dovetailing of contexts' which I experienced is really very common

46

in psychosis. People frequently make statements similar to that which the psychotic is thinking, or say things which are quite reasonable 'replies', partly because the lowering of the threshold of consciousness in madness makes one sensitive to the associative connections and relational schematic processes which go on beneath overt speech. In this way the psychotic is very sensitive to other people's unconscious or preconscious processing and not only can 'read' people very closely, but can, at times, predict them. Schizotypals and other borderline personalities also have this (often disturbing) power to a lesser degree (see, for example, Claridge 1985: 172). Although this in no way explains *all* the coincidences I suffered, this kind of capacity also helps to provide the bizarre cement or matrix to the grains of genuinely uncanny happenings.

SITUATIONAL FACTORS

Moving from an intellectually rich university environment to a working-class district was very stressful. This should not be underestimated. The life change made me feel chronically uncertain and insecure. I did not know 'the rules'.

Using Selfridge's (1955) example of the importance of context in identification:

$$THE\ CAT$$

where the same shape means something quite different in different contexts (see also Neisser 1967: 47), it was as if I previously had been an 'H' and was now an 'A'. In a sense I was 'the same' person yet I was changed by my totally different environment.

Gradually the underpinning processes and procedures that mediated my behaviour were undermined. Expectations were repeatedly refuted, for example: when one man said 'I can't write' I rapidly discovered that it did *not* mean that he could not write like a D. H. Lawrence, it meant that he literally could not write at all. When I said to someone that I was always writing because I was after 'the answers', he replied in all sincerity that, when he was at school, 'You could get books with the answers at the back; why don't you get one of those books?'

From being regarded as an exciting and stimulating person to talk to I discovered that many 'ordinary people' actually found me *boring* to talk to. My whole programming was changed. Various if–then statements were no longer applicable. A certain facial expression on another's part no longer meant 'Well that's a tough proposition to swallow'. It now meant 'I can't understand what you're talking about'.

I could no longer happily and easily anticipate what would get a conversation started. The cognitive style appropriate to my new environment was not one that emphasized principles, ideas and concepts but one that emphasized anecdote, narrative and description. Interaction changed from being dialogue characterized to being dualogue or monologue characterized. I sensed a distinct unwillingness on the part of so-called 'real people' to listen with the same attentiveness as I; they 'already knew'.

Ideas did not get an airing. There was no opportunity to internalize the jogs, jolts, blocks and refutations that one usually receives in a university environment. My cognitive style changed from self-correcting, self-monitoring and conversation seeking to self-satisfying, confirming and conversation avoiding.

My rule system for interaction no longer worked. Instead of negotiating a topic in discovery fashion by small steps, the system necessary and expected seemed to be based on a rule of mutual self-assertion – as if the implicit communication in discussion was 'here are my opinionated views, now give me yours'.

And yet if all I had had to do was to move along existing dimensions (e.g. from cautious to risky or from giving two-sided arguments to one-sided arguments) or if I had had merely to explain myself a little more slowly and clearly, there would have been no problem. The whole system I had in my mind was, however, 'all wrong' in this context. There was no consistency as I had known it. This was a 100 IQ environment. A different world with *its own* situationally appropriate knowledge structure and behavioural style. One could not merely change the values of the parameters in the equations; different equations were needed. As I was far too busy with my research I was really unprepared for all of this and I gradually withdrew from everyday socializing as I found it too stressful and boring.

MYSTICISM AND DELUSION

As Lenz (1979, 1983) has argued: the early stages of delusion may be characterized by 'super-rational' or mystical thinking such as I experienced (Table 5.1). There seems little doubt that mystical and delusional thinking are, or can be, related. This is a theme that will be mentioned a number of times in this book. Although my 1979 experience 'turned bad' eventually I did find peace and thus, in my own way, found God, by giving myself over into the hands of positive, life-enhancing and loving influences which I sincerely perceived as coming from beyond myself.

My suicide attempts in 1979 were unnecessary and were not really required of me. But the way my life has evolved since, make Jesus's words ring true: that 'he who loses his life for my sake shall find it'. Since September 1979 I have gradually climbed out of my spiritual pit, found love and the capacity to love and generally fashioned my life

Table 5.1 Similarities between the experience of mystics and religious leaders and those of patients in the early stages of delusion (after Lenz 1979: 189, Table 1).

Irrational experience	Patients' expression	Mystics also reporting this experience*
Abnormal feeling of importance	I have reached my true self. I am enlightened, chosen, renewed. I am united with God. I am a new messiah or saint. I can see perfectly clearly. I am inspired I am saved	Ign, Jo, Ther, Zen
Delusions	I have had visions, received signs	Ign, Ther, Zen
Suddenness and passivity	It happened suddenly. It overcame me	Ign, Jo, Ther, Zen
Experience of mission	I have been given a mission. I must make a sacrifice. I take the sufferings of others upon myself. I chastize myself	Ign, Jo, Ther, Zen
Polarity of moods	I am overjoyed but it is not an earthly joy. I have sinned against God. I am in the power of the Devil. I am the active element of destructive powers	Ign, Jo, Ther, Zen
Suspension of feeling for time and space	I was not conscious of time and space	Ther, Zen
Feeling of shame	I am ashamed	Ther

*Ign = Ignatius Loyola
Jo = John of God
Ther = Theresa of Avila
Zen = Zen Buddhists

into an effective and useful one. I have no doubt of the existence of God.

The whole experience, but particularly the loving way in which it was resolved in 1981, obviously is the source of the generally positive contextual approach adopted in this book. It also sensitized me to the possible mystical precursors and accompaniments of the delusional state and to equally possible, although controversial, paranormal accompaniments. Psychotics often report thought transference and, as argued by Eisenbud (1972), Lewis (1956), Telling (1928) and Ullman (1973), this may not always, or entirely, be delusional but in some instances may be a genuinely veridical experience. Schizotypals probably are more holistic than analytic, and holistic personalities have indeed been shown to be better at ESP

(Busby 1967). My own experience has therefore made me very tolerant and open-minded about the reports of previously psychotic people and has convinced me that to fully understand psychosis we may perhaps have to have some changes in our current ways of thinking.

The early stages of the episode described in Chapter 4 may remind some readers of the Buddhist concept of Satori. This is a state of consciousness beyond duality, discrimination and differentiation. It is apparently the beginning rather than the end of Zen training. Some practitioners of Zen are also said to have developed clairvoyant, precognitive, telepathic and psychokinetic powers although they must never use them to further their 'self'. An interpretation of my altered state in Buddhist terms might therefore be fruitful. The relevance of this approach seems to be particularly striking in the light of these remarks by Gabb (1944): 'All Enlightenment is gradual, but its eruption into consciousness may be sudden in cases where its appearance has been obstructed by an over-active intellect or excess of sensuality.' This could well have been written of me. Similarly, Kovel (1977: 152) writes:

> The transcendent state potentially permits a spectrum of experiential states to occur. At one end is the attainment of the blissful state of reunion and unity; while the other faces the terror of repressed demonic forces. The situation is very much the same as having a good or bad drug trip.

Zaehner (1957) is cutting; he writes that true mystical experiences lead to 'sobriety' (of course), false ones to 'drunkenness' and are a form of madness, specifically mania. Zaehner, however, continually tries to make absolutist claims about the validity and meaning of different types of mystical state but simultaneously has to admit, along the lines of Muslim doctrine, that the *real* test is the effect it eventually has on the person's life. He also has to admit that different types of mystical experience, for all their pitfalls, may yet heighten spiritual sensitivity. Personally I doubt that we should assume that tranquillity and serenity are always the affective characteristics of the 'true' mystical experience or that God will only touch us if we come to Him from a spotlessly clean path.

In 1979 I was desperately searching beyond rationality. My social situation and the state of mind my life had led me to produced an experience of torment comparable to that of the Zen student trapped by multiple koans, such as the famous 'what is the sound of one hand clapping?' Humphreys (1986) states that the Zen hopeful has to need Enlightenment and illumination like a man stuck underwater needs air. With this I would concur. One has to be *squeezed* into the mystical state by one's thinking, being unable to turn either left or right, either up or down. Only when there is nowhere else to go, when every rational route is blocked, does one discover the Borderline/Satori. It is nonsense to argue that the experience is false if it is accompanied by exhilaration.

Buddhist and related literature therefore certainly 'talk the same language' as I, but there are differences. On page 46 of Humphreys (1986) we find,

> Zen is therefore a matter of experience . . . it has a subject but no object. It is impersonal, undirected, purposeless. There is no reference in the vast literature of recorded satori to union with the Beloved, or to union at all. Zen is a zip-fastener between the opposites, it passes and they are no more.

For me there was an experience of access, union, of self-loss, of renewal *from* somewhere, perhaps someone. Although there was Enlightenment there was enrichment from a source. My experience therefore had both Zen and Christian flavour.

Although we see discrepancies, then, from the satori experience there are parallels with the impression of 'dual unity' described by Grof (1975: 178–9) as a feature of the LSD experience, i.e. the paradoxical coexistence of a sense of unity with that of simultaneous awareness of one's own identity. Transpersonal experiences are also described as effects of LSD: the transcendence of distinctions such as self/other, past/present/future and time/space. There can be spatial expansion of consciousness, temporal expansion and experiential extension beyond the framework of objective reality.

Given the association of such experiences with delusion this provides sustenance to Claridge's belief (1978, 1985: 183) that the LSD experience is a closer model of schizophrenia than is amphetamine psychosis.[2]

THE PSYCHOLOGY OF 'COSMIC CONSCIOUSNESS'

Given these various parallels, what has mental science to say of these uncanny experiences?

Within psychology, extant theories of the middle ground have, for the most part, not attempted to encompass such experiences and phenomena except to the extent of regarding them as totally subjective at best and pathognomic at worst. They have been likened to Freud's 'oceanic feeling' and to be merely manifestations of regression (e.g. The Group for the Advancement of Psychiatry's 1976 report on mysticism – devastatingly criticized and shown, in effect, to be worthless by Deikmann 1977). Deikmann (1966, 1977) and Ornstein (1986) do not take such a dismissive view of their significance.

Another exception is the theoretical superstructure developed by Jung under the heading of Analytical Psychology. In a number of places above I have raised Jungian concepts and ideas. Jung was not naive, of course, to the phenomena one encounters in altered states of consciousness. His alas rather nebulous ideas have, however, been given substance and form and have been developed by Progoff (1973). Progoff discusses the kind of experience I had in terms of 'a lowering of the mental level'. His description of this state clearly maps one-to-one onto my own experience and so will be quoted at some length. This 'lowering', he says,

> Opens the very deep stratum of the Self, the Psychoid, to whatever factors are present in the continuum of the Self. In this condition the psychoid level of the psyche is open to influence of every possible kind. It is accessible to whatever forces and factors happen to be present at a given moment in the continuum of the Self, whether these are factors operating within one's own psyche, within the psyche of others, or whether they are forces of any kind active in the universe.
>
> Considering this, we recognize that in opening the individual at the psychoid level, the process of mental *abaissement* makes a person psychically vulnerable at the same time that it greatly enlarges the range of his psychic possibilities. The specific effect upon him depends on the nature of the other factors and influences that are present in the continuum of the Self within the range of his personal atmosphere. They may be affirmative or negative; beneficial or destructive; they may assist the life of the person, or they may distract from it by giving false leadings and confusions.

Progoff goes on:

> Each experience has to be appraised on its own merits, especially since its effects upon an individual depends a great deal upon the state of inner development within that person. In principle, the factors that exert influence during the condition of *abaissement* are of the greatest diversity. They may range from petty subjective anxieties to large visionary awarenesses of prophetic scope. They may reflect some small cranny of an individual microcosm or they may reflect the large wisdom of the macrocosm. Any of them may be reflected at the psychoid level when *abaissement* takes place.
>
> (Progoff 1973: 113–14)

Again on page 115 we find:

> When the 'lowering of the mental level' increases the sensitivity of the psyche to the reflections of the pattern [of being], the individual becomes capable of perception or cognition that goes beyond space and time in our usual causalistic sense.

Progoff interprets such events in one's life as the experience of an archetypal symbol. This:

Results in a sense of relationship to the interior workings of life, a sense of participation in the movements of the cosmos. The individual at such moments feels his individuality to be exalted, as though he were transported for an instant to a higher dimension of being. Clearly the situation that is established when an archetype becomes active in human life is more than personal. It is felt to have what Jung speaks of as 'cosmic character' and this is derived from the fact, as he says, that it appears in the individual as a 'complementary equivalent of the "outside world"'. It is experienced with a great intensity, and it brings an awareness of a special light, a numinosity carrying a sense of transcendent validity, authenticity and essential divinity.

We may not agree with Progoff's interpretation (that is, if we can understand it); indeed, the concept of archetype is generally rejected by most academic psychologists through its untestability. However, the important feature of these quotes is that Jung and Progoff *are taking such experiences seriously* and attempting to understand them in terms of a theoretical structure which can also be deployed to understand the less portentous experiences of the average person in everyday life. In those terms the experiences of the normal, the mystic, the borderline psychotic and the psychotic may exist on a graded continuum. This is an invitation to us all to be accepting, tolerant, patient and, most important of all, to listen to those who report the uncanny.

Jung's and Pauli's concepts of synchronicity and of the archetype stand outside of contemporary science. My approach, however, is to build on current scientific theories and use current scientific techniques – pathetic though we may feel they may be in the face of the task that confronts us – to eventually reach an understanding of the experiences that I, and the other people reported in these case studies, had. In doing so we may eventually up-date Jungian ideas and incorporate them into a coherent scientific framework.[3]

In this sense, I am rejecting the Buddhist advice not to try to understand the Tao but to just 'be' with it. I am rejecting also the Christian's advice to revere faith more than understanding. Indeed, as Josephson (1977) argues, a limited conception of God may well come within the purview of the theoretical accounts of modern physics in the foreseeable future. The next great unification may well be that of science and religion (Josephson 1987).

FORGIVENESS

The final resolution of my crisis was brought about essentially by an act of surrender. I was beaten; I asked God for help and he seemed to reach down, put a hand on my shoulder and say 'OK lad, you've had enough'.

When one sees oneself as having been *unfairly* treated over a long period this evokes immense anger, and the 'kindling' produced by such sustained anger can dangerously weaken the very fabric of one's psyche. (The importance of perceived 'unfairness' in psychosis is also mentioned in Curran *et al.* (1976).) Indeed, suppressed anger has been linked with psychokinetic rappings by Watson (1974) and with Gilles de la Tourette's syndrome by Shapiro and Shapiro (1968) and Prabhakaran (1970), a very mild form of which I also suffered for a time – although I chose to omit this in Chapter 4. There is no question that what certainly seemed to me to be the spiritual solution to my anguish in 1981 has enabled me to find the necessary forgiveness in my heart without which a sustained recovery, I believe, would have been impossible. One has to see the part one played *oneself* in one's own persecution and maltreatment. It is not true that 'everybody else is to blame' and in madness, far from denying this, one eventually faces it to a greater or lesser extent. I am naturally an androgynous man who generally relates slightly better to women than to 'regular guys'. In expressing that self so obviously and blatantly in chauvinist machismo cultures I was basically risking the wrath of the world down on my own head – which in a way is what actually eventually happened.

In seeing the way psychologically critical life events involve *interactions* between self and other and seriously involve one's *own* input, not the evil of others, the path is open to peace within. This is so. The world inside my head in 1979 was like the Second World War; now (slightly amusing though this may sound) it is like a meadow in spring. For people who have experienced sufferings similar to mine, this spiritual aspect to recovery from psychosis should never be ignored.

CONCLUDING REMARKS

My own case, I feel, solidly demonstrates that mental illness can only be understood and treated within a multilevel, multifactorial framework.

Cognitively I was easily distractible but, as is often the case with such people, rich in ideational fluency. My first PhD (in Geology) was a condensed 900-page three-volume tome researched and written in only two years. For years my associative flexibility worked to my advantage ('good idea Pete' my colleagues would often say) but under the stress of hunger and of my situation the looseness became maladaptive.

My home environment was highly critical and also characterized by massive emotional overinvolvement. (When I first made (unsuccessful) moves to get married (at 21) my mother reacted with ferocity and very seriously threatened to kill herself unless I dropped the girl concerned, which, wretchedly, I did.)

At a social level I was a complete misfit and had no support whatever –

no money, no home, no career, no future, no security. Keeping going under these conditions is quite difficult.

Spiritually I felt totally contemptible. Both masculine men *and* sometimes feminine women had posed as spiritually superior to me all my life. My life was peppered, here and there, with Roman Catholic girlfriends to whom I related not as people but as human bars of soap or detergent ('mind washers') to cleanse myself of my feeling of inner shamefulness. Needless to say they were all non-smokers, did not wear backless dresses, and did not take sugar.

On this issue Roy Schenk writes that 'an attitude of moral superiority is the worst form of violence that people can do to each other' (Schenck 1982: 36). He also cites Langdon Gilkey (1966) who was writing of a Japanese concentration camp experience: 'that sharpest of all hostilities of one human being to another – that nonacceptance which springs from moral disapproval and so from a feeling of moral superiority' (p. 172). Such behaviour is very much the fruits also of puritanism and of the (compensatory) *religion* of macho masculinity.

It is difficult to comment on genetic factors. There is no history of psychosis in my family as far as I know, but there is a history of creative achievement. The cognitive processing in psychosis and creative work may thus be equivalent (Keefe and Magaro 1980). Creativity was the solution to my feelings of spiritual devastation. If I could communicate my own unique vision, then that at least would validate my identity: I was 'good for something'. That something was *ideas*. I could also be myself with women, although their spiritual superiority ('I'm his better half'), as I say, was at times overbearing. (Schenk's important book (1982) on male oppression attacks this assumed spiritual superiority of women head on and discusses its occasional destructive consequences at length.)

In 1978 I also discovered, on the floors of West End discos, that I could fully be myself and express myself through *dance*. This was really quite an incredible experience. After years of dry, positivistic, mechanistic, empirical work I put colour, rhythm and beat into my life by dancing. My movements were like those of a flower unfolding. I had to express *beauty*, a beauty within – almost totally crushed and despised by puritans – unfurled exquisitely on those dance floors. The power of beauty galvanized every sinew of my being. Gay men, renowned for their dancing ability, would actually come up to me after I had left the floor and compliment me on my 'fantastic' dancing, saying that I should 'go professional', etc. Enchanting lesbians would dance beside me and at the end of the music would leave with words such as 'thank you, that was beautiful'. Dancing was so healing. Never was I more fully myself than when I was on those floors.[4]

It is perhaps worth finishing these two chapters on my own case with a sobering thought. Even though my own experience was bizarre and spectacular it is worth mentioning that in psychiatric terms I was not really very ill. At all times I was continually fighting to make sense of my experiences and these efforts at integration are clearly a sign of health. Although experiences such as mine may capture the reader's imagination and attention, it is the mute, still, withdrawn, emotionally flat psychotic who really most deserves our sympathy and needs our help. I was back to normality in a flash once the medication took effect; those people never get better – and they may soon be all cast into our midst to fend for themselves. They will be lucky to stay alive, let alone write books.

6

ALANA J

'I'm dancing as fast as I must'

INTRODUCTION AND FIRST 'EPISODE'

In Chapter 1 I referred caustically to the negative bias in research on schizophrenia which propels researchers forwards in the hunt for the schizophrenic deficit. Claridge (1985: 152–3) also bemoans this sad state of affairs. There is however a parallel negative bias in research on the, perhaps related, area of sexual variations. I shall deliberately attempt to counteract this bias in this study of a schizoaffective infantilist and fetishist: Alana J.

Psychoanalytic investigations suggest a borderline, narcissistic or out-rightly psychotic level of personality functioning in sexual variants of gender disturbed and/or fetishistic orientation (e.g. Bak 1953; Lewis 1963; Ovesey and Person 1978; Payne 1939), findings consonant with the results of some psychometric research (Taylor and McLachlan 1963; Bentler and Prince 1970a, b) but not all – see, for example, the generally low psychoticism scores reported in Beatrice (1985).

The direction of causality problem, however, is a very serious one in this context – for example, when neuroticism scores have to be interpreted or when scores on paranoid sensitivity are assessed. (Note the total neglect of this vital issue in Beatrice (1985).)

Although there is much search for high scoring patterns on scales reflecting pathology, there is a singular absence of investigations into the intelligence, creativity and imaginativeness, abstract thinking capacities, vitality, daring and capacities for pleasure of the variant groups, all of which, I think, would repay enquiry. In this case study we shall therefore 'turn the coin over' and examine the other side of the link between sexual variation and psychotic functioning.

It frequently is said in the literature of human sciences that fetishism is virtually unknown in women. Gosselin and Wilson (1980), for example, base their entire study of this variation on men. This, despite the obvious pleasure women obtain from wearing clothes in fur, taffeta, chiffon, silk and satin. The intensity of the experience may be less than the male equivalent but a sensuous delight in the caress of such materials obviously is so endemic in the female sex that nobody would ever consider that there was anything 'abnormal' about it.

Alana's fetishism was more ostentatiously sexual. She was, from her earliest years, stimulated by transparent plastic baby pants and nappies. The reader may initially find this rather amusing and indeed she expected laughter and ridicule from people were it ever to become known. It was her great secret, kept from everyone, including the psychiatrists and social workers who tried to help her. Unknown to all, Alana would masturbate with a plastic sheet wrapped around her hips and buttocks. Later she did this while wearing plastic incontinence pants, a nappy, and sometimes surrounded by transparent PVC clothes. At other times she would at night fantasize about a warm-loving older woman who she liked to think would 'mummy' her.

Alana had very strong lesbian tendencies. She had been raped three times as a teenager and every boy she went out with seemed only interested in her 'for sex'. This had not helped her to realize her, undoubtedly present, heterosexual capacity. Nonetheless she had felt a conscious sexual attraction to older women ever since the age of 4. Alana's greatest pleasure was to be bathed and powdered by an older woman, have a nappy and plastic pants put on, and then be allowed to suckle at the woman's (preferably large) breasts. She had longed for this since childhood but only eventually realized it at the age of 37, many years after her episodes.

Alana described her first 'breakdown' as a kind of anxiety attack at the age of 23. She cried uncontrollably for a week. One problem was her hair, which had been very long and she had had it cut short. She was very upset by the result: it made her look like a man. (Looking and feeling rather like a man was a long-standing problem for her right up to the time we first met.) Another problem was that she was in love with another woman but could not make a sexual relationship with her. She believes that the frustration of both these problems and of her sexual situation in general was what made her break down. She had a professional job at the time and was referred by her doctor to a psychiatrist – but she did not go back after the first meeting because she thought the really important issues were her fetishism and lesbianism and she was not prepared to discuss those desires with him.

Her first psychotic experience was in 1974 when she was 26. Before that, she describes her life as having been terrible. She used to lose her temper frequently, get drunk (usually on whisky) and cry a great deal. Anything she did not enjoy made her feel that she was wasting time. She could not make friends or communicate with people and she wished desperately that she could have confidence and be an interesting person. The only thing that really gave her pleasure was training to be a dancer.

Eventually she found she could not sleep and became very depressed. She jumped out of the first-floor window of her flat ('as a cry for help') but that act really, she felt, brought on the psychosis. She then started noticing colours and felt that they had some meaning. Her mind was racing: 'There were too many thoughts in my head,' she said. Everything that happened had a meaning; she could not eat and her thoughts kept 'going round and round'. She visited her GP who prescribed soluble aspirin plus something 'to relax her stomach' with the aim of enabling her to eat.

She started to think that she was being followed and watched. When a car went past, especially if it was red, it had been sent 'to keep an eye on her'. All this time she was 'madly in love' with her dance teacher. A piece of lemon skin in a glass had been left by this teacher as a message that she'd be back to see her – because the skin 'reminded her of the sun'(?). Everything David Hamilton said on the radio was directed at her and all the songs had meaning relevant to her situation. Then the TV programmes and the contents of *Woman's Own* also became directed at her. She was convinced she was going to go on Broadway.

Despite all this she did not go into hospital and had no treatment (her mother, not entirely unwisely I think, put everything down to malnutrition) but the strange experiences nonetheless subsided after 6–8 weeks. Then she made a critical decision: to give herself *one year* to somehow 'make it' as a dancer. Eleven months later another episode overwhelmed her.

BACKGROUND

The story so far is fairly standard. Every psychiatrist knows of the high incidence of sexual problems and variations in people diagnosed as schizophrenic or schizoaffective, etc. All of Alana's experiences thus reported also fit easily into established categories of 'delusions of persecution', 'ideas of reference' and 'interpenetration of thoughts'.

The superficial impression of Alana herself may seem to the reader to be one of low self-confidence, inability to communicate and poor social skills, temper tantrums, unrealistic dreams, drunkenness, 'perversion' and madness. It would be all too easy to view her in that way, elementary and effortless to weave interpretations from her life history data which would present her as an inadequate fantasizer. Yet having known her for seven years (I met her at about the same time as I met David B, with whom she was friendly) that is not, for me, the story that emerges at all.

When I first met this young lady I found that, when she was relaxed and at ease, she was an extremely entertaining conversationalist with a considerable knowledge of dancing and the world of dance and a remarkable aesthetic sense. We went together to see a documentary film about the working life of models and her comments on it revealed tremendous sensitivity to the models' non-verbal behaviour and a finely tuned sense of what is good art and what is not. I rapidly realized that this girl's failures to communicate were due to mixing with people who were completely unsuited to her. She would really have been much better off in a school of art.

Convinced that, as with Shafiq, I was dealing with a very talented person I gave her the Wechsler Adult Intelligence Scale. She scored no less than 146 on verbal ability and 114 on the performance scale, with an overall IQ of 133. And this was an ex-hotel chambermaid. After Thurstone's finding that verbal fluency correlates 0.69 with full-scale IQ score (Thurstone and Thurstone 1941) it was not surprising to find that Alana obtained the second highest fluency score in the experimental investigation out of a sample of 59 people. (She was only beaten by a modern languages graduate.) This test involved generating as many words as one could think of that began with a particular letter. Later, to check that the result was not a fluke, I tested her again against myself on letters other than the one used in the experiment. She out-performed me every time.

Psychopathologists may expect me to state that Alana's thinking was 'disordered' or confused. On the contrary, she demonstrated exceptional clarity of mind and excellent planning and organizational ability. One social worker who was friendly with her even repeatedly took advice from her and would praise her 'remarkable powers of common sense'. This high ability had not been entirely dormant in her earlier years. Throughout her time at school she had always come top or near the top in history, art, geography and biology (but was totally nonplussed by physics and mathematics). Generally, however, she had found her school rigid, puritanical and authoritarian, obviously totally unsuited to her liberal-minded intuitive and divergent thinking personality. She left with only two 'O' levels.

It is clear that Alana was not only intelligent in the conventional sense but that she also had high 'bodily kinaesthetic' intelligence in the sense of Gardner (1985). Although she had talent as a dancer her real wish was to be a choreographer. A very secondary wish – not uncommon among bisexual girls – was to be a stripper. Once she gave me a display in her flat of one of her erotic routines. It was quite remarkable. I sat through the entire performance with a solid erection.

She had been keen on modern dancing and ballet many years before it became fashionable, and she had excellent dress sense. She attempted to write a lesbian novel and created some passages of literary merit but could not, alas, achieve integration, in book form, of her ideas.

As a child she had been told that she ought to become a comedienne. Indeed, she could create hilariously funny dance routines with the same skill that she could generate erotic ones and she also had an enormously amusing repertoire of voices and faces. Everyone who knew her liked her; of her, one man said 'Alana can talk to anyone, she's a gem'. Her lover, an older woman, described her as 'a sweet and loving girl'.

Given this very positive picture of Alana, how did she stumble across the psychotic state?

Although we must assume that Alana had a long dormant capacity for psychosis, the great source of what we might call 'tonic' stress in her life was her mother. She was a small, rather tight-lipped woman with a 'strong' personality who rather dominated her husband (a warm, caring man) and had very fixed ideas about right and wrong, good and bad. She once said to me, with almost a threatening expression, 'I'm a Big Royalist and a Big Tory.' She was very much 'against blacks', thought Mary Whitehouse was 'a wonderful woman' and if any sexually tinged scene appeared on television would complain vociferously. She always preferred Alana's sister, and indeed showed this in no uncertain terms in her will.

Alana's unpredictability and disobedience was an anathema to her. Alana had very much a mind of her own, was perhaps best described as 'a raver' in her earlier years and was not mindful of the Victorian values that her mother prized so highly. Her sister (Barbara) was a very hard-working girl, a teacher, who, although not totally averse to crossing swords with their mother, was not really the kind of person who would follow Alana into the (then) underground world of lesbianism (1971–) and, dangerously, amphetamine 'pill popping' (1966–7). Her persistence and grit was much to her mother's liking. Generally when the family went out on walks, Alana would walk with their father and Barbara with their mother.

Alana's mother explained: 'I used to give Alana and Barbara a job to do and I'd come back five minutes later to find that Alana had gone off somewhere and left Barbara to do the job on her own.'

Interestingly, one summer, when Alana was about 7 and her sister 6, Alana had come out of the garden and told her mother: 'Barbara's dead!' Her mother had rushed out, found it was untrue, and gone 'absolutely hysterical' at Alana's deception.

There was not a single point or aspect of life on which Alana and her mother saw eye to eye. The only thing they had in common was that they were both talented artists. So 'strong' and immovable was her mother that Alana reacted frequently by erupting into temper tantrums and screaming rages which, of course, only made matters worse in the long term. Of her, her mother said to me: 'She's given me Hell!' Alana had even once stuck a fork in her mother's arm.

The tapestry we are weaving so far depicts a colourful creative Alana, very much of Dionysian spirit, pitched against a stoical Apollonian Victorian mother whose mind was dominated by the protestant ethic. From afar off that was how it seemed. But Alana was not all peaches and cream. Like David B, and possibly Shafiq, there was a definite problem in what I referred to earlier as 'behavioural modulation'. She would move from being 'very sweet' into a state of barely controllable fury after taking only a few light and rapid steps through a narrow middle ground. I saw Alana's temper a number of times: it was indeed quite terrifying – and could reach frightening proportions in a few tens of seconds. Similarly, she would show high motivation and enthusiasm about a task or topic and then, almost in an instant, lose interest completely and become apathetic and lethargic. Her life seemed to be an oscillation between passion and depression, between believing what she wanted to believe (especially about the chances of a loved woman reciprocating her affections) and plunging into a state where she felt totally unlovable, pathetic and useless. This modulation problem was the source of her unpredictability and must have evoked great discontent in her mother who, by her style, was totally ill-equipped to handle her.

Alana said that she had never felt loved by her mother, whom she perceived mainly as a restrictor of her spontaneity and imagination. From her sexual variation it is possible to infer that she *had* felt loved as an infant but that this love had been withdrawn as she gained more independence. The birth of her sister, eighteen months her junior, had probably not helped in this respect. Her fetish for plastic, which apparently another (male) member of her family has, was probably genetically 'prepared'. Fetishes are not random, they tend to be for soft, smooth, shiny materials, perhaps reminiscent of skin and glistening bright eyes.

Her mother was not a warm woman. Alana does not remember being cuddled even once by her mother, and when Alana's father died of heart trouble in 1976 Alana felt totally alone.

She had moved to London in 1971 to join 'the gay scene'. (Her mother had reacted with total silence when she admitted her lesbianism to the family, although her father was more sympathetic. Her sister had said, 'You always think you're the only one who's got problems.') Alas Alana was looking for a warm feminine lover but she describes the scene she found as full of feminists, intellectuals and dykes. Trousers, shirts, jumpers and short haircuts abounded on cold-faced, bitter, word-spinning women whereas she sought and craved a human, caring woman in dresses, high heels and perfume. Such a person could not be found.

She did have a relationship with a woman of similar age to herself, but this woman, although she undoubtedly loved Alana, was highly critical of her and emotionally overinvolved with her. The relationship seriously damaged Alana's already fragile self-esteem and, she believes, 'softened her up' for madness.

From talking to Alana about the way this came about and from discussions with other contacts it seems that continued criticism and emotional overinvolvement and overprotectiveness are particularly pathogenic because of the emotively significant *implicit communications* involved rather than because they are 'cognitively confusing' as suggested by MacCarthy *et al.* (1986). These implicit communications in a sense take us from Leff, who has done most work on this combination of stresses (see Chapter 12), to Laing. Unconsciously the identified patient is receiving the messages: 'I am in a position to repeatedly criticize you, I am your superior, I am right, you are wrong. You are the "looked after" one, I am the "looker after". I am dominant, you are submissive, I talk, you listen, I am adult-like, you are child-like, I know what's best for you, you do not, I can deal with life, I can face life, you cannot. I am masterful, competent, you are not.' In the extreme this becomes: 'You are my punch bag and my looked-after lump of custard pie. As long as you are around I will be right, adult, in charge, competent, able to get by in life, "good and right". I will be the willer, you the willed. Thus I exist, am substantial, you do not, are empty, implodable. I am, you are not.' Clearly such behaviour could come from a range of sources, not only the family or the mother. I have known people suffer such 'psychotogenic' stresses in offices, in the army, the police force, at school, etc. (It is time really that theorizing ceased being 'locus obsessed' in this respect, and became process oriented. In other words, in this context, it is time it grew up and 'left home'.)

In Alana's case the source of this so-called 'high EE' or high 'expressed emotion' was her girlfriend. The overall effect was apparently a great increase in 'nervousness' and feelings of inner emptiness. In despair she took more and more, over time, to her fetishism in which she indulged with great guilt and which induced considerable subclinical paranoia. She was not able to practise it very often and her frustration and loneliness eventually built up to an intolerable level.

One ray of light in her life was her (for once) sustained love of dancing and of her dance teacher – a very creative, feminine woman who, apart from her rather small breasts, was everything Alana had ever dreamed of and ever dreamed of being. It was in this context of a history of puritanical authoritarian restriction, and a number of 'phasic' kindling stresses[1] – such as rejection, sexual passion and frustration, guilt, paranoia and love – that Alana accessed the psychotic domain.

THE SECOND EPISODE

She had given herself a year to work her way into a professional dance group. After eleven months she half-realized that this was not going to happen; but her enthusiasm for dancing remained undiminished. In fact she said that at that time she lived for it; it was 'something special' in her life.

Penniless, unloved, vastly underemployed as a chambermaid, mixing in her time off with butch lesbian women whom she hated, she would regularly dance herself high. The music of Stevie Wonder, famous for its spiritual character, plus various other artists such as Earth, Wind and Fire, The Average White Band, Bob Marley and The Pointer Sisters would, with her dancing movements, transport her as if into another dimension of being. Time and space would be suspended; she would be filled with a sense of idyllic beauty. Her little room, boring job, butch lesbian acquaintances and distant mother would all be left behind as she danced herself into an ecstatic state of union with Pure Love.

The episode happened very quickly. She sat meditating in her room (a state known to produce low autonomic but high cortical arousal: Banquet (1973), Hirai (1974), Orme–Johnson (1973)). She heard a chorus of Hallelujahs in her head. She heard a baby cry as if it had just been born. She was convinced she had been born again and that this was a turning point in her life. At about the same time she thought she had ESP.

Alana continually heard her dance teacher whispering her name. She was deeply in love with this woman and in a deluded way believed that the woman was also in love with her. This seems to have been a pure wish-fulfilment delusion – what we might call an 'optatic' delusion after the Latin *optata*, which means 'according to one's wishes'. Her reasoning seems to have been: 'I am a lesbian, therefore she (I wish and hope) is a lesbian. I love her, therefore she (I wish and hope) loves me.' When I presented this obviously very straightforward interpretation to her she said, 'Yes! Yes, that's it exactly!' Other delusions, however, do not fit this pattern so easily. She thought, when she lay on the floor of her room, that 'people' were taking photographs of her through the ceiling. Her head kept going from side to side and she felt that she was in some sort of trance. Psychotic experiences were exacerbated at night whenever she lay on her back in bed and was drifting off to sleep. She felt quite 'normal' and rational during the day.[2]

Eventually, back in her hotel room, in a state of intense doubt, she, like myself, experienced uncanny taps and clicks and, again like myself, discovered their code of one click or tap for Yes, two for No. This lasted for about a day. Her own mind was as if externalized. The housekeeper brought a doctor to see her because she could not sleep nor wash nor even go to the canteen. She was admitted immediately. Once she left her room she forgot all about the clicks and they never returned. She was put on medication and never 'relapsed' again.

Alana now rarely talks of her episodes. This, I think, is a good sign. Perhaps I was able to help her: I was narcissistically gratified one day when she said, 'I've been happy since I met you.' She now has a good job and a relationship with a feminine older woman who she loves deeply. She still takes medication which she feels helps her to handle anxiety and depression. It is the latter, more than anything else, for which she still needs verbal support. Her relationship and identification with her love – a successful businesswoman – has at last given her the motivation to work and the tenacity to hold down a job.

REFLECTIONS ON ALANA J

Comparing Alana's experiences with mine, reported in Chapter 4, we can see some parallels. Apart from our shared battles with puritans, she seems to have accessed a mystical state, though transiently, through dance and *possibly* suffered acoustic paranormal phenomena. (Whether her belief in her ESP was veridical or not we shall, of course, never know.) This Borderlining state, as in Lenz's cases (1979, 1983), sadly collapsed into delusion. Perhaps if there is a motivation to leave an intolerable reality, one cannot immediately use what one has discovered at the periphery of sanity to enrich one's own life and that of others, and one ceases to be effective in the world.

Her access to the mystical state was achieved in a state of high arousal and under great stress. Possibly repeated excitation, in a person who cannot anyway modulate it easily, weakens an inhibitory mechanism (as suggested by Malmo (1957)) permitting excitation to rise eventually to disruptive levels.

Callow reductionists will merely state that Alana suffered a biochemically mediated altered state of consciousness with no objective reference. In contrast I suggest that her experience, like my own, reveals that the mind in certain states can mediate the intuitive awareness of a deeper reality usually only revealed to mystics.

Alana's crises, like those of all the people so far discussed, have stimulated her religious sensitivity. She was confirmed in 1983 and has no hesitation in going for a half hour of silent prayer at times of inner turmoil. This in itself reveals how, for some people, Borderline experiences touch the very heights and depths of their being, revealing macroconscious as well as unconscious capacities and perhaps an extra-dimensional aspect to reality.

Now, in a generally calmer state of mind and having found what she was looking for sexually, Alana is consolidating all she learnt from her episodes and is moving forwards into what looks like a highly productive and happy future.

It would be wrong to end the study of Alana with the implication that she can be validly pictured now as walking off into the sunset with her lover. Affairs between lesbians or bisexual women are just not like that, if any affairs ever were – no doubt there will be other 'older feminine women' in her life. However, although Alana still suffers paranoid and depressive thoughts from time to time she does get on with her life and has improved her situation, through her own efforts, out of all recognition compared to its dishevelled state in 1979/80. In this imperfect world it is not possible to rearrange someone's psyche so that he or she comes to think and live like a thoroughly analysed psychotherapist (even were this to be desirable, which I very much doubt). The solution to Alana's despair has been a combination of anti-psychotic medication, perhaps a little validation and understanding from myself, and the love of an older feminine woman. These control the arousal disorder, repair the feeling of wretchedness and make good the developmental disorder and the sense of early symbolic mother loss. These are not ideal solutions but they work, and together they get Alana through life.

7

CHRIS

'Out of this world'

INTRODUCTION AND BACKGROUND

A classic example of the popular notion of an 'undiscovered genius', Chris describes himself, with humility, as 'a drawer' rather than an artist. Yet every drawing he reveals evokes immediate gasps of admiration from every person I have known who has seen his work. He has had some illustrations published but I cannot display his work to the reader without prejudicing his future – his style is so distinctive that it is easily recognizable – and there are still many people who steadfastly believe that anyone diagnosed as schizophrenic cannot produce great art. Chris secretes fantastic, highly original images onto paper like – to put it pithily – a cow secretes milk. He has had very little formal instruction in drawing techniques; his is a raw, largely untutored, talent.

His images have always been 'other worldly'. Asked to represent a particular shoe or nude he has not usually done a better-than-average job. He has had a long-standing interest in science fiction, which caters for his wide-ranging iridescent imagination and his penchant for 'free style' production. This preference for a largely unconstrained atmosphere for creative endeavour he shares with David B, Shafiq and Alana J. Chris is an extreme manifestation of it; given the whole field so that he can exude that which is within, he produces striking work. Narrow the array and make demands and his efforts deteriorate. Yet there is no doubt that there is a more-than-average talent there.

Twenty-one when I first met him, in 1980, he was a very pleasant, friendly and attractive young man with a tremendous sense of humour. He would regularly generate hilariously funny analogies and far-fetched witticisms demonstrating verbally the same level of creativity that he did visuo-spatially. If, however, as Mednick (1962) argues, creativity is demonstrated in the production of useful *contextually appropriate* remote associations, then Chris was even more genuinely creative in the verbal sphere.

I always regarded this young man as rather like a breath of fresh air. His wit, axiomatically unpredictable, and his colourful interests would always blow any gathering cobwebs out of my mind, sharpen my perception and produce plenty of belly laughs. He was (judging from their remarks) also attractive to women because of his great sense of humour, his unassuming, perhaps rather hesitant manner with them, his pleasant fresh-faced appearance and his light, entertaining but warm conversation.

Chris would often say that his problem areas lay in the territory of self-assertiveness and self-confidence. Although attractive to women he did not really believe himself to be and the task of asking girls to dance would fill him with great apprehension. Although enjoyable to talk with he was shy and spent a lot of time on his own. A talented drawer, he downplayed every production, compared himself unfavourably with recognized artists and displayed his creations only with reticence. The picture is rather similar to the 'avoidant personality' of DSM–III (1980); similarly, whereas hypomanic people overestimate their ability, Chris would habitually underestimate his resources and performance in virtually every area of life in an almost 'hypodepressive' manner. Such tendencies are, in part, indicative of such a personality.

He had two elder brothers, one of whom, Michael, was also diagnosed as schizophrenic. His father was a retired jobbing builder and greengrocer. He was a regular gambler and was also very partial to a drink. He seemed not to have made a close relationship with Chris. In contrast, his mother, who worked as a cleaner, was an exceptionally caring and loving woman who was very concerned for his welfare. Rather like David B's mother, warmth and affection exuded from her. In many ways, especially through the psychotic episodes of her two sons, she carried the household on her shoulders, worked hard and was difficult to anger. Although it might be said that she wanted her sons to leave home and be independent, yet spoilt them in such a way as to keep them there, I really cannot see that she was double-binding them in this way any more than do millions of other loving mothers nationwide. If Chris's mother was the pathogenic core then half the nation's children would currently be in psychiatric units.

FIRST EPISODE

His first experience of psychosis occurred in 1980 when he was living with his parents. He had left his job as a clerical assistant and was unemployed. He spent a lot of time on his own, reading, watching television and listening to music. He would argue a lot with his father because the latter came home drunk most nights. Chris would go on long walks, especially to parks, and spend the whole day there. He felt depressed and anxious and suffered from tachycardia and pains in the chest. He would go to the cinema on his own (seeing both 'The Exorcist' and 'Alien' twice), severed all contacts with friends and spent a lot of time at Speakers' Corner – where he was 'affected' by one particular speaker who used to quote a cocktail of Nietzsche, Hitler, the Bible and Idris Shah (*Caravan of Dreams*) with remarkable accuracy.

His pre-delusional state involved strange feelings devoid of concrete thoughts, a kind of 'meaning feeling' (see page 91). Some content then crystallized: 'people looked strange'; he was 'not at one with society'; 'things were coming to a head'. He was a Kafkaesque figure, different, tormented. Then through a kind of gestalt synthesis he crystallized a delusion from the solitude of his room that there was a war on. A 1984 regime of a neo-Nazi character was in power. He even thought he was Jewish and that the regime would, as he put it, bungle him away into a concentration camp. Under this delusion, which he described as 'the funnel through which everything flowed', even an otherwise trifling event such as a visit to the post office took extraordinary courage. Outside, the streets looked different, old and decayed as in the Second World War. Chris was taken to hospital by his father after he impulsively threw himself out of the first-floor window of his parents' flat. He said that he did this 'because of frustration and anxiety' and because he wanted to escape from his situation. This event seemed to mentally awaken his father to the fact that all was not well with his son.

There is a pattern in the approach to Chris's episode demonstrative of my early expectation in this research noted on pages 2–3. Not getting on with his parents and not feeling that he really articulated well with his friends and with society, Chris withdrew. This withdrawal meant he placed himself in a situation which gave him licence to entertain himself with his own imaginings free from the jogs and corrections one usually receives to one's ongoing thoughts when one indwells in the world. Free from constraints and from the modificatory feedback one receives through airing one's ideas to others, Chris indulged his undoubtedly original mind such that he came to see patterns in the clouds of his own fantasies.

Before he crystallized his '1984 delusion' he became interested in many things but was committed to none. His attention would flit from one topic to another as if driven by a craving for mental excitement. His idea that 'things were coming to a head' probably reflected his feeling that he could not entirely control the incrementally rising arousal of his own brain. Again a form of modulation problem raises its head.

The delusion itself was a creative leap. Through it he understood why the world was strange and different but he had done it without anyone telling him. With his own imagination he had worked out 'what was going on'. Via his delusion he was transacting with a world with which he could not normally communicate. This I think is generally true: the delusion is an arcuate leap towards productive integrated functioning. By constructing a world on their own terms, deluded individuals can, at last, transact with it. They may be persecuted or be the centre of attention or both, but at least in a sense they are 'in' the world and no longer outsiders. The delusion is a vehicle for a social process; now the people 'understand' the world; they know how it is structured; the rules are laid bare. No longer are they puzzled and confused, uncertain and hesitant, they are plunged right into the middle of a network of relations which makes them very much at one with ongoing life.

On this view Maher's belief (1974: 104) – which is very relevant in Chris's case – that the delusion enables the person to say implicitly, 'Now at least I know the worst', is nonetheless a corollary to the central concern.

Chris, like all the people discussed so far, was an inveterate enquirer, seeking the truth behind appearances; the projector loaded with film behind the screen and its fleeting images. Carl Sagan (1977: 183) has argued that science is a paranoid pattern seeking process applied to nature; conversely, paranoia is the result of a scientific attitude operating to find patterns in inadequate data.

Just as visual illusion is more likely when impoverished degraded stimuli are looked at with one eye by an expectant observer, so, I think, delusion is more likely when an impoverished social situation is viewed by an active questing mind. Since information is never complete, visual illusion, to some degree, accompanies all of our perceptions and so a limited measure of delusion is also a fact, almost an inevitable fact, of life. (See, for example, Charles MacKay's book on popular delusions (1841) and the research on the very common delusion to the effect that 'people get what they deserve' – the so-called Just World delusion: Lerner (1970, 1974), Rubin and Peplau (1975), Wagstaff (1982, 1983), Wagstaff and Quirk (1983).) That ambiguity and ignorance may facilitate delusion has also been suggested by Miller (1951: 277).

We see clearly in Chris's case how a delusion is a creative thought, and I would concur in a general sense with Freud's (1911) belief that it is a creative action in the service of self-cure. Just as our understanding of the 'how' of the creative process itself is limited, so is our understanding of the initiation of delusional belief. The consequences of delusion, however, are more transparent. While Chris's thought gave him a world context in which he at last found a place, the actual effect of that thought was the reverse of the unconscious motive that preceded it. (Hence the result of a delusion need not be the cause of it.) A delusion could be said to take a person one step forward towards the world and then two steps backward away from it. Chris was mortally terrified of the world that he then perceived. He knew the world but did not like the consequences of his own belief. He sought a locale in society and found hell in his own mind. Not surprisingly, he leapt through a window into oblivion.

SECOND EPISODE

This occurred two years later when he was living in a hostel. He had felt that he was being 'pushed and pulled' by the other people who lived there. He started to withdraw; refused to eat or talk with other people except to snap at, or argue with them. At the time he felt a lot of anger towards his father, who was often drunk. Chris wanted to be left alone and did not want to say anything to anyone.

He heard a record by Clock DVA entitled 'Thirst' and took it to mean that 'the way out' was to de-vi-ate. A phone-in programme on the radio 'sounded strange'; he was sure it was all a hoax and even tried taping it to prove it. Eventually he found that his brain was 'going at ten million miles an hour'. If he said anything it would set off a shock wave of double, triple and quadruple meanings; thoughts were racing and ricocheting around his mind.

He became unable to sleep and lay on his bed for two days with his bedside lamp lit. He felt he was in a cellar; the walls of his room were grainy and seemed to be very dirty. There were insects, so he thought, crawling about on the walls but when he looked hard they disappeared. He thought that the hostel was on fire; he could smell burning. The rest of the people who lived in the hostel were having sex with the Jewish girl who lived in the next room. There were security cameras everywhere, and he was being constantly monitored. Being a smoker he needed tobacco, but the effort required to go to the shop to get it was gargantuan. Still he went. When people said to him that he had 'got to get out of this state' he took that to mean that he had got to get out of town.

Eventually a doctor was brought and he was admitted immediately to a psychiatric unit.

BRIEF UPDATE AND OVERVIEW

Chris has kept out of hospital since 1982. Although he has not yet settled down into stable full-time employment he has done quite a number of further education classes in English, Art and Study Skills and worked full time as a security guard for several months.

He married in December 1983, a woman seventeen years his senior, but alas the marriage only lasted six months and was marred partly by his extreme jealousy. They are still good friends, like each other, and both accept that their decision to get married was made impulsively.

Chris once went for psychotherapy but, like Shafiq, gave this up, in disgust, after two sessions. He now is a keen computer user and wishes to embark on courses in computer graphics. The use of a computer as an instrument for his inventive visual imagination would seem to promise results of great interest and vitality.

In the first three to five years of this study I sought hard for evidence of unconscious hostility (after Knight 1940), unconscious homosexuality (after Freud 1911), defences against shame and humiliation (after Colby 1976, 1977), evidence of the suffering of early sadism (after Cameron 1959) and various assorted communication distortions within the families of these people, Chris included. Despite looking for the subtlest hints in non-verbal behaviour, slips of the tongue, fleeting facial expressions, indeed for anything that might be revealed in an unguarded moment, I was genuinely unable to sustain these basically negatively toned theories.

In Chris's case, as in them all, any troubling hostility was overt and fully conscious, homosexuality trivial and impotent as a force, his family caring and his school and early days devoid of trauma. When I began to look on the positive side it became evident that Chris was a man able to look at the world in novel ways and I sensed that this angle looked more promising.

In this case, as in all the studies reported so far, we see the results, in psychosis, of a creative mind alienated in some way from society and under stress. We see difficulties in modulating arousal, conscious hostility to a parent, particularly a parent of the same sex, a rapid search for data that confirms a speculation – which thus acts (to use Chris's words) as 'a funnel through which everything flows'.

We see a conflict between conscious and unconscious mentation, an unconsciously motivated move into the world via delusion but then a consciously mediated move out and away when the force of the consequences of that delusion is fully apprehended. In this sense a delusion, even if spectacular, may give transiently calming order and feelings of unity with society (plus in *some* cases aggrandisement of the self) but when considered over time it is a system with rapidly diminishing returns.

Whereas an appropriate, carefully articulated belief, based on a great deal of evidence, enriches a person's life, puts him or her into the world in an effective productive way, and makes sense without great effort, an idiosyncratic spectacular belief based on very fragmentary data, although transiently exciting (in a 'what heats me cools me' fashion), alienates one person from others, decreases that person's effectiveness in the world and requires progressively more and more remote associations to be generated and selected to sustain it.

Chris shows a definite pattern of an independently minded man with a very sensitive perceptive nature, perhaps attentive to subtleties that others easily miss, generative of fantastic ideas, who felt something of a misfit and who thereby was hesitant in social situations. He put his innovative capacity to the task of creating a self-styled world, but when he had conceived it he found he could live in his dream with even less effectiveness than he could in the world from which he had withdrawn. Chris was, in my view, very much a victim of his own talent.

8
ALISON
'I'm waiting'

'You . . . are a *paranoid schizophrenic.*' So said Alison's psychiatrist to her in 1980 after her first episode. Indeed these are the only words she remembered from her talks with him. They have, however, stayed with her, reverberating around her mind, ever since; words she perceived of condemnation rather than comfort.

Alison was a lovely looking young woman, about 5' 3" tall with a pert face, greenish eyes, a melodic feminine voice and an extremely polite manner. To meet her, one would never believe that she had been through any crises in her mental life; she seemed perfectly normal, perhaps a little quiet and reserved, but that was all.

Behind her consciously mediated pleasant polite 'exterior' Alison carried the, also conscious, heart and mind of a warm, indeed, passionate woman. Like Alana J she oscillated between being 'madly in love' and merely 'lukewarm'. Her first episode, late in 1978, grew out of a very brief affair with a tall, fair, handsome doctor. (Alison had a weakness for highly intelligent professional men.) She, in fact, only went out with him once but quickly developed a deep all-pervading infatuation for him and believed, on the basis of very little evidence, that he was in love with her. Rather in the manner of a woman with de Clerambault's Syndrome, or at least in a state of nympholepsy,[1] she pestered him with phone calls, letters and cards. He became very irritated with her behaviour and was rude and aggressive with her on the telephone.

As their 'relationship' turned very sour she started to believe that he was watching and monitoring her. Indeed, she did actually see him once 'hovering' around her flat in his car. This event triggered off vastly increased self-consciousness and self-awareness. She started to believe that this man was following her around – a feeling that lasted for several weeks. Any car remotely like his *was* his; any man who looked like him *was* him. Eventually her brother took her to a psychiatric unit and she was admitted.

Her second episode, in 1980, was quite different. She started to have difficulty sleeping. She would often stay awake all night thinking and listening to the radio, her thoughts, accompanied by intense subvocal articulation, racing and rambling. She lost her appetite yet experienced great feelings of energy and could easily walk for miles. Then one morning, after a dream of a similar nature, she awoke with the conviction that people were trying to kill her.[2] Outside she ran along a sidestreet off Oxford Street 'dodging bullets'. Eventually she found herself in Piccadilly Circus where she thought she heard a passer-by say to her, 'You'd better make your way to Charing Cross Hospital now.' She went there, by taxi, lying down on the back seat to avoid being 'hit', and was admitted.

After I had lost touch with her a third episode occurred, in 1982. This was precipitated by loneliness and by her ringing up her previous boyfriend, the one she had pestered. He said to her: 'Anything from you goes right in the bin.' The sound of his voice and his rudeness, she said, 'seemed to bring it all back.' This was a brief crisis and with great grit she was soon back at work.

She very quickly developed a passionate attachment to another doctor, one of extremely high status and repute, fully believing that he was going to divorce his wife and marry her. She never had a date with him and based this belief on next to no evidence at all, merely a single warm remark he made to her. This love she had, however, fortified her for three years which she quietly and patiently spent waiting for him to get divorced. 'I'm waiting,' she would say when I asked her what she was doing with her life. For eighteen months of this period she was on *no medication at all*. This is of extreme theoretical interest. This delusion clearly defensively solved all of her psychological problems. It was manifestly a control strategy to prevent more serious psychosis. She would become quite tersely ill-disposed towards people when her 'relationship' was questioned, to an extent that made people reluctant to pursue the issue further, so clearly important was it to her and so certain was she of the correctness of her belief. Given the eminence of her potential spouse this delusion obviously validated her sense of being special and must have tremendously boosted her self-esteem and feelings of being lovable by men of 'high quality' – to the extent that it is reasonable to infer that this feeling and this need were of central relevance to her psychological equilibrium.

Eventually she realized, because of his off-hand attitude to her, that her belief was ill-founded, that the dream was not going to come true. Shortly after the demise of this belief her flat was burgled, and within two weeks she was manically deluded.

On the telephone she told me she was having hypnotherapy 'at a distance' from the hospital. An unknown therapist was implanting 'suggestions in her mind', which were clearing it and 'freeing all her emotions'. She said 'they've found out that I've been repressing all my emotions since I told my mother about a sex game I was playing with my brother'. She said she was now 'full of life. I'm not a schizophrenic'. She was going swimming and dancing regularly. All through the conversation she was laughing hysterically and uncontrollably at every marginally funny remark I made.

I told her that I did not believe a word of what she thought was happening to her and she just giggled. Once again, however, she bounced back from this episode quickly and was soon working, although part-time.

BACKGROUND

Alison seems to have had a reasonably average childhood in most respects. Her home was loving and she harbours no great negative feelings towards either of her parents or to her brothers. She was not victimized or dominated or overprotected or excessively criticized; indeed, her early life seems to have been very happy. Although she reports that her brothers jokingly regarded her as the 'helpless little sister' there was nothing malign or vindictive about this. The only sadness in her life was the loss of both parents – her mother in 1974, her father in 1973. Indeed, she nursed her mother, who was dying of cancer, for a year.

At school she started going out with boys rather later than most of the other girls, at 21 in fact, and felt some mildly homosexual jealousy when she lost girlfriends to boys. However, there seemed to be nothing particularly pathological about that time in her life.

Alison was a highly intelligent woman with the equivalent of a degree in French, and for a time held highly paid jobs as a bilingual secretary. She was also extremely imaginative and a typist of exceedingly high quality.

She had no religious feelings and in none of the four episodes she had suffered, inclusive of the one in 1978, had she had anything remotely like a mystical or spiritual experience. She had no religious delusions, nor had she developed a religious attitude since her crises. Although imaginative, one would not really have described her as creative in any outstanding way and her delusions did not have the colourful kaleidoscopic quality I sensed in the reports of Chris.

Like him, however, she tended to have her four episodes or crises when she had been isolated. Reduction in cues had given her licence to entertain herself with increasingly remote thoughts or, to put it another way, contrary to a behaviouristic model nothing stimulates paranoia better than no stimuli.

All the people we have studied so far were under some kind of stress at the time they developed delusional thoughts. In Alison's case the loss of love for or from a man appears to be critical. Indeed, relationships or infatuations with men appear to have very considerable psychological significance for her. In all her affairs she had difficulty being natural and rapidly began to 'play games'. Her men had to be good looking and in positions of some status. As long as she was in love she was stable. When she lost the feeling, or the affair began to go wrong, her psychic economy started to be noticeably upset.

It is only fair to say, however, that Alison partly engineered the problems in her relationships with men which so dreadfully destabilized her. We shall see why shortly. In any normal relationship one has to negotiate a bond. In love relationships there is a lot of testing of course, but at first I think one deliberately smooths the other's path by confirming what we think the other is predicting and by experiencing confirmation of our predictions. On the edges of consciousness at the start of bond formation are thoughts such as 'I think she will . . .', 'I think that she thinks that I will . . .', 'I think that she thinks that I will think she will . . .', etc. This is not really 'knotty' in a Laingian way; one *has* to do this to enhance the operation of bonding, to navigate the bond. It is almost a kind of 'landing operation'. In relations with men Alison seemed to mischievously refute some predictions while confirming others strongly. Men would be confused. *That* is 'knotty' behaviour which really asks for trouble; *that* is 'playing games' and in Alison's case was probably a strategy enacted out of fear of intimacy.

Despite all these problems she was a woman with a very strong need to love and be loved and the absence or loss of a man in her life was a considerable blow to psychic harmony. It is possible to speculate that this had something to do with the loss of her father, perhaps it was a reactivated mourning reaction. However, I found little evidence that she had a 'complex' about her father; she spoke of him in a spontaneous, free and easy manner showing no hint of intense emotional discharge, or pent-up fury or passion.

If Alison was interested in a man *she* would approach *him* (usually, and interestingly, by letter) and this strategy, backed up by her good looks, was often initially successful. Having 'got' the man, however, her difficulty always had been in maintaining the relationship satisfactorily. Like some men who are validated by having a lady friend, Alison was validated in all that she was by loving and being loved. She was told that she would make 'a lovely mum' and I always sensed that Alison, single, was somehow half a person.

Over the last nine years, however (she is 38 at the time of writing), Alison's relationships with men were largely 'in her head' as she herself admitted and realized and she seems to have had all the trouble in her mental life since she started to so internalize her relationships.

Her manic episode (in 1985) may have been, as in the case of Chris, a step towards productive functioning. It was valuable for Alison to realize that she was repressing her emotions; indeed, she was usually only actually *lively* when she had had a few drinks. Yet, like Chris, while taking one step forward she simultaneously took two steps back into delusion.

The centre of theoretical interest in Alison's case is clearly love, sex and 'affairs with men'. After the sex game she was playing with her brother (when she was 4) her mother said angrily: 'Don't *ever* do anything like that *again*!' Unfortunately this planted the suggestion in her mind, so she says, that she should not do anything like that, ever again, with *anyone*. This made the task of negotiating affectional bonds with men extremely problematic for her and the ways in which she approached the task, as we have seen, were always rather bizarre and awkward. This was her vulnerability, her 'button'. She solved the problem by 'loving from afar'. This avoids the tangled and mine-infested territory of relationships close-up.

Alison's apparent 'stability' when she is 'in love from afar' is also most interesting. In this context let us look at the similarities between being 'mad' and being 'madly in love'. In both there is an obsessional quality, in both there is lack of control, there is inflation of self, the desperate need to 'see it through to its "logical" conclusion', the uncertainty is electrifying, the need gargantuan, the plotting and planning quite frantic. And in both there is total involvement, an oceanic quality and loss of appetite. In both there is also the wish to risk the whole self, the threat of loss of self, excitement, the desire to 'suck' the beloved or the world into congruence with one's desires. There is insomnia, euphoria, increased vitality, both madness and love are seen to 'solve all things'. There is fear, a feeling of surrender, a roller-coaster quality to the experience, an absence of feelings of mastery, a jelly-like quality to the self. The two are clearly very similar. Alison was 'sane' while she was 'madly in love from afar' because her psychotic style of thinking could be retained, but with a non-threatening central content and focus of interest. Being 'madly in love' is the nearest most normal people ever reach to the psychotic state – but I would guess that those who are very prone to this kind of experience are likely also to be more prone than average to madness itself.

Alison does not fit my overall theme of the psychotic as a creative person and/or a person who can gain access to mystical states. She *does*, however, show evidence of the behavioural modulation problem, mentioned repeatedly in this book, being either greatly overinvolved with a man or not interested at all and either manically emotional or quite reserved and cool. During her episodes of delusion there was also evidence of enhanced confirmation bias, thus sustaining her aberrant beliefs.

Her social worker and present counsellor are keen to work on her 'buried hostility', something she finds rather puzzling, boring and time-wasting. She is not for them a very keen counsellee. Personally I do not think that the Knightian theory (Knight 1940) – of repressed hostility as the key to paranoia – is particularly pertinent in this case. Alison, on the contrary, seems to me to be a woman with a great need for love and a great capacity to love. Also, she is not exactly a woman of outstanding social skills – although she does not in the least lack self-assertiveness – but instead of expressing and satisfying these needs in real life relationships she has been thrown back, partly through disappointments, on to her own vivid imagination to find that for which she so desperately hungers. In contrast, her aggressive emotions seem to be reasonably well managed. If necessary and justifiable she can express herself in a very piercing and biting way but can also be more gently assertive, again, if appropriate. Her grittiness in getting back to work after relapses, sometimes while she was still a hospital out-patient, also shows socially useful and effective aggression.

ADDENDUM TO CHAPTER 8

A Note on Simon T

For various very personal reasons Simon did not wish his (very interesting) case to be discussed in any biographical manner. However, he did 'release' certain information concerning the largely successful methods he and I used to help him, first, with outright hallucinations, second, with a special form of thought-broadcasting delusion and, third, with what is here referred to as his 'semi-hallucinations'. These methods clearly should be communicated.

He had become very isolated and withdrawn in the summer of 1978 and spent long periods in his room in a shared flat in a provincial town. He was convinced that the neighbours were talking about him but could only hear muffled noises from the flats next door and beneath him. Over a period of about a month these noises gradually took shape until one day they became clear voices. The voices were of a young couple echoing and commenting on his thoughts – the man supporting and the woman criticizing him. Within an hour or so he realized that they were hallucinations and tried getting drunk as a means of removing them – without success.

Rather than going to see a psychiatrist or GP he decided after about two days to take a brief holiday and went to stay with a close friend in a distant town. When he arrived there and settled in he rapidly discovered that the sound of Radio One drowned his voices. After the radio was turned off it would take a few seconds for them to return. He decided to capitalize on this observation and played Radio One continually from 8 a.m. until 11 p.m. at sufficient loudness to continuously mask the voices. After four days of the use of this technique the hallucinations had disappeared completely and, he claimed, never returned. During this time he took no tranquillizing or anti-psychotic medication of any kind. Simon happily referred to this as his 'Radio One Therapy'.

A similar technique was reported by Feder (1982), who used radio headphones with his patient, but it would be fair to say that Simon T was the first discoverer of auditory masking by patterned sound as a means of alleviating hallucinations without the use of anti-psychotic drugs. He said that he also found the general 'happy sound' of Radio One and its relaxed easy-going manner very therapeutic. Obviously the concern, care and sympathy of his friend also helped considerably to reduce his feelings of anxiety and panic.

It would seem therefore that a move to a place of asylum, coupled with the use of masking patterned sound, was sufficient to eliminate completely this terribly distressing phenomenon and it would be advisable, given the almost equally distressing side effects and long-term costs of anti-psychotic medication, for psychiatrists to recommend the wider use of this technique.

In 1981 Simon also reported to the effect that his own inner speech or subvocal articulations were occasionally *audible* when they were (to him) very intense and loud. Psychiatrists he spoke with clearly regarded this belief as a Schneiderian first-rank schizophrenic symptom (Schneider 1959). I suggested to the hospital that he be videoed in conversation for about one and a half hours and the video recording played back to him so that he could tell whether they were audible or not. They agreed. The articulations turned out not to be audible at all and, after realizing this, Simon's particular form of 'Thought Broadcasting Delusion' disappeared – and has apparently not returned at the time of writing (1990). This testifies to the fact that reliable feedback *is* sometimes valuable for previously deluded patients; when they are reasonably settled they do not *always* 'find ways around' contradictory evidence to sustain their beliefs. I shall take up this theme again in Chapter 12.

Semi-hallucinations

Simon was able to deal with outright hallucinations successfully, as we have seen, with his Radio One Therapy. Hallucinations, however, that were actually based on some sensory input but resulted from addition to or rearrangement of that input were more difficult to conquer. Simon would refer to these as his 'semi-hallucinations' – they were comparable to David B's 'incipient hallucinations' discussed in Chapter 2. They were basically remarks heard in the street or through walls which involved supplementation or contortion of the actual input.

As we saw in the case of Alison (page 75), a black or unopened box, stimulus–response behaviouristic approach is effectively bankrupt as a tool for understanding or helping the paranoid or deluded person. (Indeed, behaviourist treatment of deluded psychotics involving instructions to decrease deluded behaviour actually increased its rate: Wincze *et al.* 1970.)[3] Paradoxically, from the behaviourist viewpoint, a situation involving an *absence* of stimuli is an extraordinarily potent energizer of the paranoid process. Examples are abundant from Simon T's episode. He would suffer agonies and weave outrageous theories to explain unanswered letters. If he called someone and the 'phone just rang and rang then it was deliberately not being answered because that person somehow 'knew' it was Simon who was calling. The dead of night was a time fraught with great anxiety. A delayed cheque had been 'interfered with' by the pseudocommunity; a broken appointment was due to a friend or acquaintance having 'discovered' something bad about him, thus ending the relationship in a passive way. Missing items had been stolen; people who had moved had done so to get away from him, and so on.

Unclear stimuli also had tremendous potency for him, again, in contrast to behaviourist predictions, having far more behavioural consequences than direct, clear, unambiguous stimuli.

One therapeutic exercise that we used in this context was to try to create examples of likely 'mishearings' of unclear stimuli. Table 8.1 gives some of the results. This helped Simon T to realize that many, if not all, of the 'overhearings' he had suffered could well be based on remarks that were quite different from what he had thought had been said. Simon's own experience of 'delusional mood' (Conrad 1968) seems to have arisen from misoverhearings of this nature – through which he developed the uneasy feeling that he may have been being referred to in the misperceptions that he had – hence the resultant feeling was 'something is going on'.

It is clear from the asterisked example 6 in Table 8.1 – which was a misperception that he actually did make – that his mind was doing

Table 8.1 Auditory misperceptions that could sustain or elaborate malign delusional thought

Actual remark	Could be misheard as:
1. Physics	He's sick
2. That's it	That's him
3. We're going to the market tomorrow	He's a marked man from now on
4. He might have gone	His mind's gone
5. He's going to Essex	He's going to have sex
6. Look Mam, there's a MacDonald's!*	Look Mam, there's that man they're going to knock down!
7. We'd better put the kettle on	We'd better kill that one
8. It's marvellous down there	There's Martians down there
9. It's the twenty-fifty of this month	There's plenty of filth in this punk
10. There's thirty days ahead	There's thirty days 'til he's dead
11. He's a flirty type	He has a dirty mind
12. He must have taken it	His mother was to blame for it
13. I only go to church at Christmas	A turd like him should be killed off
14. His wife just rambles	His life is just a shambles
15. It does look likely	It does look like him
16. He's meant to be in	He's masturbatin'
17. He's a participant	He's a Paki bastard

preconscious mental acrobatics of Olympian quality to make out of the actual stimulus what he experienced. In his semi-hallucinations he leapt like a gazelle to the conclusions he wanted to reach – as if to be right and consistent in his terrifying beliefs was more important than to be at peace or to be happy.

Simon's delusional thinking was, I think, fed far more by such semi-hallucinations than by outright hallucinations devoid of external input. He did, as did David B, have a tendency to avoid circumstances where they were likely to occur such as shops, crowds, minimarkets and buses where people could be speaking not *quite* out of earshot. Alison, who lived on a busy, noisy road, also feared them and always slept wearing earplugs so as to avoid or reduce them. Semi-hallucinations were an ever-present threat to the well-being of all these people.

Many clinicians interpreted Simon's reports as evidence of outright hallucinations, but this was not really so, and he himself had insight into this – although not sufficient to eliminate all of his seemingly aberrant beliefs. We also discussed the fact that his conviction in the validity of his overhearings tended to *rise* with time since experiencing them. This 'post-event cementation' of his confidence levels suggests that the subsequent higher level cognitive processing of the perception which embedded it, with consistency, in his belief system was largely or partly responsible for his high conviction even though the real-time evidential basis, of a more peripheral, perceptual nature, was realized to be very slender. Discussions along these lines were also very helpful for him.

Simon used a wide range of avoidant behaviours to evade his tendency, which he felt was automatic and involuntary, to 'make something out' of degraded or poor auditory input. He insisted on net curtains so as to eliminate the possibility of a couple looking in during the day, seeing him, then saying something which he might partially overhear and 'elaborate' on. He never switched the light on, in the evenings, in his front room unless opaque curtains were drawn, for the same reason. (It is quite likely that many 'normal' people share these fears to some degree.) He tended to live in the back of his flat, thus avoiding the front room which was a 'danger zone locality' for partially overhearing comments of people passing by in the street outside.

It is evident both from the experiences of Simon T and those of the other case study volunteers, that semi-hallucinations are an ever-present threat to psychotics, perhaps even more so than are outright hallucinations, and clinicians should realize this and be sympathetic about this, often chronic, problem. Other possible techniques, feedback-based, which may help to alleviate the anxiety associated with and caused by this enhanced cognitive processing of impoverished input, are discussed in Chapter 12.

9

OVERVIEW AND REFLECTIONS ON THE CASE STUDIES

Thinking on delusional thinking is changing. The stock textbook image of a person invariantly and rigidly holding on to a certain belief has been challenged by Garety (1985). Similarly, the assumption that a deluded person can *never* be argued out of a held belief has been invalidated by Rudden *et al.* (1982). Early emphasis on the *content* and deviance of the belief (e.g. Jaspers 1962; Freedman *et al.* 1975) has been replaced by emphasis on the *evidence* for it, how it relates to the person's intelligence, education and background and on the manner in which the belief is held (Moor and Tucker 1979). The dichotomous view, i.e. that a person either has delusions and hallucinations or does not (rather as a woman is either pregnant or not), has been quashed by Strauss (1969), Chapman and Chapman (1980) and Chapman *et al.* (1982). Delusions, like hallucinations, exist on continua from arguably justifiable and mildly paranoid or eccentric thoughts which could be entertained by anyone (and probably are) through to examples of fully blown bizarrity and impossibility based on little or no evidence. The traditional search for deficit and disadvantage in paranoid and deluded patients is now being counteracted by some research that shows them to have areas of superiority over normal non-psychiatric controls (e.g. La Russo 1978; Magaro 1981; Claridge 1988) and which argues that they possibly carry a survival advantage (Jarvik and Deckard 1977) – see also Heston and Denney (1968) and Karlsson (1972).

Delusional thinking is not then, it seems, conceptually distinct from normal thinking. One of the themes of Meissner's book (1978) is that paranoid processes are on a continuum with daily human functioning; paranoid mechanisms are utilized by everyone. We are, however, far from an understanding of normal thinking and our explanations for delusional thought are still very incomplete.

Like normal thoughts, delusional thoughts can assume many many different forms. It is, however, wrong to think that paranoid people have but one delusion: their thinking is usually suffused through with dozens of inappropriate and invalid inferences covering almost every area of their lives. It is nonsense, however, to seek different explanations for every different delusion just as we cannot have a different theory for every different dream or joke.

Just as I state in the note to Figure 2.1 (see pages 16 and 157) that we should move towards a rapprochement between research on auditory hallucinations and that on normal auditory perception, so I think we should thus coalesce our efforts on normal and on delusional thinking and not have the phenomena investigated in different camps. In this context the works of Chapman *et al.* (1978) and Eckblad and Chapman (1983) are particularly valuable.

MAGIC

The task facing us is nevertheless enormous. There is a rational aspect to delusion: I see it as a risky thinking style in the long-term interests of caution/self-protection/survival (a massive preference for Type 1 errors); but its *content* is undoubtedly magical and irrational. Because of this it may always elude an understanding in logical or rational terms. Wilson (1983) encountered the same barrier in attempting to understand magical thinking in fiction. In this respect the psychotic and the sexual variant, groups I have compared before in this book, are in the same pool. I find it to be no surprise that sexual variations are present in the psychotic sample. For example, the magical power that material has for the fetishist is beyond reason, beyond sense. I have known satin fetishists who claim to 'worship' the material and, as Wagner was, are creatively inspired by it. Both the psychotic and some sexual variants seem to have an access to a magical, irrational form of experience long repressed and condemned by our materialistic society but which nonetheless lives on, waiting, available and unextinguishable. (The 'repression of the irrational' is also discussed by Pauli in Laurikainen (1988).)

Similarly in the mystic, the psychotic and the masochist we see a capacity for Dionysian abandon. Abandon to forces beyond themselves, a capacity to 'let go', 'give in' and to let what will be, be, and what will happen, happen. This probably is the reason why mystical experiences can indeed turn into delusional experiences. It is, however, very much an aspect of life and of being which we have eschewed in our Baconian Apollonian efforts to master and control nature and human nature. All of these people are indulging in the magical, the 'mad', forbidden territories of the human psyche. All, even masochists, comment on the spiritual nature of their experiences. To understand them in terms of the commonplace and down-to-earth may therefore prove impossible, our scientific interpretations may forever be partial and we must face this.

With these cautions in mind I have adopted the attitude that we must loosen our thinking to get our minds around the phenomenon of delusional thought; we must be audacious, we must dare. Very early in this investigation I decided to start my attack on the nonsensical in this spirit with a nonsensical question and this was it: *What colour is madness?*

When one does ask such questions of people – for example, 'What colour is Tuesday?' – replies are received which demonstrate a certain degree of consensus. (Tuesday tends to be yellow, I find!) I asked the 'madness' question to each of the people discussed in the case studies independently and of myself with reference to my own 'episode'. I was surprised to find that all but one of us regarded our experiences as *purple*. (Alana J initially also said this, but a few years later changed it to red.) Lüscher (1971) has this to say of violet, which is the nearest to this colour in his scheme: a preference for it (p. 71) implies

> A high degree of sensitive intimacy leading to complete fusion between subject and object, so that everything which is thought and desired must become Reality. In a way, this is enchantment, a dream made fact, a magical state in which wishes are fulfilled . . . . The mentally and emotionally immature . . . may prefer violet. Violet occurring in first position suggests a pre-adolescent immaturity carried forward into adult life. In this event the person will tend to be unrealistic and have difficulty distinguishing the practical from the visionary.

This is clearly a very intriguing and apposite quote in this context. (I now find that purple is a colour that has long been associated with the mystical experience, further, albeit slender, evidence that the mystical and at least the acute psychotic states are related.)

In Lüscher's terms the violet-preferring person may in some sense be immature but that person's vision is hardly 'unrealistic' when one considers what Schrödinger had to say of reality in 1955: 'Subject and object are only one. The barrier between them cannot be said to have broken down as a result of recent experiments in the physical sciences, for this barrier does not exist.' Bohr also stated that an independent status could be ascribed neither to the physical nor the mental realms, and Pauli was of the belief that to know reality we shall have to fuse the physical and the psychological (Laurikainen 1988).

The immaturity of the enchanted person is also given a different slant by the work of Barron (1972). He commented (p. 85) on the way that creative people are not so much characterized by a capacity to 'regress' as to carry their childhood sense of wonder with them into adult life. Creative people may show a hint of immaturity in their behaviour, but it is underpinned by a process that they put to great societal use. All of the people in my sample who suffered psychotic episodes were of great imaginativeness and, in the cases of Chris and Alana J, this issued forth in work that could be truly regarded as creative. Where, then, did they go wrong?

Table 9.1 Characteristic features of the psychotic

Feature	David B	Shafiq	Volunteer Alana J	Chris	Alison	Simon T
1. Unusually emotional home environment	×	√	×	×	×	√
2. Parents unusually critical *and* overprotective	×	√	×	×	×	√
3. Training in bizarre and/or magical thinking	×	×	×	×	×	√
4. Living at home at time of first episode	√	√	×	√	×	×
5. Difficulties in leaving home	√	√	×	√	×	×
6. History of psychosis in the family	√	√	×	√	×	×
7. Spoilt by parents	√	√	×	√	?	√
8. Arrogant/feeling of being 'special'	√	√	√	√	√	√
9. Guilty conscience	√	√	√	√	√	√
10. Highly creative individual	×	√	√	√	×	√
11. Withdrawn and isolated at time of episodes	√	√	√	√	√	√
12. Behavioural modulation problems	√	×	√	√	√	√
13. Amplification of confirmation bias	√	√	√	√	√	√
14. Low socio-economic living conditions	×	×	√	×	×	√
15. Unemployment or underemployment	√	√	√	√	√	√
16. Low self-esteem	√	×	√	√	√	√
17. Physical unattractiveness	?	×	×	×	×	×
18. Low intelligence	?	×	×	×	×	×
19. Anti-social behaviour prior to crisis	√	×	×	×	×	×
20. Poor social skills	√	√	√	√	√	√
21. Low on self-assertiveness	×	√	√	√	×	√
22. Difficulties in relating to opposite sex	√	√	√	√	√	√
23. Repressed homosexuality and/or hostility	×	×	×	×	×	×
24. Poor relationship with same-sex parent	√	√	√	√	×	√
25. Indulgence in sexual variations	×	×	√	×	×	√
26. Unmarried at time of first episode	√	√	√	√	√	√
27. Age <35 at time of first episode	√	√	√	√	√	√
28. Overt homosexuality or bisexuality	√	√	√	×	√	√

29.	Under stress at time of episode	√	√	√	√	√	√
30.	Racing thoughts before episodes	√	√	√	√	√	√
31.	Loss of appetite before episodes	√	√	√	√	√	×
32.	Difficulty in sleeping before episodes	√	√	√	√	√	×
33.	Great capacity for excitement	√	√	√	√	√	√
34.	Mystical experiences before or during episode	√	×	√	?	×	√
35.	Possible ESP before or during episode	×	×	√	×	×	√
36.	Anhedonia	×	×	×	×	×	×
37.	Manic tendencies	√	√	×	×	√	√
38.	Depressive tendencies	√	√	√	√	√	×
39.	Gender identity problem	×	×	√	×	×	√
40.	Deterioration over five-year period	×	√	×	×	×	×
41.	Evidence of hallucinations	√	√	√	×	×	√
42.	Evidence of delusions	√	√	√	√	√	√
43.	Said that the colour of madness was purple	√	√	×	√	√	√
44.	Prone to obsessions and/or compulsions	√	×	√	×	√	√
45.	Prone to phobias	√	×	×	√	√	√
46.	High on neuroticism	√	√	√	√	√	×
47.	Introverted personality	×	×	×	√	×	×
48.	Impulsive personality	√	×	×	×	×	√
49.	Highly aroused at time of episode	√	√	√	√	√	√
50.	'Very imaginative'/ great love of fantasy	√	√	√	√	√	√
51.	Low on venturesomeness	?	√	×	√	√	×
52.	Difficulty modulating hostility	×	×	√	√	×	√
53.	Phobia of breaking down again at the same time of year	×	×	×	√	√	√
54.	Believed in delusions with absolute and complete certainty	√	√	×	√	√	×
55.	Suffered 'the meaning feeling' before delusional thoughts crystallized	√	√	√	√	√	√
56.	Considerable number of 'life changes' prior to first episode	√	√	√	×	√	√
57.	Persecutor was once loved	?	×	×	×	√	√

58. Paranoid pre-morbid personality	√	×	×	×	×	×
59. Schizoid pre-morbid personality	×	×	×	×	?	×
60. Avoidant pre-morbid personality	×	×	×	√	×	×
61. Schizotypal pre-morbid personality	×	√	×	?	×	√
62. Borderline pre-morbid personality	?	×	√	×	×	×
63. Looked young for their years	√	√	√	√	√	√
64. Delusion encroached extensively on person's life	√	√	√	√	√	√
65. Delusion was bizarre	×	√	×	×	×	×
66. Delusional thinking was very disorganized	×	?	×	×	×	×
67. Delusion was very preoccupying	√	√	√	√	√	√

Note: 54 and 64–7 dimensions taken from Kendler *et al*. (1983).

THE 'TYPICAL' PSYCHOTIC EPISODE

In Table 9.1 I list a number of features commonly thought characteristic of the psychotic; features also of importance in precipitating, sustaining or predisposing to psychosis and some that have emerged from the present investigation. If we consider those characteristics applying to five or to all six of the people listed and discussed in earlier chapters, we arrive at the following description.

They were all young (less than 35 years of age), unmarried, rather neurotic people, with perhaps a poor identity through an inadequate relationship with the same-sex parent. They were unemployed or under-employed (and therefore bored), imaginative and with a great love of fantasy, had a great capacity for excitement, and found that they could not relate to other people particularly well, especially members of the opposite sex.

In these circumstances, lacking a close validating relationship, a certain degree of paranoid sensitivity developed. Without such a relationship, which would have made them feel 'basically OK', they sought validation in the world with the ever-present threat of rejection from people whose ties to others were stronger than they were to them. They were unsuccessful. Hence, as a result of their poor social life they withdrew more and more and replaced a life in-the-world with a life of reverie. In personality they tended to have a view of themselves as somehow very 'special', yet at the same time their esteem was not high and they also were rather prone to guilt feelings. Usually some stressful event occurred, one 'fitted' in a malign way to some particular vulnerability. This would agitate and arouse their already rather fanciful, meaning-seeking minds and, rather than discussing and airing their thoughts with close ones, they instead, alone, embarked on a private mission of self-protection, justification and enhancement. Rather than join the world they attempted to model the events of the world in their iridescent imagination, free from the jogs of verifying or corrective feedback that could have been provided by others. (Through this they preserved 'the magic of the secret'.)

In that state they felt distanced and alienated from life. They started to have difficulty sleeping, their appetites became poor, and their thoughts were racing. They felt isolated and full of doubt. Life and the world became 'different', strange, they felt that 'something, somehow was going on'. They suffered a kind of 'meaning feeling'. As a step towards health, a step towards life-in-the-world, they crystallized a spectacular, exciting hypothesis which indeed placed them in that world, a delusion. This was not best thought of as a 'projection'; it was a thought that happened to solve simultaneously many current problems such as boredom, feelings of alienation and of unpredictability, etc., and which, in a rather Gregorian fashion, 'made sense' out of their current situation. It was conceived in great doubt, a thought of a mind unable to find the middle ground, viz.: 'When in doubt, fear the worst!' This conception, or rather its realization in a particular form, rocketed them from the state of being a complete outsider to that of being 'the centre' (the Medius Complex). Yet quickly they found that the costs of this thought were greater than its immediate benefits. Though now free of doubt and very much part of 'the action' in-the-world the *implications* of their particular conception eventually made their new situation even more unliveable than the old one. Conceive a delusion and something is bound to happen to confirm it. Like a cognitive virus spreading implications as disease through the system, confirmatory instances occurred in positively uncanny profusion. Rapidly they found that their view of the world implied a portentous form of victimization; events were happening all the time that not only sustained but elaborated their conception. Events did not only have significance and meanings with reference to what they thought was going on but, like Epsom's poetry had double, triple and quadruple meanings. Fast though they tried, self-protectively, to anticipate or 'second guess' their adversaries, machinations seemingly beyond their control were happening faster. Hard, indeed frantically, though they worked – with the vigilance of a threatened beast – they found that they could not even keep up, let alone be ahead.

Eventually their world 'imploded'; on the brink of 'the worst' actually happening, they were admitted to psychiatric units and their (eventually) self-defeating conceptions were medicated out of awareness.

The above is a brief bird's-eye-view of the psychotic and the psychotic episode. It may seem to paint the psychotic in negatively hued colours, but between the strokes is a positive view. It depicts a sensitive perceptive meaning-seeking mind that may indeed find everyday (often coarse) social life too much. It is the kind of mind that can either write a penetrating perceptive novel laying bare the many facets of its characters or, if stressed too far, implode into oblivion.

Far from finding that the people I dealt with were bravely sustaining false selves or personae in the face of an adverse world, I encountered them as the very personification of genuineness and perceptiveness. They were all refreshingly direct and open and could read my mood in a flash. Far from finding them to be concrete and literal, they were easily able to abstract and go far, indeed in some cases too far, beyond the information given. This is the very essence of humanness and they were indeed quintessentially human.

PARANOIA WITHOUT CLASSICAL PROJECTION

The Knightian (Knight 1940) and, in part, Freudian (Freud 1911) notions that the deluded paranoid projects their unconscious hostility onto the world (classical projection), I found no evidence for. This book is very much a discussion, therefore, of paranoia without such projection. The empirical evidence for projection being the characteristic defence of the paranoid is also rather weak (Cooper and Kline 1986: 30). There was no doubt however that these people felt very different from the common stock of humanity. They could hardly have been expected to have used the rule: 'When in doubt assume a stranger is the same as you.' Instead, as we have seen, they slot-rattled to 'when in doubt, fear the worst'. Hence the hostility they inferred that they were suffering was seeded in caution, doubt and a feeling of difference from the bulk of their associates, not consequential on a projective defence. In all these people aggression was easily expressed when the situation reasonably could be said to have called for it, although in Chris, Alana J and Simon T it tended to be overdone or 'poorly modulated'. These people could be regarded as both repressing *and* expressing their hostility, but psychoanalytic theory, strictly speaking, calls only for its repression in these cases. This was not so. Also in the cases where aggression and hostility could not in any view be regarded as repressed – David B and Shafiq – the hostility inferred in others was still considerable. (Even some psychoanalysts, e.g. Bonime (1979a, b), question that projection is involved at all in paranoia.) At best we can defend a view of conscious or 'naive' projection (Horney 1939: 26), otherwise known as 'attributive' projection (e.g. Sherwood 1981), but not of classical or, to use Cameron's (1959) words, 'disowning' projection of *unconscious* hostility or homosexuality. This naive projection, however, in no way reduces stress (see Holmes 1981: 465) and hence its *defensive* role is highly questionable.

To check, empirically, the possibility of naive projection I rank ordered the volunteers in the case studies in terms of the malignity of their delusional systems. This rank order correlated perfectly with my rank ordering of the intensity of their *overt* hostility. As a check I asked my wife Jill, who knows all the subjects well, to also rank order them in terms of their overt hostility, although when she did this she did not know why I was requesting that she do so. The outcome is shown in Table 9.2.

Table 9.2 Rank ordering of the volunteers in the case studies

Malignity of delusional system	Overt hostility
(Most)	*(Most)*
1. Simon T	1. Simon T
2. Alison	2. Alison
3. David B	3. David B
4. Shafiq	4. Chris
5. Chris	5. Shafiq
6. Alana J	6. Alana J
(Least)	*(Least)*

This gives a Spearman rank order correlation of 0.943, which is clearly highly significant ($p = 0.01$, one tailed).

It would be unwise, however, to argue that no defensive behaviour of any kind is involved in delusional thinking. The more malign delusional states, assuming (importantly) mood congruence of the delusion (see Winters and Neale 1983), are characterized by the emotions of anger, fear and guilt. Now research in the context of attribution theory has shown that negative affect mediates a perception of control as external just as positive affect mediates a perception of control as internal (Weiner 1986). The person's argument tends to be 'if life is lousy it's not my fault' and 'thanks to my own efforts I have a good life'. The shift to an external locus of control (which schizophrenics in treatment do tend to have: Cromwell *et al.* 1961) may have the defensive function of attributing negative life circumstances to an external source. This perception of negative outcomes as due to external factors under the control of others is also and exactly the perception that would then lead, in an attribution theory conceptualization, to high anger (Weiner 1986: 135–49). The psychotic therefore does not project *unconscious* anger outwards but shifts control of outcomes to an external source.

In these circumstances conscious anger would be expected to escalate in a positive feedback mode both due to it inducing and resulting from the ascription of negative life-event outcomes to this external source. (This escalation of anger in positive feedback fashion also is discussed by Melges and Freeman (1975: 1039).)

Were Colby correct in his view that the paranoid is defending against shame (Colby *et al.* 1971; Colby 1975, 1976, 1977) this defence (if successful) would eliminate the theoretical need for, and the psychological presence of, an external locus of control – which is blatantly present.

Given the anger (and coincidence) induced and the anger resulting presence of this external locus, the psychotic is then forced self-protectively to adopt a highly risky criterion, in signal detection terms, to evade or anticipate any persecutors; hence the importance of feedforward, look-ahead and planning in paranoia so emphasized by Melges and Freeman (1975) and Federn (1977: 232). They are prepared to suffer false alarms or Type 1 errors (delusional interpretations) in order to maximize hits (correct interpretations) and to feel safe in the knowledge that they 'know what is going on'. On this top-down processing view their much researched hypervigilance, extensive scanning and, sometimes, overinclusive thinking detected after admission are largely caused *by* the delusion and the processing style necessary to sustain and elaborate it and are not, in gross measure, a cause *of* it. (In effect all the psychotic is doing is adapting in a quasi-rational, if frenzied, manner to a dangerously changed conception of the world.)

Emphasizing an attribution theory approach to the deluded person's mentation (see also Kaney and Bentall, 1989) implies axiomatically that the understanding of causal conscious thinking is a more profitable way of accounting for paranoid disorders than is the postulation of purely unconscious defensive thinking. But positive symptom schizophrenia certainly involves causal thinking. Events happening close together in time are causally connected to an extent bordering on frenzy. Schizophrenics also search for the causes of all the coincidences that happen to them – constructing a pseudocommunity to 'explain' them. The globality (across situations) assumption causes preoccupation. The stability (across time) assumption causes despair. The externality assumption in part causes the delusion and the delusional pseudocommunity. The negative outcomes, inferences of intent and external controllability cause the anger and fear.

Were Colby's very simple defence-against-shame view correct, people would also be being admitted to psychiatric units for clinical paranoia in their millions. The disorder is, surely, far more complex than this.

THE 'MEANING FEELING'

We therefore can accommodate the processes involving negative affects within an attribution theory framework. Delusional thinking, however, cannot be explained by one or two processes, it is a result of a whole orchestra of processes playing in sinister harmony. There are affects in psychosis which are less tangible than those discussed above and these need a different conceptual grid to cover them. Of critical importance here is what I have so far called rather vaguely the 'meaning feeling'. All of my volunteers could empathize very easily when I described this to them. It is a phrase of my own designed to capture the flavour of some of my own experiences in 1979.

The meaning feeling is contentless. To describe it I have to use words which imply content but the experience is, like Garnier's spatial poetry, beyond language. There is a feeling of significance, of portentousness, of foreboding, of multiplicity and wispy insubstantial ambiguity. The affect[1] is primary; delusional thoughts can give solidity to this feeling, but such cognitions (e.g. the contents of the so-called 'delusional mood' or trema (Conrad 1968) to the effect that 'something strange is going on') are secondary.

The meaning feeling is the affect character of the Borderline/mystical state. The collapse from it into delusion is again through an *attribution* of its source to an external worldly factor. This 'misattribution process' is therefore worth closer inspection.

PARALLELS WITH THE MYSTICAL STATE

In earlier chapters and previously I have made a great deal out of the similarities between psychotic and mystical states, and indeed out of the outright occurrence of mystical experiences before and during the psychotic crisis. Both mystical and well-systematized delusional thought are forms of thought 'hyperorder' rather than disorder, hence it is not surprising that they are related. However I have failed to find anything remotely resembling such phenomena in the cases of Shafiq and Alison. The mystical experience is closely related to Maslow's 'peak experiences' and instances of B (Being) cognition (Maslow 1968, 1971). He notes that these are more endemic in those of more poetic and artistic temperament (Maslow 1970) and not so common in the more down-to-earth self-actualizers. This may be the reason for the absence of anything mystical and/or paranormal for Shafiq and Alison, both of whom were rather pragmatic, hard-headed characters. (I once called both of them 'tough little nuts'.) David B, in contrast, was both tough-minded *and* poetic.

Nonetheless, I feel that this theme needs to be explored just a little further – largely because of the positive feedback I have had when discussing it with the others. There are great similarities in *theme* between the mystical state such as I experienced it and certain aspects of the psychotic state which I shall outline below in the form of parallels between the two:

The mystic: *I am in touch with everyone*
                is paralleled by
The psychotic: *Everyone can hear my thoughts.*

The mystic: *The world is not as it is commonly seen*
                is paralleled by
The psychotic: *The world has changed, there's a war on.*

The mystic: *There is a great harmony and oneness between all things*
                is paralleled by
The psychotic: *People and the world are all together in communication against me.*

The mystic: *Nothing is trivial*
                is paralleled by
The psychotic: *Everything means something, even street signs and car number plates.*

The mystic: *No one is a stranger*
                is paralleled by
The psychotic: *Everyone knows me and is plotting against me.*

The mystic: *I am both supreme and insignificant*
                is paralleled by
The psychotic: *I am the Christ and the Devil.*

The mystic: *I am passive, floating, at one with the universe, open to all*
                is paralleled by
The psychotic: *I am dissolving, decaying, penetrated by rays, penises.*

The mystic: *Meaning is everywhere/all is meaning*
                is paralleled by
The psychotic: *Everything I do or that happens has double, triple or quadruple meanings.*

The mystic: *I do not think, I am thought*
                is paralleled by
The psychotic: *I do not think, thoughts are planted in my head by computers/hypnotherapy at a distance.*

Parallels seem to obtain but there are also differences. The certainty of the psychotic often carries with it great aggressiveness; the certainty of the mystic does not. The mystic opens himself to that which is beyond himself and remains unharmed; the psychotic is very nearly destroyed. The mystic uses irrationality productively; the psychotic destructively. Taking Kierkegaard's existential leap the mystic finds Nirvana, the psychotic Hell, the mystic swims, the psychotic drowns.

We see, nevertheless, from this brief comparison that some of the higher order characteristics of the mystical state are reflected at a lower order, more tangible 'real' level in the delusional. The deluded person differs not only in the ways discussed above but also in putting everyday worldly meanings to the cosmic intuitions of the mystic and then searching for isolated events that confirm the more mundane interpretation. In a sense, perhaps, the deluded does not hold the mystical state but falls down and back from it. I believe that the mystical intuitions may indeed be the frame at a kind of 'deep structure level' for the delusions which thereby exist at 'surface structure level'. The collapse into delusion from the state of uncertainty, from the 'meaning feeling', is not a collapse from abstract to concrete thinking but from holistic global intuitions to local analytic ratiocinations and perceptions.

Psychotics may also be interpreting in everyday terms a level of transcendent interconnectedness which they have intuitively accessed but cannot put into words or re-present to themselves in a meaningful way – simply because they have no medium of expression for what has touched them. Outrageous though it may sound, psychosis is thus partly an educational problem. Were we to prepare people for such states of consciousness they would be less likely to misinterpret them in delusional terms. The therapeutic relevance of this is that people's initial strange perceptions and/or feelings could well be accepted, or at least not questioned, without danger, while their attributions could thus be the focus of change efforts. Successful therapeutic intervention along these lines, within an attribution theory framework, has been reported by Johnson *et al*. (1977).

THE UNCANNY

This radical but positive view of psychotics allows us to see their experiences in a very different light and to search in our thinking, theorizing and experimenting for very different phenomena and patterns than usually are sought.

All of the psychotics I have discussed spontaneously remark on the extraordinary frequency of confirmations; that they were far beyond what would be expected simply on the basis of their own enhanced awareness or confirmation-seeking attitude. That they were, in a word, uncanny, as if the world was orchestrated to 'drive them mad'. Although I have not conceived of any way of testing this, perhaps they are right; maybe a state of psychic excess does, as if acting in part like a kind of semantic field, produce coincidences. Maybe the subterranean levels of the mind structure the meaning domain shared by other minds so as to bring about comments, remarks and events that have meaning in the particular terms of the thoughts of the psychotic person. This may sound, at first, to be a rather 'cranky' hypothesis but we know so little of the *capacities* of the psychotic mind that we should not dismiss it out of hand.

Though the hypothesis is dangerous I think we need to face the possibility that the psychotic cannot, at times, tell the difference between reality and fantasy because, again at times, he or she has accessed a realm where there *is* no difference between reality and fantasy. Perhaps there *is* a 'psychoid realm', a 'point of potential to kinetic conversion' where the physical and the psychological are not totally differentiated out, where *res extensa* and *res cogitans* become merged and unified. This is the realm that Pauli always sought and would in part explain the rampant coincidences and 'ESP leakage'.

This realm must, however, also be a structuring of events, of physical processes; this is not merely a psychic intervention. This is very close to the 'source' or 'fount' of transcendent thinkers, where within and without are one. This is the portal of direct access. Near the portal is the meaning feeling, the feeling of contextual connectedness, of relations as libretto to the music of the transcendent emotive state.[2] In this scheme of things, reality, deep reality, is symbolic. It is a purposeful reality in which even objects could be eventuates of meaning. Such a reality, if not entirely psychic, is of mind and requires minds for its apprehension. Such a 'deep structure' is at least indicated and, I think, permitted by experiences in psychosis and at the Borderline, if not demonstrated and required.

It is a disturbing yet, paradoxically, sobering thought that the type of person we have always regarded in the western world as 'reality oriented', 'well adjusted', 'straight' and 'sensible', the type of person we have seen as a good tool for the uncovering of what really is, may not in fact be of temperament appropriate to the accurate perception of reality at all. While we have encouraged people to be or to become of this ilk, our inducements could well have been profoundly misguided. In contrast to the grey rationalizer, the purple magicians already know that 'the ultimate answers to existence are not to be found in intellectual concepts and philosophies, however sophisticated, but rather in a level of direct non-conceptual experience which can never be limited to the dualistic nature of language' (Blythe 1976).

COMING DOWN TO EARTH

Strenuously I have tried to observe the long neglected positive side of the psychotic. I have always given them the benefit of the doubt. I have, over these eight years, resisted every tendency to infer pathology unless it was heavily forced upon me. Even in outright pathology I have sought generatrices which are not outwith a positive conceptualization. In adopting this attitude I have been led to making audacious claims in the defence of the psychotic and to reconstruing them in ways markedly discrepant with that demanded by the medical model of orthodox psychiatry – a model which has considerable influence also in the research field of abnormal psychology.

It is now time to organize our thinking, to thrust into the experimental phase of the enquiry. If, as seems to be the case, psychotics are not only rather selfish and spoilt but are people of talent, originality, courage and grit, genuineness, perceptiveness, sensitivity and vision, then is it possible to demonstrate or confirm this in standardized tests? Does human worth somehow slip through the nets constructed in the service of objectivity or is our positive view fundamentally mistaken? We shall see.

10

THE EXPERIMENTAL STUDY

The theories and how they
were tested

The experiment reported in this and the next chapter chiefly investigated two processes which I believe are amplified in the deluded psychotic: confirmation bias (the tendency to seek and accept data that confirm one's hypotheses at the expense of data that refute them) and creativity (as defined and assessed by tests of so-called 'divergent thinking'). I was critically interested in the effect of *arousal*, or general state of alertness and energy mobilization, on these processes as the acute psychotic episode is at least in part a disorder of overarousal.

It is not possible to claim that the process operations tapped in an out-of-context experiment using quite artificial stimuli really totally explain delusional thinking. In this chapter we are seeking only *tendencies* which, when considered as operating over a long time span and in a real-world context, could *permit* or encourage delusional thought.

The thrust of this chapter is, however, not only a negative one. Psychosis touches both Abaddon and Nirvana and can thus only be appropriately characterized if we appreciate its double–edged nature and, perhaps, deeper significance. The delusional and, I believe, related area of mystical thought are both forms of cognitive hyperorder. Hence their study may yet give us insight not only into aberrant brain processes but into the deepest (or highest) levels of reality. This, of course, is a grand aim, but if we cannot as yet understand the nature of the transcendent realm or of the 'point of potential to kinetic conversion' of Chapters 4 and 5 (if indeed such a realm has any meaning) we can perhaps understand the workings of the device (the mind–brain system) that could possibly apprehend that domain. This chapter then has both a moderate-level aim, very much rooted in mainstream scientific research (where my feet are firmly on the ground) and a high-level aim which reaches towards a science of the future, a science which tackles Newton's ocean, Pauli's irrational, Malevich's non-objective and Jung's Psychoid (here my head is obviously reaching towards the clouds).

Before I begin, a problem that arises from a form of Cartesian thinking must be eliminated. In the same way that one can understand the structure and function of a tool – e.g. a spade, a hand, a pair of scissors – one cannot, surely, then say that one understands that which the spade digs or the hand grasps or the scissors cut. Yet in the mystical-creative, the Borderline and at times in the delusional state one has *direct* apprehension, one feels 'at one' with the Truth. This is quite different from the realm of discourse appropriate to talking about a spade digging. The person in the mystical or the related delusional psychotic state is not doing but being, not operating but resonating, not diving but floating, not changing or manipulating but experiencing an essence, mapping onto, establishing an absorbed state of parity. Here there is no demarcation between *res extensa* and *res cogitans*. Given the quality of the experience it is possible that some insight into how this is permitted and into what happens when it occurs will give us a glimpse of what we are resonating to or what we are establishing an absorbed parity with. In this endeavour the study of psychology may take us to what Niels Bohr (e.g. Bohr 1958) often referred to as deep truth. Bohr, for political reasons (Laurikainen 1988), ostensibly preferred to avoid this, but Jung and Pauli did not. Here, then, we shall take some steps towards a gradual encroachment (contra Camus) on the Borderline.

AROUSAL, CAPACITY, CONFIRMATION BIAS AND DELUSIONAL THINKING

The theory to be articulated is that the vastly increased arousal of the psychotic increases confirmation bias and exacerbates the delusional state because, at high arousal, attention is funnelled evoking in consciousness a preoccupying central dominant idea and then resources or capacity are decreased over the range from high to very very high arousal. Because of this there is insufficient capacity to cope with the rejection demands posed by myriad external and internal stimuli and patterns, which thus take on cognitive consequences for the psychotic through being simply assimilated to an ongoing idea. In other words, the idea is established at high arousal and is then entrenched at very high arousal. Anecdotal evidence suggests that under distracting conditions effort is required to maintain flexible adaptive thinking. This would imply that the screening out of irrelevancies is an active, albeit unconscious, process. (Spare capacity may, of course, also decrease under high *anxiety* because of the distracting effects of worrying thoughts: Eysenck (1982).)

Refutation bias, which Popper (1959, 1963) has argued is the strategy that people *should* use in problem solving, may however, even in normal people, overload cognitive capacity. It may be extremely difficult to test a chosen hypothesis *and* seek alternative hypotheses at the same time. Indeed, volunteers in scientific inference experiments who show refutation bias do not generally progress rapidly (Mynatt *et al.* 1977). I therefore expect all the volunteers in this experiment to demonstrate some measure of confirmation bias and, indeed, a certain degree of it may be necessary for good performance.

For the psychotic the problems presented by greatly amplified confirmation bias may, however, be exacerbated. Disconfirmatory input presumably requires and provokes more thorough and extensive internal search to accept or reject. If it imposes these greater demands, and if capacity is decreased by extreme hyperarousal, disconfirmatory information may well be relatively neglected if the person is simultaneously faced with the tasks of storing their ongoing idea, testing it, elaborating it and vigilantly scanning the external array all at the same time.

Hyperarousal may also promote attention to dominant or probable signals (Broadbent 1971) provoke retrieval of dominant responses and attention to sources that will most readily repay the allocation of effort (Eysenck 1982). This would be expected to *help* produce the preoccupying central delusion of the psychotic, as delusions, at least judging from my own case study work, tend to reflect important cognitive themes of great emotive significance in the psychotic's life. If hyperarousal promotes openness to and retrieval of evidence and ideas which confirm a delusion that high arousal itself has helped bring about through previously strengthening dominant habits, then a vicious circle-positive feedback system is produced which would be expected to push arousal even higher over time.

If arousal is moderately high the external and internal 'beam of attention' (Wachtel 1967) may be narrow (Easterbrook 1959). Hence the scanning of the situation, in the early stages of delusion, prior to formulating an initial position, may be hasty and incomplete and undeflectable by 'secondary' concerns which might otherwise enrich ideation. The psychotic is liable to foreclose on a position and not 'tolerate ambiguity'. Hence the initial sampling of the internal and external array will be restricted and very partial. This will lead to very selective, narrowly focused thinking. High drive previously has, of course, been shown to increase rigidity in problem-solving tasks (Maher 1957; Glucksberg 1962, 1964).

Hyperarousal also tends, even in normal volunteers, to influence software strategies so that confidence levels polarize or shift towards risk (Broadbent 1971). In the psychotic the latter seems to be demonstrated to an extreme degree. In ambiguous and stimulus-impoverished situations the psychotic adopts an extremely risky criterion which also maximizes (valuable) hits and minimizes (costly) misses. Hence any stimulus pattern that can even remotely be assimilated to the delusion is generally detected and accepted as 'positive' while patterns that disconfirm it are ignored. This, therefore, produces high false alarm perceiving.

The above 'bottom-up' in the sense of mechanistic, rather quantitative arguments, taken with the generally 'top-down' in the sense of motivational, qualitative arguments articulated in Chapters 1–9, lead to the view that there is an orchestra of processes in delusional thinking acting on different levels. These operate together in harmony in the direction of producing speedy, risky confirmation-seeking thought which acts under extraordinarily high incentive but which can only perseverate a central dominant idea and elaborate rather than undermine it.

The felt arousal of the psychotic, which obtains under tremendous incentive, is, I believe, an additive mixture of a hyperfunctioning passive (Eysenck 1982) or tonic (Claridge 1967) arousal system and an effort system (Kahneman 1973). Unlike Kahneman, however, I do not think it appropriate to equate capacity with effort. If acute psychosis is, in part, a hyperarousal phenomenon then at some point capacity, 'processing space', or capacity to perform simultaneous or parallel operations actually decreases while effort or capacity devoted to the central task continues to increase. The psychotic ends up putting increasing effort into progressively simpler styles or modes of thinking. As one counsellee said: 'I felt that I was going like a rocket yet at the same time that I didn't have much space to move in.'

In as much as the pseudocommunity or persecutors seem always to be one step ahead, the psychotics feel that they themselves are performing suboptimally. Hence they are continually faced with the necessity of boosting performance – thus using Broadbent's (1971) upper (compensatory) mechanism. Their task is: 'find out what is going on and take evasive or counteractive action.' But they are never quite up with ongoing events. Thus they continually need to expend more effort. Alas, the psychological consequences of doing this only exacerbate their situation. The more alert, fast and vigilant they become in performing their delusional task, the more 'evidence' do they find – which increases incentive further and justifies still more speed and vigilance.

The effort system, which I see as, in part, a form of conscious arousal modulation device, does however function. The unconscious (I assume) involuntary arousal modulation system (of Claridge 1967) may well break down. This must have consequences at the voluntary level – the person may be able to boost arousal more easily than dampen it.

Although this position seems broadly similar to that of Hasher and Zacks (1979) who discuss normal cognition, there are differences, some of which refer to phenomena that I infer make their appearance at *very very* high arousal. Contrary to Hasher and Zacks (1979), who also argue for reduced capacity at hyperarousal, fairly simple forms of effortful processes may, I believe, be enhanced in the very aroused state. One such process is subvocal speech. Innumerable contacts of mine who have suffered psychotic states report intense subvocal speech having accompanied their 'racing thoughts' as their crisis was intensifying.

Hasher and Zacks also argue that high arousal has no effect on word-meaning retrieval as this is an automatic process. If, however, acute psychosis is a hyperarousal phenomenon then it would seem that the processing of the semantic implications of words, either in visual or auditory form, is actually enhanced.

High arousal seems to make it easier to inhibit the operation of automatic processes when this is useful for efficient task performance (evidence from the Stroop test: Eysenck (1982)). However, at very very high arousal, at least when this has been sustained for long periods as in acute psychosis, this success in inhibition may break down. Furthermore, while effort increase usually leads to capacity increase (Dornic 1977), in acute psychosis these constructs seem to diverge.

The general approach here, however, does attach some of the phenomena of the acute psychotic episode to those that obtain in normal people. Although there are differences, the scheme is consistent with a view of schizophrenia and active psychosis as existing on a continuum with normal mentation and not as a group of qualitatively different entities.

A general arousal and capacity approach does not permit me to make differential predictions of the magnitude of confirmation bias on visual and verbal tasks. However, the work of Magaro (1981, 1984), Gur (1978), Gruzelier (1978, 1981) and, in social psychology, Drake (1983) all suggest that at least the paranoid delusional syndrome, which is certainly characterized by Drake's (1983) 'belief perseverance', is a left hemisphere dysfunction. One might imagine that this could well be the case given the generally linear sequential processing style of the dominant hemisphere (Ornstein 1986). Magaro argues, from the basis of the *highly* controversial distinction between 'controlled' and 'automatic' processing (Shiffrin and Schneider 1977), that the paranoid is 'conceptually driven' with a dominance of controlled left hemisphere processing while the non-paranoid is 'data driven' with a dominance of automatic right hemisphere processing. Drake (1983) argues that high arousal generally activates the left hemisphere (see also Powell 1982) and that hyperarousal of the left hemisphere produces perseveration of belief and focusing of attention on the self. Drake's hypothesis therefore makes different and more differentiated predictions than a global capacity model in that performance will differ depending on whether tasks are left or right hemisphere mediated. Drake and Bingham (1985) provide experimental confirmation of Drake's arguments: students showed more attitude change after persuasive messages aimed against a currently held belief or opinion were input to the left ear (right hemisphere processing) than when input to the right ear (left hemisphere processing). In the latter case their previous beliefs persevered. Rausch (1977) also found that patients with right temporal lesions (overaroused left hemispheres (?)) showed lose–stay responses (confirmation bias and belief perseverance) while left temporals (overaroused right hemispheres (?)) showed win–shift responses (refutation bias) (Drake 1983).

If these arguments are valid it is possible that if paranoids have overaroused left hemispheres, they will show particularly high confirmation bias in verbal tasks (left hemisphere). If the non-paranoids have over-aroused *right* hemispheres and thus show win–shift responses rather than lose–stay responses, they will show particularly *low* confirmation bias on *visual* tasks given that visuo-spatial information is predominantly processed by the right hemisphere (Kinsbourne 1982). Confirmation bias on verbal *and* visual tasks should therefore be higher in paranoids as compared with non-paranoids, but arousal should in general correlate *positively* with verbal confirmation bias and *negatively* with visual confirmation bias since the more aroused is the right hemisphere the more refutation bias it demonstrates. Cacioppo *et al.* (1982), for example, demonstrated that during relative right hemisphere activation in right-handers there is biased attention towards persuasive messages with which one *disagrees*.

Confirmation bias was examined in this experiment in both a visual and a verbal mode. In the visual mode a Slide Viewing Task (SVT) was employed. The procedure, similar to that deployed by Draguns (1963) and Bruner and Potter (1966), was to show slides of everyday objects (such as a roundabout, a stapler, etc.) first very much out of focus and then, gradually, in focus. Volunteers were requested to guess what the slide depicted at each stage of the refocusing sequences and give a rating of confidence in their hypothesis on a scale from O ('Pure guess') to 5 ('Certain'). The frequency with which volunteers 'hung onto' *incorrect* hypotheses across focusing position changes while more and clearer data were becoming available (as a function of the total number of incorrect hypotheses) was the measure of 'visual' confirmation bias.

Confirmation bias was hypothesized to be influenced by very high arousal via the latter's effects on capacity, and hence arousal was also measured in a number of different ways.

First, autonomic arousal was measured via pulse and via systolic and diastolic blood pressure determinations. Assuming that high cortical arousal will lead to amplification of stimulation and drop in thresholds, the spiral after-effect duration should increase with increase in cortical arousal and thus be a tentative measure of this parameter. Similarly stronger inhibitory or modulatory processes should result in shorter after-effects.

General felt arousal was assessed by the MacKay *et al.* (1978) and Nowlis (1965) self-report measures.

It was expected that the confirmation bias score – which for each volunteer was the mean number of focusing position changes through which incorrect hypotheses were maintained – would be higher in the psychotics than the non-psychotics and higher in the paranoids than the non-paranoids and, due to increasing rigidity at high arousal and decrease of capacity at *very* high arousal, confirmation bias would show a positive correlation with arousal.

A critical disambiguating test is possible here: if the Drake (1983) hypothesis is correct, visual confirmation bias should correlate *negatively* with arousal.

In assessing confirmation bias in the verbal mode, two tests of associative thinking similar to Mednick's Remote Association test (RAT: Mednick 1962) were employed. In one, volunteers were presented with two word items and requested to find a third word which was an associate of both the previous two (2–3 test). In the other they were presented with three word items and were requested to find a fourth word which was an associate, in a more general sense, of all the previous three (3–4 test): e.g. atomic, sex, shell; answer, *bomb*. Pilot experiments with these tests with 35 volunteers revealed that people first did a search and retrieve operation (through a nodal network?) and then serially tested possible solutions against the given words until a solution which 'fitted' all the test items could be obtained.[1] Confirmation bias was therefore demonstrated when, say, a volunteer found a possible solution word which fitted with *two* of the three test words but not with the third. I infer that the third word is either being ignored or is being associated with the solution word only in a very tenuous convoluted fashion. Either way, confirmation bias is manifested.

Psychotics were expected to show higher confirmation bias than non-psychotics in both the verbal tests, paranoids higher than non-paranoids and the scores were expected to show a positive correlation with arousal on both the capacity model *and* the Drake hypothesis. It was expected that confirmation bias on the 2–3 test would correlate positively with that on the 3–4 test.

In measuring cognitive capacity it seems to me inappropriate to separate capacity itself from that which has capacity; inappropriate totally to separate upper compensatory processes from lower passive or tonic processes; and inappropriate to separate arousal from arousal modulatory processes. All the members of these pairs, I think, overlap and are interdependent.

Capacity is notoriously difficult to define and measure (Kahneman 1973, but especially Allport 1983a, b) and although I am arguing that it decreases at very very high arousal it may be possible that some operations such as similarity perception are actually enhanced at these levels. I shall take perhaps the least controversial processing entity and assess the capacity of working memory (Douglas 1967; Baddeley and Hitch 1974; Baddeley *et al*. 1974). I shall assess the capacity simultaneously to store and perform operations on that which is stored using the backward digit span task from the Wechsler Adult Intelligence Scale (Wechsler 1958). The more capacity a person has, the longer will be that person's backward digit span.

It was predicted that psychotics would show shorter backward digit spans than non-psychotics and that the difference between forward and backward digit span would be greater in the psychotics.

Verbal reports of volunteers in pilot runs of this test suggested that backward digit span makes considerable demands on capacity as the person has to both rehearse the digits 'forward', visualize them and scan the image backward before it fades. The person then renews the image by rehearsal, visualizes and scans again. The digits are never reported in one flow, the person has continually to make an image reappear in order to scan it and report. It is thus virtually impossible to perform any other task (such as balancing a dowel rod) while performing backward digit span.

Since confidence ratings were obtained at all focusing positions in the Slide Viewing Task it was possible not only to record mean confidence levels (which is what is usually done on tasks of this kind) but to perform a signal detection analysis and obtain a non-parametric measure of bias to risk or caution, the B index (McNicol 1972: 123–9) on this task. An incorrect hypothesis held at a high confidence level is a false alarm and a correct hypothesis held at a very low confidence level is a miss.

It was expected that the psychotics would show significant differences in mean confidence levels and B index values from non-psychotics, but no prediction was made as to the direction of these differences. Since paranoids are more sensitive to non-verbal cues (La Russo 1978) it was considered a possibility that they might be more sensitive generally and, at least, show higher d' values than the non-paranoid group.

AROUSAL, CREATIVITY AND PSYCHOSIS

That highly creative people may possess a high loading on an underlying personality dimension related to psychosis has been noted many times since the idea first appeared in the writings of Aristotle, Seneca, Diderot and Schopenhauer (e.g. Kretschmer 1929; Barron 1953, 1972; Cattell and Drevdahl 1955; MacKinnon 1961; Cattell and Butcher 1968; Andreasen and Canter 1974; Eysenck and Eysenck 1976; Woody and Claridge 1977; Keefe and Magaro 1980). That creative production may in part be a control process which is required to keep psychopathology at bay has been suggested by Storr (1972) and that creative people differ from uncreatives in their dispositionally high resting cortical arousal levels has been shown by Martindale (1975). Martindale also comments on the hypersensitivity to distraction that this induces in high creatives and points out that this has also been noted in schizophrenics. Receptivity to information on the unattended channel has been found in both schizophrenics and high creatives (Dykes and McGhie 1976) and highly creative writers have been found to be overinclusive on a test designed to assess this phenomenon in schizophrenics (Andreasen and Powers 1975; Keefe and Magaro 1980). (It should be noted, however, that overinclusion is not invariably demonstrated in schizophrenics' performances on such tests: see Payne (1973).)

The work of Martindale on the relations between arousal and crea- tivity (Martindale and Greenough 1973; Martindale and Armstrong 1974; Martindale 1975) indicates that high creatives can boost arousal easier and better than they can reduce it. Martindale and Armstrong (1974) found that high creatives, as assessed by the RAT, were better at quick control of alpha but were not better at alpha increase. Instead they were better at alpha suppression. Hence the creative's real forte is the focusing of attention (arousal boost) necessary to move from primary to secondary process modes of thought. Pine (1959) and Pine and Holt (1960) had also previously suggested this.

The difficulty that high creatives have in dropping arousal and their sensitivity to distraction means that they also have to modulate their arousal using external tricks and strategies such as finding secluded places to work or, as Bosuet apparently used to do, wrapping their heads in furs, lying in bed or disconnecting the doorbell to cut down sudden arousing distraction (Martindale 1975). This high dispositional arousal and difficulties in arousal drop in high creatives seems also to obtain, I think, in psychotics prone to delusion. The latter also seem to withdraw into isolation partly to titrate their arousal level but the very isolation then gives them licence for unconstrained fantasizing, which eventually exacerbates their state.

It is possible to speculate that high creative production is mediated by either very very low (Blum 1961) or very very high (Bachtold 1980) arousal. This has also been suggested by Martindale (1975) who regarded the extremities of arousal as the zones of primary process thinking (mystical states, reverie and free association), with middle levels of arousal best for rational serial secondary process thought. That the shift from primary to secondary process thought may be an arousal shift was also suggested by Blum (1961) and Martindale and Armstrong (1974). Martindale's work concentrated on the benefits of arousal drop (as measured by increased alpha) as a facilitator of creativity (Martindale 1975) and Martindale and Greenough (1973) found that high arousal decreased creativity on the Remote Associates and Uses of Objects tests. However, in deluded psychotics we seem to have cases where remote associations are facilitated by arousal of extreme magnitude; hence, in this thesis we are searching the opposite end of the spectrum investigated by Martindale.[2]

An inverted-U relation between creativity and arousal is reminiscent of drive theory research in this domain (Mednick 1962) where it was argued that, as drive increased, response hierarchies at first steepened – making dominant (usually common) responses more likely – and then flattened again so that more remote associations became available (as they had at very very low drive). An excitation-inhibition theory would make the same prediction: if creativity depends on the balance between excitatory and inhibitory processes and inhibition increases (very slowly at first) with excitation until the latter floods the system and inhibition breaks down, then a non-inverted-U relation between arousal (which may *tend* to rise with excitation) and creativity would result (Figure 10.1).[3]

Inhibition could be transiently released, say, by alcohol, but repeated strong excitation may weaken inhibitory mechanisms (Malmo 1957) producing a relatively more chronic state in the psychotic. Oppenheim, in an early work (1890), suggested a failure in neural transmission modulation to account for hysteria and Claridge (1967) and Epstein and Coleman (1970) all suggested that a modulation problem (albeit of arousal itself) was critical in explaining acute schizophrenia.

The general pattern relating arousal to delusional thinking, therefore, seems to be as follows. 'Quite high' arousal helps mediate the emergence of a dominant idea and the search for evidence to confirm it. The confirmations themselves, through their portentous implications, boost arousal further thus facilitating creative elaboration and ramification of the delusional system. Confirmation seeking and creative thinking go hand in hand during the ontogeny of the delusional episode, both facilitated by high arousal which perhaps operates by enhancing relational judgement/similarity perception. Ideas coalesce internally (creativity/similarity perception) and are matched and enriched by external stimuli (confirmation bias/assimilation/similarity perception). *The delusional and the mystical states could thus be said to be two modes of vastly enhanced similarity perception, the summit of relational judgement.* Repeated boosts of

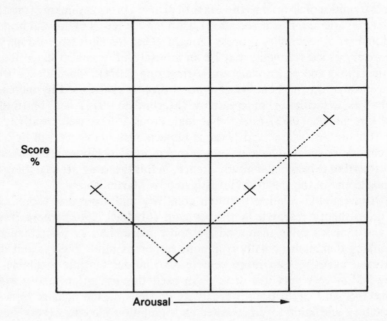

Figure 10.1 The non-inverted-U relation between creativity and arousal

106

excitation weaken inhibitory mechanisms pushing arousal to intense levels such that, without modulation or control, the organization, fine tuning and differentiation are lost. At this stage the psychotic does not have delusions or confirmation bias; delusions and confirmation bias have the psychotic.

It would be wrong to argue that the psychotics lose control completely; many aspects of their thoughts and behaviour may show selectivity and differentiation, and they do not emit the same response to all stimuli – which would be the result of a complete breakdown of inhibition (Milner 1957). Furthermore, their crisis itself may represent the results of unconscious intent, and during the crisis a preconscious intent of the form 'I'm in great danger, give me more power' may, to speak dualistically, be operating. Perhaps through a genetically mediated capacity, the psychotic's brain *can* respond to this instruction but the end result is a kind of 'hyperfunctional malfunction'. Capacities for associative thinking and verification are amplified but these put the psychotic in an ever more threatening position, leading to ever more excitation and arousal boosts being necessary to cope with the escalating dilemmas.

The limitations of an excitation-arousal approach are, however, fairly clear. Being a bottom-up intrapsychic approach it cannot explain similarities in theme in delusional thinking between patients, which would seem to be partly due to environmental formative factors (e.g. vague knowledge of the power of computers, folklore about evil spirits, etc.). Many aspects of the organization of delusional thought are thus left unaccounted for (Lapidus and Schmolling 1975).

Obviously the total global picture of delusional psychosis cannot be explained by hyperarousal. The arousal model contains no environmental information and reduces the functions of an executive ego, which would deal with *tolerance* of stress, anxiety and arousal and *control* of impulses, to a vaguely specified 'inhibitory mechanism'. The problem structure of a delusion cannot be described entirely in terms of internal representations, dynamic structures and processes or local brain processes. Delusions may shift in content and style dramatically on the basis of the most 'trivial' environmental stimuli or patterns which are totally outside the predictions of a cognitive, AI, psychoanalytic or arousal theory. We must ask not only what is inside the psychotic's head but what the psychotic's head is inside. The context within which the psychotic is living is not 'much the same as for everyone'. It is vastly, even uncannily different from that of the common stock of humanity and is considerably changed by their presence. Hence, in looking at arousal processes we are looking merely at *tendencies*, at local patterns operating in a massive network of mutually interpenetrating relations which extend far outside and beyond the psychotics themselves.

To be more specific, the creativity measures used in this experiment were:

1 Uses of a brick test (Christensen *et al.* 1960; Wilson *et al.* 1975) given with a gentle constraint – a time limit of two minutes. This was scored for both fluency and originality.
2 A fluency test – the volunteer was requested to write down, in two minutes, as many words as possible that began with the letter S.
3 The Drawing Completion test (Barron 1962), in which the volunteer is given a fragment of a pattern and asked to 'complete' or 'make something out of it', thus creating a picture (no time *limit* although the volunteers were timed).
4 and 5 The 2–3 and 3–4 verbal thinking tests mentioned previously with no time limits (although again the volunteers were timed). The 3–4 test was the test on which autonomic measures were taken during and after the volunteer's activity.

The validity of these tests was assessed and strongly confirmed by comparing the scores of high 'real world' creative volunteers against those of low creative volunteers (Chadwick 1988: 301, Table 16).[4]

CREATIVITY AND PERSONALITY

Following the work of Eysenck and Eysenck (1976) and Woody and Claridge (1977) it was expected that creativity scores would correlate positively with psychometric measures of psychoticism. Three measures were taken:

1 A short paranoia scale devised for this experiment (*Pa*) but using items from the *E*, *P* and *N* scales of the EPQ (Eysenck Personality Questionnaire; Eysenck and Eysenck 1975), and items from the special psychoticism scale discussed below.
2 The score on the *P* (psychoticism) scale of the EPQ (P^E).
3 A special psychoticism scale (P^C) quite different in content to the *P* scale, again devised for this experiment, basically covering aspects of psychoticism not dealt with in the EPQ.

(When lie scores were taken into account, the *Pa*, the P^E and the P^C scales did discriminate psychotics from non-psychotics (Chadwick 1988: 294–5).)

Measures of empathy, venturesomeness and impulsivity were also obtained, for completeness, using the I_5 of Eysenck and McGurk (1980).

CREATIVITY AND THE PARANOID/NON-PARANOID DISTINCTION

In the first experimental test ever done of the creativity of schizophrenics, Keefe and Magaro (1980) found that non-paranoid schizophrenics scored higher on creativity, as assessed by the Alternate Uses test than did a group of paranoid schizophrenics and a group of non-psychotic psychiatric controls. This was predicted on the basis of Magaro's (1981) scheme to the effect that paranoids are left-hemisphere, controlled, serial convergent thinkers while non-paranoids are right-hemisphere divergent thinkers. Keefe and Magaro (1980) also offered the hypothesis, following Forrest (1976) and Prentky (1979), that schizophrenia and creativity reflect similar cognitive processes.

The present experiment offered an opportunity to attempt to replicate the important finding of Keefe and Magaro although, admittedly, with less pure samples. I predicted that a paranoid/non-paranoid difference would again be found on the Alternate Uses test and indeed in all of the creativity tests, with the non-paranoids being the higher scorers.

It would also be expected that in all the creativity tests non-paranoid psychotics would score higher than the non-psychotic groups.

A direct 'clean' attempt at replication of the Keefe and Magaro experiment was alas not possible as my previously psychotic sample contained four (out of seventeen) volunteers who had suffered predominantly from mood disorders with delusions, rather than from schizophrenia. However, the general pattern found by Keefe and Magaro was expected to emerge.

THE VOLUNTEERS FOR THE EXPERIMENT

There were fifty-nine volunteers who participated in this experiment, seventeen previously deluded psychotics (five women and twelve men), twenty-one people who scored highly (≥ 13) on the N (neuroticism) scale of the EPQ (nine women and twelve men) and twenty-one people who scored low (≤ 12) on this scale (also nine women and twelve men). The so-called 'high N group' I recruited to act as an overaroused control group for the psychotics as Depue (1974) had found that with a highly aroused, rather than normal, control group a schizophrenic effect in an information-processing task was completely eliminated. It proved impossible to find a control group of recovering psychotics who had had no trace of delusion during their illness. Fifty-seven of the fifty-nine volunteers were right-handed, two were left-handed.

The psychotics contained nine people with a paranoid diagnosis and eight with a non-paranoid diagnosis. Those diagnoses, which were very clear-cut in this respect, were reviewed and confirmed. All but one of the psychotics were on medication at the time of testing.

The fifty-nine volunteers in this experiment did not include a single undergraduate psychology student; they were all working or unemployed men and women.

The ages of the volunteers ranged from 19 to 64. Overall there were twenty-three women and thirty-six men and their occupations ranged widely from secretary, social worker, teacher and interior designer (for the women) to food technologist, radio journalist, film-maker, clerk and salesman (for the men). The sample was thus a fair cross-section of society although fifteen volunteers were unemployed – a quarter of the sample. Interestingly, none of these were from the low N non-psychotic group; in contrast, 19 per cent of the high N group and 65 per cent of the psychotic group were unemployed.

Having divided the volunteers into the three groups (previously deluded psychotics, high N and low N non-psychotics) the groups were matched for sex, reasonably closely for age, and less closely for number of years of education. An attempt was made to match them also on the level, and in some cases even the exact nature, of their occupation although this was difficult. Overall the volunteers averaged around 35 years of age with about 13 years of education. Seventeen of the volunteers were friends of mine; six of these were in the psychotic group, five in the high N group and six in the low N group. (Further details are given in Chadwick (1988).)

Since many of the creativity measures in this experiment were verbal, the three groups of volunteers were also matched overall in vocabulary score on the Mill Hill verbal intelligence test (Raven 1976). No significant differences were found in mean Mill Hill score between the three groups.

COMMENTS ON THE RUNNING OF THE EXPERIMENT

My approach in running this experiment was to try to set up conditions where the volunteers, despite knowing that they were under evaluation, could behave, think and feel freely and honestly. Despite the artificiality of the situation I wanted to pick up their spontaneous natural style. To this end every attempt was made to help the volunteers feel relaxed, safe, valued and appreciated.

In the delusional crisis the psychotics give of their best partly in order to survive; hence it was necessary to try to reproduce this 'best' in another context where survival was not involved. I decided that the only way to achieve this was to try to create a warm, accepting and rewarding atmosphere where the volunteers could operate in an authentic way.

The experiment was therefore not run in a university laboratory or cubicle setting but in the kitchen of my fairly comfortable West London flat. Volunteers were requested to arrive at around 6 p.m. and my wife, who by any standards is an exceptionally warm and friendly person, was always on hand to greet them and help make them feel at ease. Volunteers were told beforehand that the experiment involved 'some personality questionnaires, word games, drawings and slides'; that it was basically fun and would be 'a night out with a difference'. The atmosphere was very informal and during all the performance tests my attitude was generally encouraging and rewarding. Hence I would make such statements as 'Yes, you've got the idea', 'You're doing OK', 'That's fine', etc. The exception to this was my behaviour during the Slide Viewing Task where, to avoid confirming or refuting volunteers' evolving hypotheses, I had to remain bland and quiet.

Given the above comments regarding the non-structural features of the experiment, the following procedure was adopted for every volunteer.

The evening began with a pre-experimental chat. Following this, details were noted of the volunteer's age, date of birth, education, and profession and details of any tablets being taken were also jotted down. In addition I recorded whether the volunteer was a smoker or non-smoker. (Because the arousal measures were such important independent variables and because nicotine is such a powerful stimulant, smokers were requested to refrain from smoking at the beginning of the experiment when resting blood pressure and pulse readings were taken, as were state measures, and also to refrain during the 3–4 test where blood pressure and pulse readings were taken while they were on task.)

For the previously deluded psychotic volunteers, information was obtained on the number of episodes they had suffered; the age at which they suffered the first episode; their diagnosis and its date; brief details of their delusions (if they were willing to talk about them); and their current medication, if any.

The experiment was conceptually divided into two parts: the first part involved assessing the volunteer on the independent variables such as vocabulary, arousal, digit span, etc., and the second on the performance variables (creativity and confirmation bias scores).

After the experimental tasks were over I usually had a general chat with the volunteer and asked for his or her reflections on the experiment. These chats were very useful. The vast majority also said that they had, in effect, found the evening interesting and enjoyable. (A description of the actual running of the experiment, at a very detailed level, is given in Chadwick (1988: 255–88).)

11

THE EXPERIMENTAL STUDY
Results and analyses

As the reader can probably tell from the previous chapter, this was a very long and detailed experiment. In fact each volunteer was eventually assessed on no less than 167 variables. Obviously I shall have to be very selective in the data I report as 13,861 correlations were obtained in total. I shall therefore focus, in general, only on those results for which predictions were made, although some other patterns of theoretical interest will be mentioned. A great deal will, however, have to be omitted. Throughout this chapter I shall relate the findings to the overall themes of the book so that the reader is not merely confronted with figures and significance levels.

AROUSAL, CAPACITY AND CONFIRMATION BIAS

When volunteers were grouped into four equally spaced categories of arousal (low, moderate, high, very high), as measured by the Nowlis inventory (1965) – this having the highest correlations with the other arousal measures – and their backward digit spans computed, the pattern was an inverted U (scores being 4.75, 5.36, 5.43 and 5.24). Very tentatively, then, it seems that capacity first rises and then falls, as generally expected, at very high arousal.

With reference to the relations between arousal and both visual and verbal confirmation bias,[1] the correlation of Nowlis Activation score with visual confirmation bias was *negative* at −0.135 and with verbal confirmation bias was only very low positive (+0.031). The same pattern, however, is found with the MacKay *et al.* (1978) arousal measure: a negative correlation with visual confirmation bias (−0.305) and a positive one with verbal confirmation bias (+0.210). Again using the measure of dispositional arousal, the *N* scale score, the same pattern emerges: a *negative* correlation with visual confirmation bias (−0.177) and a positive one with verbal confirmation bias (+0.115). Slight effects in the same directions occur when correlations of reported stress with confirmation bias are studied: a positive correlation with the verbal measure (+0.047) and a negative one with the visual (−0.079).

It was expected that if capacity decreased, at least at very high arousal, then confirmation bias should accelerate at that level. Considering the scores of volunteers in the four levels of arousal categories the highest level of verbal confirmation bias was indeed in the very high arousal category (11.77 per cent). The mean verbal confirmation bias score over the three lower levels of arousal was only 7.39 per cent.

The predictions of confirmation bias via a capacity model therefore only appear to apply, and then only tentatively, for verbal confirmation bias.

The results described above do, however, confirm in a more general sense the predictions of the Drake model – that is, if one regards self-report measures of arousal as roughly indicating general cortical arousal. General cerebral activation should, on Drake's (1983) theory, cause increased verbal confirmation bias (left hemisphere) (lose–stay responses) but decreased visual confirmation bias (right hemisphere)[2] and hence a negative correlation between arousal and visual confirmation bias. The pattern of the results is in accordance with such a scheme.

If we consider smoking as a stimulant likely to operate on both hemispheres (?) the same patterns should emerge in correlations with confirmation bias, and they do: smoking correlates positively with verbal confirmation bias (+0.225) but negatively with visual confirmation bias (−0.361).

The spiral-after-effect correlations were the reverse of this pattern (+0.075 with visual confirmation bias and −0.200 with verbal). However, being involved in 'where' perception as well as 'what' perception, this after-effect may heavily involve subcortical as well as cortical structures (e.g. Sekuler and Blake 1985).

If we consider the visual and verbal confirmation bias scores[3] across groups, where it was expected that the psychotics would be higher on such biases, the general picture is in accordance with these predictions. The verbal confirmation bias scores on the 2–3 and 3–4 tests were very similar (correlation +0.579, $p<0.001$, one-tailed) hence the two scores were pooled by taking the total confirmation bias score on both tests, dividing it by the total number of questions completed and multiplying the result by 100. This is, in this chapter, the 'verbal confirmation bias' score.

The psychotics are much higher on verbal confirmation bias (18.77 per cent, SD 12.50) than the high N non-psychotics (7.84 per cent, SD 6.88) and the low N non-psychotics (2.87 per cent, SD 3.25) ($F = 18.746$, $p < 0.001$). The psychotic mean differs, as expected, from the mean for the low N sample ($F = 39.413$, $p < 0.001$, df 1.52) and hence, there is a linear trend in these scores. The paranoid psychotics were, as expected, higher than the non-paranoid psychotics on verbal confirmation bias (24.04 per cent, SD 13.08 compared to 13.51 per cent, SD 10.03, r-phi = 0.435, $t = 1.808$, $p < 0.05$, one-tailed, df 14) (see also Figure 11.1). If the above findings were merely due to carelessness or haste in responding on the psychotics'

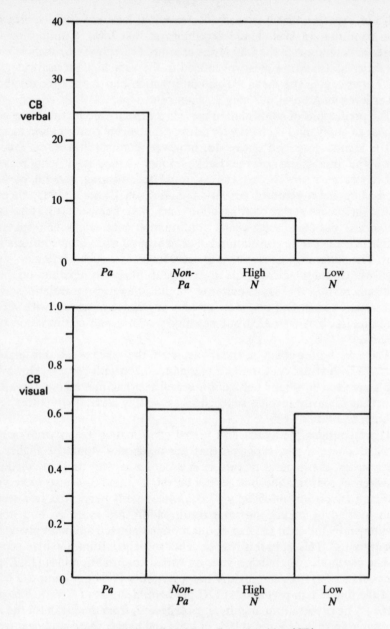

Figure 11.1 Verbal and visual confirmation bias (CB) scores

Pa: paranoid psychotics ($n = 9$)
Non-Pa: non-paranoid psychotics ($n = 8$)
High *N*: non-psychotics high in neuroticism ($n = 21$)
Low *N*: non-psychotics low in neuroticism ($n = 21$)

part, one would expect to see evidence of this. In fact relative to those questions attempted, the psychotics had, if anything, *fewer*, not more, incorrect answers on the Mill Hill vocabulary test than the other groups (11.35, SD 7.08, compared to 12.52, SD 8.27, for the high Ns and 12.19, SD 6.18, for the low Ns). They also had longer, not shorter, mean response times on the Mill Hill, the 2–3, the 3–4 and the Drawing Completion tests. They were also slightly *less* impulsive, if anything, than the high N group, not more impulsive (10.29, SD 3.24, on the Impulsivity scale compared to 11.86, SD 4.44, for the high Ns. The low N group was slightly lower at 9.43, SD 4.52). These group means are, of course, not significantly different ($F = 1.903$, $p = 0.159$, two-tailed) but are in the opposite direction to what would be expected if the psychotics were performing more thoughtlessly.

Backward digit span was, as expected, shorter in the psychotic group (4.76, SD 1.39) than the high N (5.38, SD 1.56) and low N groups (5.333, SD 1.07). These differences, however, are not significant ($F = 1.242$, $p = 0.148$, one-tailed). (Forward minus backward digit span was also greater in the psychotics ($+2.12$) than the high N ($+2.05$) and low N ($+2.09$) groups, but again not significantly so ($F = 0.012$, $p = 0.494$, one-tailed).)

In visual confirmation bias (total number of focusing position changes through which hypotheses are maintained divided by the total number of incorrect hypotheses) the psychotics do score fractionally higher (0.641, SD 0.315) when compared to the high N group (0.536, SD 0.302) and the low N group (0.594, SD 0.319). These differences, however, are not significant ($F = 0.529$, $p = 0.30$, one-tailed). The paranoids are, as expected, also slightly higher than the non-paranoids (0.669, SD 0.417, compared to 0.612, SD 0.192) but not significantly so (r-phi $= 0.0934$, $t = 0.351$, df 14) (see Figure 11.1).

All of these values are *less* than unity and hence reveal that on the Slide Viewing Task volunteers usually changed hypotheses at each new focusing position. Hence these scores are not really measures of confirmation *bias* so much as confirmation *scores*. The low values also lead to the possibility that group differences are underestimated due to floor effects.

Since the confirmation measures only show any relation with capacity on the verbal tests it would seem wiser to interpret these findings in general in accordance with the Drake model since the latter receives wider empirical support.

The inflated scores of the psychotics, especially the paranoid psychotics, indicate that their left hemispheres are *more* aroused than those of the non-psychotics (higher verbal confirmation bias) but that their right hemispheres are perhaps slightly less aroused than those of the non-psychotics (less tendency to shift hypotheses on the Slide Viewing Task and hence higher visual confirmation score). This hemisphere imbalance would seem to be greater in the paranoids than in the non-paranoids. (Interestingly, backward digit span was shorter in the paranoid psychotics compared to the non-paranoid psychotics (4.33 compared to 5.25) and their arousal was also higher, as assessed by the Nowlis (6.00 compared to 5.62.)

The fact that the non-paranoids showed higher verbal confirmation than the non-psychotics shows that the Magaro model (1981), which represents non-paranoids as data driven, is mistaken. The non-paranoids are *also* conceptually driven, like the paranoids, but rather less so than the latter.

The relation of verbal and visual confirmation bias to cortical arousal seem to be reasonably clear and it may be that the actual psychological process that mediates the link between cortical arousal and verbal confirmation bias involves a capacity drop at least at very high arousal.

Relations with *autonomic* arousal were assessed by correlating verbal and visual confirmation bias score with pulse and blood-pressure readings (Table 11.1). Although no guiding predictions were available to assist evaluation of these data the overall pattern of the correlations suggested that high verbal confirmation bias is related to low autonomic activation and high visual confirmation score with *high* autonomic activation. The theoretical significance of this pattern is unclear but the association of low autonomic and high cortical activation that may produce high verbal confirmation bias is similar to the arousal pattern associated with mystical experiences.

The imbalance which produces high verbal *and* visual confirmation bias in the same person would therefore seem to be an imbalance at both cortical and subcortical levels in both hemispheres.

Perceptual sensitivity measure d'_e was also used to assess the groups. It

Table 11.1 Correlations of verbal and visual confirmation bias with autonomic arousal measures

	Verbal CB	Visual CB
Resting pulse	−0.089	−0.044
Mean pulse	−0.045	−0.051
Pulse during thinking test	−0.171	+0.117
Pulse after thinking test	−0.023	+0.023
Resting systolic BP	−0.158	+0.117
Mean systolic BP	−0.287	+0.154
Systolic BP during thinking test	−0.335	+0.197
Systolic BP after thinking test	−0.371	+0.154
Resting diastolic BP	−0.181	+0.034
Mean diastolic BP	−0.322	−0.020
Diastolic BP during thinking test	−0.370	+0.111
Diastolic BP after thinking test	−0.388	−0.122
(Spiral-after-effect duration	−0.200	+0.075)

BP = blood pressure; CB = confirmation bias.

was expected that the psychotics having difficulties in at least everyday reality testing would generally be less sensitive, and this was confirmed: the mean d'_e values for the psychotic group was 2.47 (SD 0.63) compared to 2.75 for the high N group (SD 0.65) and 3.17 for the low N group (SD 1.0). These group differences were significant ($F = 3.839$, $p = 0.014$, one-tailed). The mean for the psychotic sample is significantly different from that for the low N sample ($F = 7.177$, $p = 0.005$, one-tailed, df 1.52) and hence there is a linear trend in these means.

The paranoids were perhaps slightly more sensitive than the non-paranoids (2.61, SD 0.53, compared to 2.32, SD 0.72) (r-phi = 0.238, t = 0.916, df 14) but clearly were not more sensitive than the non-psychotics (see Figures 11.2 and 11.3).[4]

The perceptual sensitivity measure $\triangle_m$ also was used to assess the groups (both d'_e and $\triangle_m$ are advisable replacement measures for d' when signal and signal-plus-noise distributions are not of equal variance: McNicol (1972: 88–90)). Again psychotics were expected to be lower in $\triangle_m$

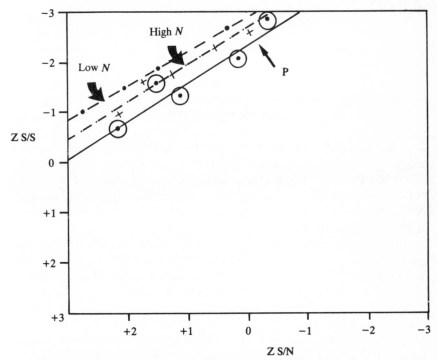

Figure 11.2 Signal detection analysis of the Slide Viewing Task

ROC lines (fitted by eye) of the three groups:
Low N: non-psychotics scoring low on neuroticism
High N: non-psychotics scoring high on neuroticism
P: previously deluded psychotics

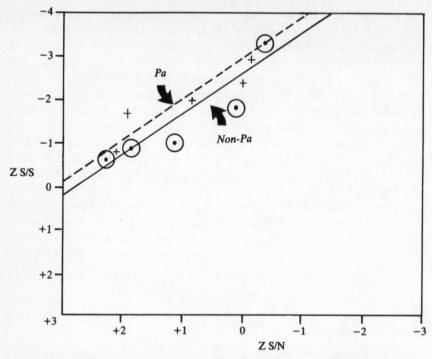

Figure 11.3 Signal detection analysis of performance in the Slide Viewing Task by paranoid (*Pa*) and non-paranoid (*Non-Pa*) psychotics

and this was confirmed. Mean $\triangle_m$ for the psychotics was 2.76 (SD 1.02), that for the high N group was 2.98 (SD 0.72) and that for the low N group was 3.80 (SD 1.08). These group differences are significant ($F = 7.350$, $p = 0.001$, one-tailed). The psychotic mean differs from the mean for the low N sample ($F = 11.610$, $p < 0.005$, one-tailed, df 1,52) and hence a linear trend again exists in these means.

Again the paranoids are slightly higher in sensitivity than the non-paranoids (2.87, SD 0.89 compared to 2.65, SD 1.19) but are not more sensitive than the non-psychotics. (Paranoid/non-paranoid $\triangle_m$ difference is, however, not significant: r-phi $= 0.110$, $t = 0.414$, df 14.)

In addition to performance and sensitivity measures on the Slide Viewing Task, volunteers were also assessed on their degree of bias in their judgements on this task on a dimension from risk to caution. In B index terms (McNicol 1972: 123–9) the psychotics seemed to be fractionally more risky (B = 3.46, SD 1.29, compared to 3.35, SD 1.27 for the high N group and 3.09, SD 0.89, for the low N group). The differences are, however, not significant ($F = 0.412$, $p = 0.664$, two-tailed).[5]

There is no confirmation of the idea that riskiness is due to high arousal, the correlation between the Nowlis score and the B index is −0.131. (The correlation of B index with reported stress was also in the wrong direction: −0.034.)

The paranoids are the most risky group of all, however, as expected (B = 3.72, SD 1.60), and the non-paranoids the most cautious (B = 3.20, SD 0.93). Clearly, however, the differences between groups are all very slight.

It was expected that the previously deluded psychotics would be more likely to hold incorrect hypotheses at confidence levels of 4 ('almost certain') or 5 ('certain'). This was confirmed: the percentage of total incorrect hypotheses held at a confidence level of 4 or 5 was 11.32, SD 11.26, in the psychotic group; 9.69, SD 14.20, in the high N group; and 4.34, SD 4.40, in the low N group ($F = 2.313$, $p = 0.05$, one-tailed).

Because all volunteers were asked to record a measure of their confidence at each focusing position for each slide it was possible to see how mean confidence level in hypotheses constructed changed as the slide was brought into focus (Figure 11.4). Here it can be seen, interestingly, that the psychotics are *more confident* in hypotheses held at high (very-out-of-focus) focusing positions, than the non-psychotic groups but *less* confident than the latter groups at numerically low focusing positions – where stimulus factors are more dominant. Hence, as in their delusions, they are more confident than non-psychotics in hypotheses enriched by internal factors but less confident than non-psychotics in hypotheses held when the hard evidence is actually clearer. Medication obviously does not eliminate this bias. The crossover interaction in Figure 11.4 is significant ($F = 3.23$, $p < 0.001$, two-tailed).

Perhaps not surprisingly given the pattern in Figure 11.4, it was found that psychotics had *more* confidence in incorrect hypotheses than did non-psychotics (these tend to be held at higher focusing positions) and *less* confidence in correct hypotheses (which tend to be held at low focusing positions) than did non-psychotics (Figure 11.5). The crossover interaction in Figure 11.5 is also significant ($F = 4.73$, $p = 0.013$, two-tailed). Psychotics therefore have less insight into the accuracy of their own decisions than do non-psychotics. This confirms the findings of Mintz and Alpert (1972) who obtained a similar pattern in an auditory analogue of the Slide Viewing Task.

So far, one clear pattern seems to be emerging. On most variables there is a monotonic trend from psychotic group scores to low N group scores with the scores of the high N group being intermediate. Even though the psychotics are reasonably matched on arousal with the high N group, there the similarity ends. The picture that tends to be emerging then is that, at least on these objective tests, high N volunteers are on a continuum between stability and psychosis and the scores of the psychotic group are not only due to an arousal factor but to a psychoticism factor in addition to the contribution to performance provided by high arousal. There is, however, little doubt that, despite medication, the psychotics *are* highly aroused and share more similarities with high N non-psychotics than they do with low N non-psychotics.

PERFORMANCE ON CREATIVITY TESTS

Contrary to expectations, the previously deluded psychotics taken as a group did not score more highly than either of the non-psychotic groups on any of the creativity measures or tests. In all cases the low N non-psychotics produced the highest scores followed by the high N non-psychotics, with the psychotic group third. From this analysis it would seem that both neuroticism and psychoticism are damaging of creativity.

Similarly, when the three measures of psychoticism used here were correlated with all the six creativity measures, thirteen out of eighteen of the correlations were negative (see Tables 11.2 and 11.3 on page 122). The highest positive correlation is +0.128 which is the correlation between S

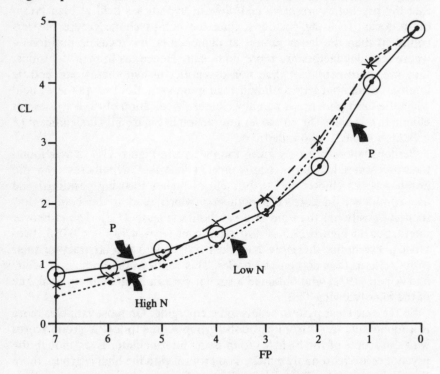

Figure 11.4 Change in confidence level (CL) with which hypotheses were held as focusing position (FP) changed in the Slide Viewing Task

Focusing position: 7, very out of focus; 0, in full focus
Confidence level: 0, 'Pure guess'; 1, 'Almost a guess'; 2, 'Possibly'; 3, 'Probably'; 4, 'Almost certain'; 5, 'Certain'.

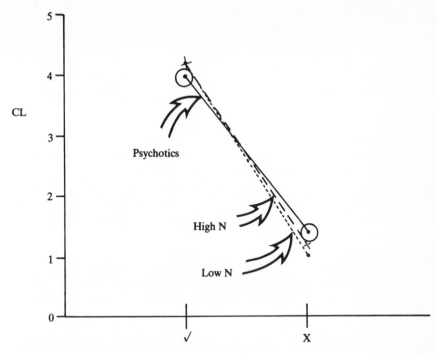

Figure 11.5 Confidence levels in correct (✓) and incorrect (x) hypotheses held
in the Slide Viewing Task

test score (a fluency score) and Eysenckian psychoticism (P^E). These findings
clearly fail to confirm those of Woody and Claridge (1977), who used a
sample of Oxford undergraduates. (Keefe and Magaro's (1980) method of
scoring the Uses test on the basis of the strikingness of the offered uses
(their 'graded measure') was not deployed as, here, inter-rater reliability
was only +0.07. Keefe and Magaro alas did not assess reliability in their
study.)

At first glance the perhaps rather romantic association of psychopathology and creativity seems to be totally and utterly destroyed. The
association starts to seem more plausible, however, when we examine
separately the scores of the paranoid and the non-paranoid psychotics.
When this is done it emerges that on every single creativity measure
the low scores of the psychotics are largely due to the scores of the
paranoids. The non-paranoid sample are in fact on a par with the two
non-psychotic groups. The paranoid psychotics never outperform the non-
paranoid psychotics (Table 11.4). The fact that the non-paranoids do not
outperform the low N non-psychotic group (although they do score higher
than the high N group on three of the six measures) may be due to the fact
that the non-psychotics contained some really quite talented people and

Table 11.2 Mean scores of psychotic (*P*), high *N* (*N*) and low *N* (*S*) groups on creativity measures

	P	N	S	p(two-tailed)
S test (fluency)	23.41 (7.07)	26.29 (6.54)	28.05 (6.28)	0.145
Uses (fluency)	4.47 (2.40)	6.38 (3.06)	6.80 (2.14)	0.032
Uses (originality)	32.08 (12.19)	36.71 (8.12)	39.39 (4.90)	0.056
2–3 score	16.12 (7.16)	21.91 (5.52)	23.14 (5.02)	0.003
3–4 score*	34.31 (15.14)	40.19 (12.70)	49.10 (11.60)	0.006
Drawing completion test (originality)	52.70 (6.47)	53.63 (2.52)	54.31 (2.26)	0.394

*Correlation of scores on this test with self-rating at verbal games was quite low at +0.117.

may have presented quite a stiff challenge to the (medicated) psychotics. Considering that they were on medication, the non-paranoids did very well by any standards.

The low scores of the paranoids (and the usually negative correlations of creativity with psychometrically assessed paranoia) support Keefe and Magaro's (1980) findings even though different scoring methods and more measures were deployed here than in their study.

When, as was intended, creativity score was plotted as a function of four levels of arousal – to test the predicted non-inverted-U relation between arousal and creativity – the result is as shown in Figure 11.6. The Nowlis

Table 11.3 Correlations of measures of psychoticism with measures of creativity

	P^E	P^C	P_a
S test (fluency)	+0.128	−0.176	−0.295
Uses (fluency)	+0.078	−0.181	−0.050
Uses (originality)	−0.134	−0.310	−0.348
2–3 score	+0.032	+0.013	+0.078
3–4 score	−0.212	−0.159	−0.161
Drawing Completion test (originality)	−0.041	−0.051	−0.138

Table 11.4 Mean scores of paranoid and non-paranoid psychotics on creativity measures

	Paranoid	Non-paranoid	t	p (one-tailed)
S test (fluency)	20.11 (5.01)	27.125 (7.47)	−2.298	0.017
Uses (fluency)	3.00 (1.50)	6.125 (2.17)	−3.492	0.002
Uses (originality)	27.08 (14.11)	37.70 (6.59)	−1.944	0.037
2–3 score	14.56 (8.05)	17.88 (6.03)	−0.952	NS
3–4 score	29.25 (11.85)	39.38 (17.09)	−1.426	NS
Drawing Completion test (originality)	51.65 (8.78)	53.89 (2.15)	−0.700	NS

Activation score was used to measure arousal, and creativity was assessed by reducing every volunteer's score to a percentage of the maximum score obtained on a particular test. Figure 11.6 is based on creativity scores averaged over the four best measures: Uses (fluency), Uses (originality), 2–3 score and 3–4 score. All four tests showed the same trend with arousal as that shown in Figure 11.6 except for one reversal on the 3–4 test.

Creativity does then seem to vary with arousal, as predicted, except at the highest level of arousal where it *decreases* instead of continuing to increase. The chances of the obtained pattern occurring, given the predicted pattern at bottom, are 1 in 64 ($p = 0.016$), which is reasonably satisfactory. Creativity therefore does seem to relate to arousal in part as predicted, but the full relationship may be cubic with a decrease in creativity at very high arousal levels. With only four levels of arousal as the independent variable it is not possible to comment further on this.

Overall the best predictors in a positive sense of creativity test score are: forward and backward digit span; Mill Hill score; MacKay arousal; Nowlis Activation; and Nowlis Concentration score.

On the other hand, the negative predictors are scores on Paranoia, P^C, Impulsivity and Nowlis Scepticism.

Hence, if a person is bright, alert (though not too alert), trusting, stable, careful and tries hard he or she is likely to do well on these tests. This is not exactly very surprising.

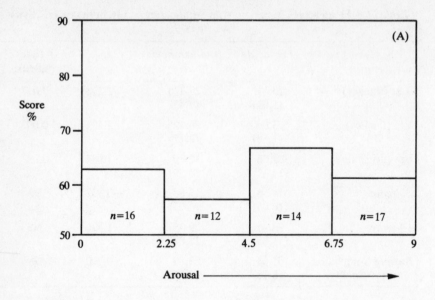

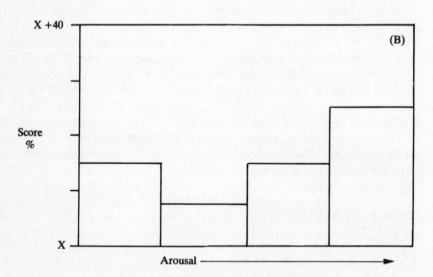

Figure 11.6 Relationship between arousal and creativity scores

(A) Arousal measured by the Nowlis (1965) nine-point scale. Creativity score is the mean score over four creativity measures: the Uses (fluency) score, the Uses (originality) score, the 2–3 and the 3–4 scores. (*n* = number of volunteers in each arousal level category.)

(B) Expected relationship between arousal and creativity where creativity scores range over 40 per cent and arousal over four categories.

CREATIVITY, CONFIRMATION BIAS AND PERCEPTUAL ACCURACY

It was argued earlier that confirmation bias can be a positive constructive phenomenon; indeed, its universality is a testament to its adaptive value as an almost anti-entropic dynamism in nature. I have also argued that many differently named phenomena, such as similarity perception, overinclusive thinking, assimilation and confirmation bias, were basically manifestations of relational judgement and the accessing of data and ideas to current knowledge structures. If the above is valid we would expect to see positive correlations between confirmation bias and creativity in that creativity involves the grouping together or synthesizing of elements from disparate realms.

Since scores on creativity and confirmation bias were not independent on the 2–3 and 3–4 tests, correlations with confirmation bias were computed for the remaining tests and are presented in Table 11.5. Generally, confirmation bias and creativity are indeed positively correlated although scores on the Drawing Completion test (DCT) depart from this pattern. The pattern fragments which form the seeds of drawings in the DCT are not really *related to* the whole as if from a different domain, nor are they disembedded from one context and placed in another; they merely act as catalysts for any number of elaborations, the final products of which they have no meaningful relation to at all.

Table 11.5 Correlations between creativity test scores and confirmation bias (CB)

	Verbal CB	Visual CB
Uses (fluency)	+0.246	+0.226
Uses (originality)	+0.490*	+0.140
S test (fluency)	+0.131	+0.008
Drawing Completion test (originality)	−0.112	−0.275

*$p < 0.01$, one-tailed.

Although no predictions were made with respect to the relations between confirmation bias and accuracy, the overall patterns of the correlations shown in Table 11.6 suggest that although confirmation bias may be associated, as expected, with creativity it is damaging of perceptual accuracy and tends to be also associated with an attitude of slight risk. It would seem that if a person is to be constructive and creative, he or she may have to trade this for some degree of loss in observational veridicality. (Indeed, in science it is difficult to find people who are both good theoreticians *and* good observers. On Brunerian and Gregorian schemes the two should go together, but in practice they do not.)

Table 11.6 Confirmation bias and perceptual accuracy on the Slide Viewing Task

	Verbal CB	Visual CB
Recognition position	−0.067	+0.043
d'_e	−0.208	−0.218
$\triangle_m$	−0.172	−0.266
B index	+0.295	+0.112

CONCLUSIONS FROM THE EXPERIMENTAL STUDY

A bias for seeking and accepting information that confirms ongoing ideation at the expense of that which refutes it is present to a greater degree in previously deluded psychotics than in overaroused non-psychotic controls and stable non-psychotics. This bias is particularly clear in verbal tasks but is arguably present although less in evidence in a visual task. Confirmation bias is also stronger in paranoids than in non-paranoids in both verbal and (possibly) visual tasks, less in high N non-psychotics and least in evidence in low N non-psychotics. It is nonetheless present in non-paranoids who thus are also conceptually, not data, driven.

Verbal confirmation bias is interpreted to be associated with high left-hemisphere cortical activation (perhaps involving a capacity decrease) but with low left-hemisphere limbic activation. Visual confirmation bias may be associated with low right-hemisphere cortical activation but high right-hemispheric limbic activation. Hence the degree of balance between left and right limbic and cortical activation states is greater in non-psychotics, and psychotics have progressively more intra- and inter-hemispheric imbalance.[6]

Although creativity and psychoticism, as measured psychometrically, may be associated in students (Woody and Claridge 1977) this does not seem to be the case in working and unemployed adult men and women. If anything, both psychoticism and neuroticism are damaging of creativity. However, non-paranoid psychotics are comparable in creativity to high and talented low N non-psychotics but paranoid psychotics seem to be markedly uncreative (at least in the divergent sense used here).

Paranoid psychotics may be more perceptually sensitive than non-paranoid psychotics but are not more so than non-psychotics with whom they are roughly on a par. Paranoids *may* also be fractionally more risky in their judgemental processes than all other groups, but the group differences are all very slight. Their possible sensitivity, however, is not married with extensive creative intellectual resources and hence they may perceive more than they can rationally make sense of.

Similarly, the creativity of the non-paranoids is not married with perceptual accuracy and hence they may construct outré interpretations which are not based on veridically evaluated evidence. The paranoids therefore may notice more than they can handle and the non-paranoids may dream up more than they can justify. *In one sense* then the paranoids are, if anything, data driven, and the non-paranoids conceptually driven – the reverse of Magaro's (1981) scheme.

A summary of paranoid/non-paranoid differences in mean scores on a range of variables where differences were expected is shown in Table 11.7. A paranoid–non-paranoid distinction does hold up, not only in the psychotic group but also in the high *N* group. Alas, it is not so clear in the low *N* group.

Table 11.7 Differences in mean score of paranoid (*Pa*) and non-paranoid volunteers on seventeen variables where predictions were made. (Non-psychotic paranoids assessed psychometrically and thus divided into high and low paranoids on the basis of the mean *Pa* score for their group.)

		Group	
Test prediction	*P*	*N*	*S*
S test (*Pa* lower)	√	√	√
Uses (fluency) (*Pa* lower)	√	√	√
Uses (originality) (*Pa* lower)	√	√	√
DCT (originality) (*Pa* lower)	√	×	×
2–3 score (*Pa* lower)	√	×	√
3–4 score (*Pa* lower)	√	√	√
Verbal CB (*Pa* higher)	√	√	√
Visual CB (*Pa* higher)	√	×	√
d'_e (*Pa* higher)	√	√	×
$\triangle_m$ (*Pa* higher)	√	√	×
B index (*Pa* higher)	√	√	×
Backward digit span (*Pa* lower)	√	√	×
Forward minus backward digit span (*Pa* higher)	√	√	√
Lie score (*Pa* higher)	√	√	×
Scepticism (*Pa* higher)	×	√	×
Social affection (*Pa* lower)	×	√	√
Aggression (*Pa* higher)	√	√	×
Total (T)	17	17	17
Least Common Sign (L)	2	3	8
p (one-tailed)	0.001	0.008	0.5

P = psychotic; *N* = high *N*; *S* = low *N*
√ = prediction confirmed; × = prediction not confirmed

On the whole there were fifty-three sets of performance scores and there was a monotonic trend, at least judging from mean values, on no less than forty-one of them, from low N group scores (highest) through high N group (intermediate) to (medicated) psychotic group (lowest scores). It would therefore seem likely that psychosis and neuroticism have much in common. However, the lack of equality in scores between psychotics and the overaroused control group of high N volunteers shows that psychosis is not only an overarousal disorder.

There does seem to be evidence, from the Slide Viewing Task, that psychotics do not perceive reality as accurately as non-psychotics even when the former are medicated. They have higher confidence in incorrect decisions than non-psychotics and lower confidence in correct decisions. In this respect the high N group, being intermediate between the psychotics and the low N group, share the problem but to a reduced extent. Reality distortion therefore occurs in psychotics and high N non-psychotics even in relatively non-threatening tasks and with non-social stimili.

Creativity and confirmation bias are allied but confirmation bias and perceptual accuracy are not. The creative, theory building, confirmation seeking mind may create great novelty yet may not be so gifted at true perception at least of our everyday realm.

12

IMPLICATIONS FOR THERAPY

The purpose of this chapter is to deploy the experience and knowledge I have gained through this research (which really began as a basic research project) in the domain of application. All the implications described in this chapter are tied conceptually to issues raised throughout the book: some highlighted, some merely mentioned, but some linkages may seem more remote as they derive more strongly from my counselling experience over the time of this investigation. Essentially, then, this chapter enables me to funnel all the skills and ideas developed during this sometimes esoteric project into helping real people in real life.

BIASES IN THOUGHT AGAIN

I began this book with a description of how I stumbled across the topic of delusional thinking through being interested in biases in human thought, biases which could not only distort but imprison our minds and prevent us from achieving deep truths and taking effective action. One bias which I have not so far mentioned but which is very relevant in the context of evaluating the causes and the treatments of psychotic crises is that known as the actor–observer divergence (Jones and Nisbett 1971). This is the bias we have as actors in life to attribute the causes of our *own* behaviour to external situational factors but to attribute the causes of the behaviour of *others* (whom we observe) to internal intrapsychic factors, i.e. to their motives, personality, character structure and so on. This is especially so when the behaviour concerned is in some way a failure or a mistake. Ross (1977) proposed that observers were the ones in error in overemphasizing internal factors and underemphasizing external factors. This is the 'fundamental attribution error'.

On the dozen or so occasions when I have asked non-psychotic people if they think they could ever 'break down and go mad' they have all replied with words to the effect, 'No I'm too strong, I have too strong a personality'. Clearly these lay people (and many professionals) tacitly believe that madness is due to some factor *internal* to the psychotic such as 'weak personality' and not primarily due to their having lived in a (for them) unliveable situation.

This bias is evident also in the psychopathology literature where there are dozens of papers on 'internal' factors in psychosis to every one on 'external' factors. Indeed, were it not for investigators such as Laing, Bateson, Brown and Leff this imbalance would probably be even greater. Investigators from some schools, such as psychoanalysis, believe that there is something fundamentally wrong with the psychotic (such as their having regressed to the oral stage) independently of their social as opposed to their intrapsychic context. This bias, which also operates in the field of personality research, has resulted in our knowing very little about how best to modify the circumstances of the psychotic's life in comparison to the wealth of suggestions that we have available on how to change the mind–brain system of the psychotic. We need, however, to know not only what is inside the psychotic's head but what the psychotic's head is inside. Hence I shall turn first to those manipulations of the external environment that would seem likely to be therapeutic.

MANIPULATIONS OF THE EXTERNAL ENVIRONMENT

We know, for example (see Bebbington and Kuipers 1988), that it is best not to discharge a recovering psychotic person from hospital to a home characterized by a great deal of criticism and emotional overinvolvement (high EE homes) and/or that the receiving family should be encouraged not to behave in those ways (from the researches, for example, of Brown *et al.* (1966), Vaughn and Leff (1976), Leff (1976), Kuipers (1979) and Leff *et al.* (1982, 1985)).

We have reason to believe then that treatment of a recovering psychotic may need to involve the whole family within which he or she is merely 'the identified patient' (IP). The emphasis is both on *change* in the family system – for example, away from scapegoating the I P – and on encouraging members of the family to communicate more clearly and less ambiguously (from the researches, for example, of Liem (1974), Goldstein and Rodnick (1975) and Norton (1982)).

Few researchers, however, believe that any particular forms of schizophrenogenic family interactions have convincingly been demonstrated. Apart from the problems raised by the absence of studies of control families, this is not a surprising state of affairs since, despite inspiring work especially of Bateson *et al.* (1956), Laing and Esterson (1964) and Lidz *et al.* (1965), the interactions of a family of, say, four members are incredibly complex and this makes abstraction of salient patterns and categorization of repetitive themes extremely difficult and necessarily impressionistic.

We know also that people should avoid making a large number of changes over a short period, such as changing their home, their lover and their job all at the same time, as this is liable to greatly predispose them to some illness, perhaps even a psychotic crisis (from the researches of, for example, Holmes and Rahé (1967) and Paykel (1979)).[1] We suspect that a lower class environment will help evoke schizophrenia in people genetically predisposed to it (Turner and Wagonfield 1967) but we cannot as yet pin-point the factors to reverse or neutralize in the environments to which we discharge psychotic clients (see page 145 on this problem).

Research in the field of memory has emphasized that if the same context is present at storage as at recall, the latter will be facilitated (Estes 1972). This would imply that it would be unwise to discharge a client to the very same physical situation from which he or she came, e.g. a boarding house bedsitter, as a return to the same room in which the crisis occurred would be expected to 'bring it all back'. (Related to this: it is unwise to discuss with clients the fine detail of their delusions because of the danger of reactivating the previous state. Particularly to be avoided is the retrieval of the feeling of meaning associated with the delusion content.)

Most mental health professionals know that to avoid biasing observers or attracting undue negative attention, recovering psychotics should be encouraged to dress reasonably well and to attempt to present an acceptable appearance to the world. Despite shortage of money, this can be achieved even with jumble sale clothes. A hair-do can do wonders for a recovering client's mood and confidence and need not be *that* expensive. An unkempt scruffy appearance encourages stares, knowing looks, smirks, frowns and comments from passers-by, etc., which can only decrease self-esteem and exacerbate a mild delusional state or reactivate one that had previously been muted. For those clients who 'stand out' because of a slovenly appearance, but do not think they do, video feedback of their appearance in public might well be jolting but beneficial in the longer term.

Other environmental or 'external' manipulations, however, are generally based on intuition, guesswork or the personal flair of hostel and group home staff who have to rely on their hunches as the best solution for the person or people concerned.[2]

This is a sad and devastatingly unbalanced state of affairs. My own experience is largely in one-to-one situations and I admit that I initially approached the topic of paranoia and delusional thinking with an internal attributional attitude. However, as I hope the foregoing chapters have demonstrated, I personally believe that external factors are critically important in the genesis and exacerbation of the psychotic state. Indeed, I would go so far as to make two assertions: that *some* schizophrenics have, in a sense, no intrapsychic problems at all (as one girl said to me, 'I was entirely screwed up by other people') and that the, in part, causal relationship between low social class and schizophrenia is a vastly under-researched problem in psychologically oriented schizophrenia research.

Research is also definitely needed, in this context, on the study of people who habitually and chronically cause mental distress in others. So far only the famous (or infamous) 'schizophrenogenic mother' of Fromm-Reichmann (1948) has received any semblance of detailed attention. However, I feel certain that this concept has distracted attention away from the hoardes of dangerous people in many other categories of life who have equal or even more pernicious effects on those who live or work with them. Relationships with such people are weakening rather than strengthening; they may be sane themselves (although in my experience they cluster in the neurotic extravert quadrant) but they may help to cause even more serious neuroses and even psychoses in others. These 'neurotogenic' or 'psychotogenic' people are similar to L. G. Brown's 'carriers of mental ill-health' (1934); if community care is to be effective, we need to know much more about such individuals.

Having said all this, however, I shall have to concentrate my own suggestions for treatment into territory where I have most experience (the positive value of medication is accepted and assumed) and focus on ideas that derive from the bulk of the research reported in this book. The following will therefore often have rather an intrapsychic flavour, but suggestions for the modification of external factors will also be an important theme. At all times, however, we need external manipulations that are sensitive to the context provided by internal factors, and internal manipulations that are sensitive to the context provided by external factors. To manage behaviour or social situation alone, or perform intrapsychic rearrangements alone, is isolationist decontextualized nonsense.

MEATS AND POISONS

Any treatment and rehabilitation programme for a recovering psychotic client must be rich, varied and flexible so as to cater for the individual's needs. Rehabilitation schemes therefore need to be client centred rather than programme centred (Shepherd 1988). One person's meat is another person's poison, and one has to be prepared to waive cherished solutions and ideas in specific circumstances. In what follows I shall discuss common 'meats' and 'poisons' and for brevity I may seem somewhat dogmatic. However, my suggestions are in most cases only meant as guides and as food for thought. Just as every client is unique so every programme of help should be individually tailored.

Although Alana J's experience and those of many manic patients are exceptions to this, most delusional thinking involves a *negative* cognitive style. It is therefore useful for therapeutic effectiveness to encourage positive thinking and a reframing not only of current but of past negative experiences in as positive a way as possible. For example, memories of school may be painful but the person can usually be coaxed to retrieve some positive memories of that time in their lives, which they previously had taken for granted and allowed to become submerged. Clearly, if the construing of events backwards and forwards in time is negative one has neither hope nor nostalgia to fall back on.

In the context of encouraging positivity, a non-condemnatory and non-punitive religious outlook is also worth promoting. To find one's strength through relating to Jesus, who was an infinitude of gentleness, love and forgiveness, produces an experience which is the very antithesis of malign delusional thinking. The guilt, anger and fear which so suffuses the mind in delusion just cannot obtain such an insidious hold when one allows God into oneself as a real living force. Guilt in particular should be a focus of counselling in this context since phenothiazine medication, although it has a major effect on thought disorder and belligerence, leaves guilt feelings virtually untouched (Klein and Davis 1969).

Cathartic approaches, which encourage the client to 'discharge' pent-up hatred and loathing towards parents for example, should, I believe, be discouraged.[3] Previously psychotic clients are all too aware of their negative emotions and having them beating cushions and pillows or screaming in sound-proofed rooms can only rehearse their negative emotions even more extensively and encourage extremes of negative emotional experience of which, really, the client has already had quite enough. Psychotics, in Jungian terms, are unbalanced personalities; they have 'pushed' their negative side to a self-harming extent. What is needed is not further exploration of their negativity but an emphasis on and a development of their positive capabilities.

Similarly, free association should be discouraged. Psychotic clients generally have quite elaborate schemata tagged or coded with negative drives. Free association can only facilitate reactivation of such negative drive schemata and produce highly aversive states. What the client lacks is cultivated positive emotional schemata. To achieve these a superior–inferior relationship is to be avoided as is a relationship in which the clients trust the therapists with many details of their private mental lives while the therapists trust the clients with nothing of theirs. This form of skewed 'I'm not giving *anything* away to *you*' attitude is humiliating and counter-therapeutic.

Paranoid clients, through their great sensitivity to non-verbal cues, require counsellors and therapists who are the very quintessence of a genuine up-front attitude. A divided counsellor whose violence only 'peeps through' occasionally to be revealed in subtleties is liable to be harmful to such clients. To a paranoid, 'hints' on the surface of that kind may be taken to mean a swirling cesspit of malicious loathing, detestation and malevolence beneath that surface. (One has to remember that, to the paranoid, the world has *No Soul*.)

All previously deluded clients have a strong tendency to go beyond the information given and to infer the negative behind a positive front. Hence,

133

if one talks negatively with them about an absent person they are liable to infer: 'If with them, then with me too.' However, this tendency to leap beyond the given can be used or tempted for the clients' benefit in order to undercut the generatrix of their delusional style by inducing them to make inferences which counteract their negativity. This can be done, for example, by only talking about absent people in a *positive* way. If the psychotics infer that the same attitude will be shown to them in their absence, this is clearly trust enhancing. This procedure I call 'positive inference tempting'. Rather than directly attempting to change the client's cognitive style it puts it to work against itself.

A cynical or subtly cynical attitude on the part of the therapist is therefore highly damaging. However, most devastating of all is a dismissive attitude to the client's judgemental ability. Most therapists do not have any great trust in a previously deluded client's judgement. This cynicism is *catastrophically* countertherapeutic. After a psychotic episode a client needs to be gradually and gently rebuilt, not scorned as inept and incompetent simply because his or her beliefs do not sound plausible. To avoid undermining the client's self regard even further it is useful to seek the very early cognitions on which the delusional system was founded. These are often quite plausible. The way they were generalized to their final bizarre form can then be criticized – but it is essential that the client be able to salvage some semblance of self-pride from the episode. 'Potty' ideas do not emerge suddenly; even primary delusions are probably preceded by many weeks experience of the meaning feeling (see page 91). Very bizarre ideas are usually the result of a long sequence of actual true perceptions and, often, remarkable coincidences that might have made anyone think similarly. This is, in part, why they are so frequently resistant to argument and new disconfirmatory evidence. Hence every example of good judgement shown by the client should be reinforced. Clients are much more likely to trust therapists who appreciate their good performances than those who are cynical about every interpretation they make.

MYSTICISM AND THE PARANORMAL AS MEAT AND POISON

The mystic thinks, 'reality is weird'; the psychotic thinks, 'there's something weird happening in the world, directed at me'. The mystic/creative thinks, 'I suffer my thoughts, streams of ideas just come to me'; the psychotic thinks, 'thoughts are implanted in my mind by computers/ hypnotic suggestion at a distance'. The mystical intuitions and the psychotic cognitions are as if in ratio; one may easily transmute into the other. It seems that mystical intuitions are difficult to hold or permit without giving them some cliché-ridden reference. This I think is what can happen in delusion.

Given these similarities and ideas (see also Chapter 9) perhaps the mystico-transcendent therapies such as Yoga, Zen, Sufism and Tibetan Buddhism and variants of Judaeo-Christian mysticism would be beneficial to the recovering psychotics intent on discovery and on the validation of their capacities? Personally I think this may be so, but only after some time. The person should not be seeking 'easy highs' or a mode of cognition which allows *any* thought to be 'meaningful', 'good enough' or 'viable'. Such 'glitzy' and loose thinking styles are, in certain circumstances, actually damaging at the *hardware* level. Product can influence process via perhaps modifying the mechanisms of similarity perception and arousal modulation. Also the structural peculiarities that these thought styles induce are themselves liable to *lead to* the very thought styles which exacerbate the peculiarities themselves. This is in itself a condemnation of the type of thinking found in some forms of neurotic and psychotic religiosity.

Nonetheless, I believe there is a mystical slice between the western rationalism and empiricism justified by thinkers from Socrates to Popper and ordinary human superstition, fable and folly – a slice that is productive and illuminating. However, it is difficult to indwell there. Anyone seeking this realm needs a social, cognitive and emotional support network without and positive self-regard within. It is not for the bitter loner or the ostracized recluse. In the latter circumstances magic can be 'bad for the brain'. One cannot reach these realms without some degree of suffering and this has to be faced. We do like meaning but we do not like anxiety – but both are the concomitants of living within a range of alternatives. To find the mystical domain one needs guidance, support and strength.[4]

On the positive side, peripheral indulgence in such therapies could be useful. The narrowing of attention and the focusing on the subjective required in meditation may be of therapeutic value to people who have difficulty concentrating and whose attention is often hypervigilant to the external world. Also the relaxation and peace and, on the hardware side, general diminution of autonomic activity may well be valuable. On the negative side, the achievement of an altered state of consciousness, via such therapies, in a previously deluded psychotic could result in an internal and external attributional search which could result in the retrieval and reactivation of old psychotic cognitions and thinking styles. Hence, if a person is not enculturated into a societal sphere or is of low self-esteem, such therapies may be just as likely to harm as to improve the patient.

Again, despite the anecdotal evidence from my own case, I believe it is generally countertherapeutic to encourage clients into thinking that they have any even marginally reliable psychic abilities. Although I believe the psychotic episode can involve some paranormal factors, and so the uncanny should not be denied, this aspect is better played down in therapy. The client needs to learn to get by in life without relying on paranormal powers, without waiting for paranormal manifestations and without being 'guided' by paranormal or spiritual forces in any obvious concrete way. Religiosity is useful as a positive *attitude* and should be calmly encouraged, but a state of affairs where they think that 'God is sending me messages' is to be avoided. Recovering psychotics are intuitively aware of this anyway and all of those close to me refused participation when I suggested running an ESP experiment. In Greyson's (1977) ESP experiment the psychotics there found the negative outcome therapeutic.[5]

On the other hand, it is therapeutic to emphasize the normality and positive value of the psychotic experience. Delusional thinking is in many ways a perfectly normal cognitive activity (Rosenhan and Seligman 1984; Maher 1988) in which individuals under great 'uncertainty stress' try to make sense out of their experiences and in doing so anticipate the future. Psychotics should be encouraged to appreciate this normality of their experience and their creativity and meaning seeking tendencies which manifest themselves in delusion and to deploy them in less self-destructive ways and for the benefit of others.

In this context the strange feelings and intuitions which often preceded the delusion should, if possible, be positively connoted and accepted perhaps as mystical experiences if appropriate. Therapeutic efforts can then be directed at changing the outré or outlandish attributions that the client has constructed to account for these unfamiliar and perplexing states. (See also Chapter 9 and Johnson *et al.* 1977.)

The basic theme then to be employed in dealing with the negative side of the mystical and the distracting side of the paranormal which may have manifested in psychosis is that they should be overcome in the sense of *incorporated* rather than overcome in the sense of denied, defeated and left behind. Psychological approaches to therapy generally use the first sense of overcome; medical model approaches use the second sense above. The past should, I think, be included not excluded, merged and transmuted, so that it is compossible with the present, not cut away. Then the person can genuinely grow rather than slot-rattle to a different mentality, posing as having grown.

TIME KEEPING

Emphasis on punctuality and session length is, I feel, countertherapeutic. Some counsellors and therapists (especially those who have committed themselves to too many clients) will spend a whole session discussing why the client was seven minutes late and will not relent until they have found some intellectually exciting 'meaty' reason for the client's 'misbehaviour'. This irritates, alienates and bores psychotic clients immensely and reaffirms to them that their therapist does not really have much understanding of their mental state. Similarly, to demand that the discussion last strictly and only for fifty minutes is, in my view, pure nonsense and again alienates the therapist from the client's world.

Psychotics' thinking, feeling and behaviour is often unpredictable, diffuse, tangential and easily side-tracked to a degree that is beyond their control. In university departments highly creative staff members are similarly unpredictable and, at times, long-winded and tangential. That is the way they are. It is true that the psychotic benefits from structure and order, but to push a 'factory mind' attitude onto psychotics in which they clock-in and clock-out for therapy is monstrous. Recovering from a psychotic crisis is usually a slow and arduous affair. It is indeed a form of mourning. The psychotic's inner world has been totally slaughtered and devastated. Psychotics have had to realize that they were hopelessly wrong about the world they constructed. They feel 'down' and silly. Rebuilding has to begin from within from an empathic understanding of what they are good at and from a sympathetic realization of the chaos of their mental state. When one's whole world and self has been annihilated first in one way by a pseudocommunity and then in another by drugs, clocking-in and clocking-out for therapy or for anything else is the depths of triviality, despair and humiliation. If professionals are not prepared to expect and for some time tolerate the inconvenience of unpunctuality and protracted session lengths they should not, I believe, be in the job of helping psychotics.

A word of qualification is in order here, however: one should not always treat psychotics very gingerly. If one always behaves towards them in a very 'charily and warily' fashion, they are liable to pick up unconsciously the implicit communication 'you are very fragile' and this is counter–therapeutic. Psychotics have to accept the consequences of their behaviour, like everyone else, and if their behaviour is, in particular circumstances, enraging, so be it.

THE DELUSION AS PURE PROJECTION

A common tendency of helping agents is to assume that the client's delusional system is a projected symbolic mirror of the psyche. This is taking subjectivism to an absurd conclusion. One can only map a delusional system onto a client's intrapsychic dynamics with the aid of a great deal of intellectual acrobatics, if at all. Delusional systems are not entirely intrapsychic constructions; they depend also on thousands of events and happenings 'out there' in the world which are totally beyond the psychotic's control or expectation. To try to work back from the delusion to the client's 'mental code' or mental structures is to collapse the understanding of delusional thinking with idealism. Delusions, like scientific discoveries, are not made from 'pure thought' while sitting in an armchair and hence they reflect an external as well as an internal realm.

Having said this, however, delusions do often reflect some of the client's

137

current conflicts. This is true also of dreams (Hall 1966; Kline 1981). People do not easily give up delusions partly because to do so would be an admission that they have *wasted* months or years building up a belief system that is totally vacuous. Hence, while the psychoanalytic and existential therapeutic procedures of encouraging the person to see meaning and personal sense in his or her delusions are personally enriching, they also circumvent the 'wasted time' anxiety.

I think it is generally wrong, however, to perceive the projections of the psychotic always as defences. The psychotic projects not to deny but to *anticipate*. The plotting and planning of the deluded person never reduces guilt and shame, it merely represents machinations designed to prevent the situation *getting any worse*.

Chronic inferences of defensive projection in the treatment of recovering deluded patients also denies the validity of their own inference-making capabilities, and this can be very countertherapeutic. As one psychotic said to me, 'Talking to him is like pissing into the wind'. Psychotic clients, far from being chronic blunder-makers, can be very sensitive and perceptive. This capacity needs to be validated not thrown back in their faces.

'THE WALL TEST'

Although it is valuable to praise those demonstrations of good judgement which the psychotic shows, and to be positive and agreeable about the cognitions and feelings on which the delusion was seeded, negative feedback is also valuable. It is quite wrong to believe that challenging or refuting a recovering psychotic will always plunge the challenger into the psychotic's delusional system. Negative outcomes in ESP tests (Greyson 1977) have previously been mentioned in this context as having been beneficial. Deluded psychotics do have a strong verificationist tendency, but when recovering they are by no means totally immune to refutatory evidence.

A test which I would suggest, and which I refer to as 'the wall test' although it is still in an exploratory stage, may prove to be helpful. In this a tape of two people speaking is played behind a partition. The client has to make out what they are saying as if he or she were living in a flat next door and overhearing muffled conversation through the wall. After having done this, the client goes behind the partition and the tape is replayed so that the client can listen to what was actually said. Clients can thus be given feedback of reality, something difficult or impossible in everyday life and can thus appreciate their own mistakes in auditory perception.

FURTHER FEEDBACK TECHNIQUES

There seems little doubt from the experimental investigation that previously deluded psychotics do operate on confirmatory evidence and ignore disconfirmatory evidence more so than do non-psychotics. They also have lower confidence in correct decisions and higher confidence in incorrect decisions than do non-psychotics. Related to this, they place higher confidence on decisions enriched from fantasy and lower confidence on decisions which are more stimulus determined, than do non-psychotics. I believe that all these tendencies could be counteracted by the provision of ongoing feedback of their performance accuracy and appropriateness in test or, preferably, game-playing situations. The Slide Viewing Task reported in this book is amenable for use as a training situation of this kind. If the decisions were made within a multiple choice task format the confidence rating assigned to them could (with reference to data from non-psychotics) be fed back as too high or too low until the volunteers had learnt to *match* their confidence ratings to their decisions and to the quality of the evidence. Tasks of this kind would improve the reality testing capacities of the psychotic clients; they would counteract the clients' tendencies to trust too strongly in their own fantasies and encourage them to place more faith in strongly stimulus determined decisions.

Feedback techniques would be valuable in another quite different area. Recovering psychotics, I find, often feel that people, whose faces are in their peripheral visual field, are looking at them – for example, when they are standing near them in buses or trains. When they have the courage to 'look back', they usually find that the people are not in fact looking at them. Some psychotics also find this to be a particularly unnerving problem when walking down a busy street. Sometimes they feel that they are walking a gauntlet of eyes and stares. Again, a video of the clients walking, taken from some strategic position, would show that people actually look at them much less than they characteristically imagine. This kind of technique could be combined with work on their presentation of self. They would be likely to discover that people look at them less, or less unfavourably, if they dress reasonably well and clear their faces of, say, sullen or haunted expressions. Shafiq would certainly have benefited from this as I suspect his characteristic gait and facial expression may have exacerbated his problems in the sense that the 'attention' he obtained may well have fed his delusional preoccupations in vicious circle fashion. Video techniques of this kind would enable the psychotic to break the circle and obtain unambiguous testing of their fears without having to undergo all the stressful machinations that would be required for them to directly seek the evidence themselves – with, of course, all the attendant uncertainties that that would produce. (A similar technique could of course be used, and occasionally has been, for transsexuals who are concerned – as they all invariably are – about whether or not they 'pass' in public.)

The certainty of psychotics is a strange kind of 'twilight certainty'. It is wrong to believe that they would not like or benefit from the real solid feedback that a video could provide. Psychotics, in a sense, fear certainty yet long for it. Rather than have their brains *create* a sense of certainty through malfunctioning, it would be and is therapeutic if they can clearly receive information about their state of reality. Rather than mistrust this, as most professionals think they would, my experience is that they generally welcome it and are thoroughly relieved when they receive it.

A final technique on this theme is what I call 'the walk game'. Often previously deluded psychotics feel that when *couples* approach them in the street they look at them, and when they have walked past they then start talking about them. This can be tested. My method here is to go on walks with a client but walk about ten yards behind them. When couples or threesomes do approach and walk past I can see whether or not they are looking at the client and *hear* whether or not they are, after they have walked past, talking about the client. So far, with reasonably well presented clients (and it is obviously best that clients be so for this game) their fears have proved unfounded and I have, to their relief, been able to feed this information back to them. Again, a clear dose of reality, rather than being mistrusted, is very refreshing to a paranoid client. (If the information had been derogatory I would still have fed it back. Clarity and certainty is, I believe, *more important* than whether the content of the information fed back is good or bad.) This technique is obviously less than fully satisfactory because the feedback information depends on the follower's auditory acuity. Derogatory information in all probability would concern their appearance. If so it would be beneficial for them to attribute 'talk-about-them-in-the-street' to their physical characteristics, which are to an extent modifiable and controllable, than to scandal sheets, past moral transgressions or to the activities of a pseudocommunity, all of which are uncontrollable.

The use of feedback techniques obviously should not be rigid and predetermined. They must be tailored to the particular fears of the client. Alison, for example, as we saw in Chapter 8, slept wearing ear plugs because she believed that groups of young men were laughing at her expense and shouting derogatory remarks up to her window as they passed her block on their way home from the pub between 11 p.m. and midnight. I offered to wait in the vicinity at that time to hear or tape record what they actually were saying and shouting, and this could easily have been done. Alas she refused; with feedback techniques the client's fear of certainty *is* a problem and it requires courage on the part of that individual to participate in some of these procedures.[6] (The wall test is the least threatening in this respect.) However the point is that, although still in early stages, feedback techniques with recovering deluded or paranoid clients present a flexible medium of help and may well be useful when deployed by helpers they trust and are close to. By depicting reality with brute clarity and/or by changing attributions, they may sidestep the pernicious influence of confirmation bias and, despite the theoretical problem that one can never prove the negative, they may undercut delusional systems and calm and refresh the client.

DELUSION REMOVAL: WHO, WHEN, AND TO WHAT EFFECT?

There is little doubt that just as phobias, such as agoraphobia or school phobia, can be removed with the eventual enhancement of the patient's life, so also can delusions. It is quite wrong to assume that the 'periphery' of the system, be it a behaviour or a particular cognition, cannot be treated directly without some form of symptom substitution occurring or that delusions themselves are totally beyond intercession. Deep level intervention is by no means *always* necessary or effective. What psychodynamically oriented thinkers seem not to realize, or to be able to face, is that although a delusion may well be motivated, motivation is not all; cognitions and situational factors are also important, as are *other* available motives that the patient may have and hold importantly. All of these latter factors may work to the advantage of patients if delusions are removed in order to enable them to improve their mental state and situation without the appearance of other forms of pathology.

From my experience during this research the following guidelines concerning delusion removal may be helpful (some of these points have also been raised by other workers).

1 One has, of course, to exercise great care when challenging or refuting a patient's delusion. A routine psychodynamic position would always predict symptom substitution but, when all is said and done, this does in fact sometimes occur. Alison, for example, always became very aggressive and agitated if the nature of, or evidence for, her belief in her doctor's affections was in any way challenged. Eventually her delusion was, to her satisfaction, refuted when she had an appointment with him and, far from showing exuberant enthusiasm at seeing her, he had totally forgotten the reason for the appointment and was relatively cool with her during it. She replaced this delusion with, among other things, manic fantasies of being 'gang-banged' which were accompanied by ecstatic multiple orgasms, sometimes as many as one hundred in a night. That was clearly a very necessary delusion which enabled her, for example, to manage her heterosexual drive and boost her self-esteem.

2 Some religious experiences, such as my own, are probably just better left alone, particularly when their outcome is positive. Thousands of years of debate have ensued over the existence of God; it is unlikely that this problem and its implications will be resolved in a case conference or ward round.

3 Delusions are ripe for challenge if the patient is, as sometimes happens,

141

becoming bored with them. If a patient is very interested in the delusion, this can make him or her more resistant.

4 Hypomania or euphoria may follow *either* the refutation of an unwanted delusion or the confirmation of a delusion with a grandiose theme.

5 A delusion *can* spontaneously decay either through boredom or through threatening implications never materializing. Time *can* sometimes help even a psychotic condition.

6 People who have a love of the spectacular may become depressed if a congruently spectacular delusion is refuted. If anti-depressant medication is administered to block this the delusion may return if the medication is discontinued (anti-anxiety drugs can similarly be countereffective if used to aid implosion therapy for agoraphobia: Chambless *et al*. 1979).

7 The *evidence* for the belief is better challenged (particularly the *early* evidence) rather than the belief itself (see also Watts *et al*. (1973) and Chadwick, P.D.J. and Lowe (1990)).

8 There will be different reactions to refutation or challenge in people who consciously think 'It *must* be true but I wish it wasn't' and those whose motto is 'It's got to be true because I want it so much'. Where there is motivational and decisional conflict and ambivalence the delusion may be more vulnerable.

9 Beliefs that are not strongly held (Watts *et al*. 1973), and those that are not thoroughly integrated into the personality over years, are more ripe for challenge.

10 Younger people and people who have more 'life flexibility', are more inventive and also have greater initiative may well be less vulnerable to symptom substitution particularly if a delusion considerably restricts their life. Older people, or those with strongly circumscribed lives or who are very unadventurous in life, are less likely to take advantage of the liberation provided by a removed life-restricting delusion.

11 As in science (and love), people will not drop beliefs or shift ground unless they have an alternative to which they can move. Scientists rarely dispense with their theories simply due to an experimental refutation, and psychotics are not necessarily very different. Hence, alternative interpretations have to be provided (Watts *et al*. 1973; Chadwick, P.D.J. and Lowe 1990), and these presented for consideration gently. Simply saying that the belief is ridiculous is aggressive, humiliating and arrogant and is never effective. Indeed, the provision of a feasible alternative interpretation *alone* can be effective, as I found with Alana J, with no challenge necessarily being needed.

12 It is wrong to assume that a person who to some degree 'acts out' on the basis of their delusion, necessarily holds their belief with 100 per cent conviction. Some actings out, such as confronting people on the

street, can themselves be *tests* of an *uncertain* belief. Uncertain beliefs are, of course, more fragile.

13 The very act of eliminating a delusion via medication is in itself a *learning experience* for patients which does tend to enculturate them into a medical view of their condition. A distressingly large amount of patient-to-patient chat is about drugs, side-effects, etc. Some patients do find the 'drug removal' of their delusion to be telling evidence against its veridicality.

14 The less extensive (less 'global') a delusion's impact on a patient's life the easier it is to test and refute it.

15 The less insight people have – hence the more 'external' their attributions – the more tenacious will their beliefs be.

16 People whose delusions put them at the centre of the world and who have no other attachments to the world other than via their delusions need enculturation into a social network, 'a place for them', before their beliefs are challenged.

17 Confrontation of a paranoid delusion may increase rather than decrease a patient's belief if it inadvertently provides confirmatory data (e.g. by the therapist glancing across at a colleague or looking to the skies).

18 Arguing with patients can give them an opportunity to bolster their belief by generating new counterarguments and justifications. Watts *et al.* (1973) suggest and demonstrate the value of asking the *patients* to generate counterarguments against their belief. This, of course, is a standard attitude change procedure. Personally I see no reason, if delusional thinking is on a continuum with normal thinking, as I believe it is, why *all* the methods of attitude change, as outlined in any social psychology reader, need not be tried with deluded patients.

19 A delusion little accompanied by the meaning feeling is ripe for removal. An intense meaning feeling contraindicates intervention.

20 One has to remember that a delusion may be a person's very *last* coping device.

ROUGHAGE AND VISION

It is absolutely essential that the client reach and be encouraged to reach beyond the realm of psychological analysis. Roughage, small talk and creative activities all facilitate this. Small talk, indeed, is a welcome release for psychotics from their intense preoccupations as well as being a better sample of the kind of talk that obtains in the real world.

A continual emphasis on problems and 'mental illness' makes the client feel that they are 'a case' worthwhile only for a report in a psychiatry textbook as another instance of a theory of pathology. This is very bad. All previously psychotic clients need to feel that they have a worthwhile, valuable, special identity of their own with their own unique vision. They have to feel that what they are and can do has some public external reference beyond psychology and psychiatry; that they can give and be something to the world; and that they have a valid unique place in that world. To the extent that therapy prevents them from achieving this, it is harmful. Many seem to think that *the* answer to this is 'getting a job'. It can be, but not at all necessarily. Other achievements are or can be just as, if not more, valuable; for example, painting a picture, creating a dance routine, helping to mend a car, writing a rebellious letter to *Forum* or decorating a kitchen in a novel way (to cite a few actual examples) can take the person out of the quagmire of pathology and put him or her into the world in a most liberating fashion since these efforts can in no way be reduced to psychology.[7]

There is no best time for the above to occur. Indeed, immediately after a psychotic crisis the best 'treatment' is to avoid talk of mental illness and problems altogether. Discussion about Chelsea's latest match or the latest fashions on Oxford Street is more effective than anything deriving from a learned work on psychopathology (see Sutherland (1976) on this point also). My own personal belief is that after an acute delusional crisis a person should be encouraged, for at least a year and maybe two, to live an in-the-world life, mixing with people, building trust, dealing with practical realities and everyday issues and not retreating into any form of deep analysis. The bitter fruit of withdrawal, isolation and reverie is psychosis. Productive living afterwards should be sought not in a retiring life but in living an active outward-looking life revolving around relationships. The decrease in self-consciousness that this tends to produce is, in itself, therapeutic.

As psychotics move into the world in a consensually validateable way there usually comes a time when one feels free even to laugh with them at their delusions thereby helping them to store the previously distressing thoughts in positive humorous schemata.

NORMALITY AND ESTEEM

Madness is perfectly normal in the sense that, judging from the experimental study, many of the processes involved exist on a continuum with normal functioning without qualitative discontinuity. Many seemingly psychotic phenomena can be conceptualized in a perfectly normal and/or positive way. As we saw in the cases of David B and Simon T, it is best *not* to be eager to find evidence of 'thought broadcasting delusions' and 'thought disorder' as one can become so hooked by these labels that one fails to conceptualize behaviours that resemble them as anything other than pathological. One may then be over-eager to suggest, say, an increase in medication to 'eliminate' them. Similarly, the Borderline state and Freud's related 'oceanic feeling' are no more to be regarded as seeded on defences producing an abnormal condition than is acute hearing to be regarded as a defence against blindness. It is a released capacity – as is the mystical state. Necessity mothers the realization of dormant capacities.

In this vein reports of so-called 'thought blocking' can sometimes be normalized by counsellors rather than being an occasion for panic drug taking. Alana J, for example, once 'lost' what she was going to say twice in the space of a few minutes with me after having spent five hours being 'talked at' by a female acquaintance with verbal diarrhoea. It could well be, I thought, that this was because sentence construction requires an assumption/prediction of *output possibility*. If *A* spends hours with *B* who neither listens to nor has any interest in *A*'s contributions, it is likely that attention will be withdrawn from embryonic sentence construction, those sentence constructions would not receive the 'cathexis' that is needed and they would rapidly decay.

Having thought of the above at the time when Alana J reported that she was losing her thoughts, I explained this theory to her and related it to her recent experience. She regained her fluency of thought quite easily. Obviously if she had coupled this worry with an attribution of an external locus of control for her mental state a perfectly logical 'normal' delusion of 'thought withdrawal' would have been conceived.

The theory outlined above of Alana's thought blocking suggests one cognitive underpinning of the link between schizophrenia and invalidating experiences. The experience of mixing with people who neither attend to what one is saying nor digest it or show any interest in it may be, as mentioned in Chapter 5, a factor in the generation of unusual states of mind such as the negative aspects of the Borderline or psychotic states. Perhaps this kind of experience is also more common in the lower social classes.

CONFIRMATION BIAS

Seeking evidence or ideas that confirm a verbal hypothesis very much at the expense of evidence that refutes it seems, from the experimental study, to be a bias which strongly characterizes both paranoid and non-paranoid psychotics and also high *N* non-psychotics. It would seem reasonable, therefore, that a cognitive therapeutic intervention aimed at decreasing confirmation bias would be helpful for both psychotics and neurotics. Word games could easily be deployed for caring agents to work on the enhanced confirmation bias that patients seem to manifest, but counselling real-time *in vivo* would probably be far more helpful.

Finally: the whole treatment programme for recovering psychotics will founder if their basic self-esteem is not enhanced. Appropriate praise and listening attentively to what they say are both esteem-enhancing 'techniques' but, really, a person's self-regard is not boosted by techniques. Every person's life is an unwritten novel: unique, unrepeatable, 'un-replicable', special. One has to have a feel for things of such quality, such importance. This is particularly so with psychotics, whose experiences are so much more poignant, vivid, acute. The particular ways in which a person's esteem can be lifted by a therapist, although discussed by Rogers in the context of his client or person-centred therapy (Rogers 1942, 1951; Rogers *et al.* 1967), will probably never be totally known explicitly. The procedures via which counsellors do this are partly tacit or implicit. Whatever the procedures are, they are best deployed from a top-down attitude of care and love rather than from being focused on specifically and analytically. The understanding of how the good or great counsellor or therapist 'does it' is really a topic within the (much neglected) theme of love and cognition. This, alas, would need a further book to explicate.

13

CONCLUSIONS AND GENERAL DISCUSSION

The purpose of the scientific endeavour is to discover the order in the natural world, to discover general principles on the basis of which we can rationally understand, perhaps predict and maybe even control naturalistic phenomena. In this context the phenomenon of delusional thinking, like that of creativity, presents a tremendous challenge as delusions, like novel ideas and dreams, have a certain erratic, fickle quality which qualifies them, for some people, as deserving of the title 'irrational'. Hermann Lenz, for example (personal communication, 26 October 1987), did not believe that my experimental study was even appropriate in the first instance as he takes the view that delusions are of this irrational ilk and thus not amenable to scientific enquiry. Hausman (1976, 1985) similarly argues that creativity by its very nature involves breaking boundaries in unpredictable ways and hence the quest to predetermine creative behaviour suffers from a logical contradiction at the very outset.

Needless to say, I am not in wholehearted agreement with these theorists or I would not have persevered with this research. My thinking in answer to them has gone along similar lines to that of Perkins (1988) whose discussion centres around the quest for the mechanisms mediating creativity. Although it may be forever impossible to predict what specific delusion or delusions a psychotic may construct or suffer, it is possible, I believe, to uncover general principles which describe processes that bias, permit and encourage delusional thinking *per se*. Perkins refers to 'enabling' factors which equip a person, say, for creative achievement, without pressing that person to achieve (much as fast reflexes would 'enable' a person to be a racing driver without pressing the person in that direction) and 'promoting' factors which do have a press quality. I would argue that influences may be arranged on a series (as in Figure 13.1) and the psychologist's task is to understand all of these influences, hopefully eventually pushing their understanding as far to the right as possible.

Beyond the far left of the 'causal triangle' in Figure 13.1 are factors which merely 'leave the door ajar' to an eventual outcome with no directional

147

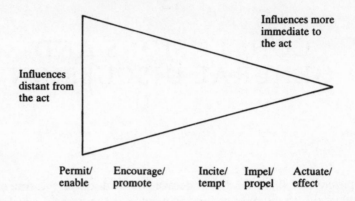

| Permit/ | Encourage/ | Incite/ | Impel/ | Actuate/ |
| enable | promote | tempt | propel | effect |

Figure 13.1 The causal triangle: at far left are factors which merely 'leave the door ajar' for an effect to eventually take place, and as we move to the right more pressing factors which are more immediate to the act come into play

implications existing at all, and beyond the far right is the act itself, solidly eventuated in thought or in behaviour.

The causal triangle exists at right angles to the usual top-down/bottom-up categorization of causal factors and in fact does not give primacy to any provoking factor. An actuating factor or a bottom-up process may indeed be temporally or structurally impotent outside a context of prior encouragements or needs.

As I argued in the introduction to this book, I shall theorize from a holistic contextualist perspective within which individual processes have always to be seen in the context of other processes, procedures and strategies if their contribution to delusional thinking is to be validly appreciated. Only language, lateral inhibition and the need for convenience segregates; basically we are dealing with relations in a context of other relations.

The theory I shall articulate here, being holistic and multi-process, sees delusional thinking as due to an orchestra of factors all working together in harmony. I shall therefore refer to it as 'orchestra theory'.

I shall start from the vantage point of bottom-up processes and then move on to other factors with the aim being to produce a fully rounded theoretical perspective in which all influences are interacting.

One bottom-up component could well, of course, be a genetically mediated overactivity in dopamine pathways (Snyder 1974), but this process, although it may tempt or incite delusions, does not actuate them as dopaminergic activity boosters such as amphetamine, nicotine and L-dopa do not automatically produce aberrant cognitions in all people in a one-to-one fashion. Overactivity in dopaminergic pathways, using an *ex juvantibus* reasoning, may also be high in highly creative non-deluded people given that dopamine blockers such as haloperidol, even at doses as low as an eighth or a quarter of a milligram in the case of the latter drug, seem to reduce the flair of people who take them (e.g. Sacks 1986).

Another bottom-up component (bottom in the sense of local and/or mechanistic) which may permit delusional thinking in the sense of giving a slight push to the flywheel of operations that eventually culminates in it, is slightly poor perceptual and decisional accuracy. Psychotics appear to be too risky in their confidence accompanying hypotheses enriched from fantasy and too cautious in their interpretations of more stimulus-enriched scenes. They have less insight into their own perceptual accuracy (which even in paranoids is slightly less than the perceptual accuracy of non-psychotics) and are poor at discriminating signal from noise events. These biases give the slightest shift towards a cognitive style which is inner rather than outer directed. The biases in no way actuate delusional thinking but predispose or permit individuals to a life enriched in fantasy and a life where they might come to rely more on fantasizing because their real-world judgements tend to be more often wrong than do those of 'normal' people, and thus more often punished.

Paranoids (La Russo 1978) may be an exception to the above in the context of *social* perception but it seems that their high social sensitivity does them little good in real-time interpersonal contexts as they perceive more than they can rationally handle. If a paranoid is perceiving another person at two levels at once (those of the person's hidden self and the presented self) this is liable to complexify interpersonal interaction very considerably. The paranoid's social feedback reception points may be too closely spaced in time, a fluent rhythm to interaction will be difficult to sustain, mentation may be interrupted by distracting worrying thoughts and hence the sensitive individual is liable to provoke discontent or puzzlement, putting them in a positive feedback system which produces more distracting cognitions and even worse timing and rhythm.

Cortical overactivity is a further mechanism which may more than leave the door ajar to delusion. Through encouraging introversion and perhaps low venturesomeness it may amplify or reinforce the preoccupation with the inner realm provoked by poor perceptual judgement. All of these processes so far, however, in no way discriminate a psychotic from a high creative. These biases could just as easily permit creative novel or poetry writing or profound philosophizing as they could eventual delusion. The paranoid might be inept in real-time but not necessarily in self-paced activity. The psychotic, like the high creative, may be better fitted for a life involving fantasy, inner enrichment and exploration and relatively sparse interpersonal engagements. There is nothing intrinsically 'right' about outer directedness and 'wrong' about inner directedness, and one can indeed just as easily construct philosophies of life in which fantasy is the centre of intellectual interest rather than social relationships (see Storr (1989) on this point also).

There does seem to be a further local mechanism 'unusuality' in the psychotics, however, or at least in high paranoids, and that seems to be a possibly filter-related difficulty in concentrating. In the context of psychosis this is usually called an 'attentional deficit' (Meyer and Salmon 1984) but in the context of creativity it is called merely 'oversensitivity' (Martindale 1975) or 'openness to stimulation'. Creatives are renowned for needing solitude and quiet and freedom from uncontrollable disturbance; again their concentration difficulty may permit this openness to stimulation, which could help produce a brilliant original painting or, via another route, a delusion. On its own, however, the defective attention model of the psychotic is a model without content, without quality.

High ideational fluency and flexibility may also be 'encouraging' factors for delusional thinking, given the latter's set-breaking character. Non-paranoids in particular seem to be quite divergent. Although the tests I gave did not show an acceleration of creativity at very high arousal this may have been because all tests involve some constraint and at that level it is totally 'free range' permuting of ideas that is facilitated, not criterion-appropriate responses. This may, of course, also explain the poor performance of the paranoids (who were the most aroused group) who may prefer not just written rather than oral responses (Lewine 1978) but a solitary self-paced environment to permute their internal representations. The paranoids, however, certainly need help in the deployment of divergent thinking in interpersonal contexts as they seem to suffer from constraint even more than non-paranoids and produce very narrowly focused responses. (I, of course, may not have been sufficiently permissive and may have been too intrusive with them.)

A process which may further encourage and perhaps even incite delusional thinking, and which in the current research was linked to cortical activation levels, was confirmation bias. In psychotics, especially paranoid psychotics, the left hemisphere may be overactivated, producing high verbal confirmation bias, and the right underactivated, producing high visual/spatial confirmation bias (the links with autonomic activation suggested a reverse pattern subcortically, but these findings were more tentative). Whereas a balanced brain mediates processes involving both confirmation and refutation, the potential psychotic's brain, especially that of the paranoid, has both enhanced pattern-detecting processes (right-hemisphere advantage over a normal brain) and enhanced serial-developing of these patterns. The result in psychosis is the 'everything means something and everything fits' experience. These biases could, of course, be highly useful (say, in scientific research) if the balance or imbalance was controllable, but if in the psychotic, perhaps in the service of some need, they become pushed to a point where they are uncontrollable the result is liable to be a dislocation from consensually validated interpretations of the world.

The psychological process accelerating at least verbal confirmation bias may be that of capacity decrease. Alas the levels of arousal reached in this experiment were hardly even 'knocking on the door' of those likely reached in psychosis and hence only a slight drop in capacity obtained at the upper end of the arousal spectrum. Tendencies in the expected direction did, however, occur. (In addition: confirmation bias on the 3–4 test, which had a higher storage load than that involved on the 2–3 test, and thus should have made more demands on capacity, was indeed rather higher (9.8 per cent compared to 8.20 per cent).)

The lack of control of hemisphere balance could be a reflection of a problem in callosal modulation (bottom-up) or a top-down effect. The brain, to speak dualistically, could be responding to strategies deployed in the service of some need and the person could be making use of the products of hemisphere imbalance to such a degree that control processes break down. Evidence of callosal transmission unusualities are difficult to interpret without a creative control group; however, my bet is that there is a problem in callosal control of hemisphere activation in psychosis but that the form of imbalanced activation state is exacerbated by the person's thinking and need-related affects (global to local effects) which calls for high similarity perception and confirmation bias to sustain the person's style of life. In many respects, the very specific perceptual and cognitive processes which have been given so much attention and prominence in the research literature on delusions are, at least in part, the *tools* of the psychotic's needs and more global emotional cognitions, not *the* singular cause of their problem.

At this point we pass temporarily from 'how' questions to 'why' questions, from brain to mind or from local brain processes to global ones. Intuitive leaps are needed here as trying to build logically from local atomistic processes to qualitative executive-guided motivational processes is like trying to snake charm a rope up a mine shaft to get to the next level.

The 'why' question has, of course, always been central to psychoanalytic thinking in this domain. The psychoanalytic theories, however, seem to be so simple that the rarity of paranoia and delusional thinking emerges as a puzzle. Whatever motives emerge cannot be seen in isolation from perceptual, biochemical and neuropsychological unusualities, and the latter cannot be seen in isolation from more qualitative aspects.

From my case study work I would agree with the general point made by Laing that the schizophrenic attempts to find a solution to, for that person, an unliveable situation, although I do not think that many of the details of the Laingian scheme are totally generalizable. For example, there may indeed be mothers (and fathers) whose behaviour is contributory to a schizophrenic decompensation (Fromm-Reichmann 1948) just as high EE families may also be, but condemning, weakening and invalidating experiences can come from many other sources.

Related to this I would agree with the Freudian (and Bleulerian) view that the delusion is an attempt at productive integrated functioning (an attempt at 'self cure'). Meissner's attempt to establish a process continuum theory linking paranoid with normal functioning within a classical psychoanalytic framework is also in parallel, at least in intention if not in content, with my own approach.

As is the case in the attempt to understand creativity, one has to understand the goals and the plans of the individuals; a study of their dopamine receptor densities, the thickness of their left-hemisphere para-hippocampal gyrus, or their hemisphere activation states alone is not enough. We must ask, in an understanding, positive way: 'What is the person trying to do?' (The answer to this in life is very different from the answer relevant in an experimental situation; the latter totally ignores the real-life goal and belief system context of the person's perceptions.)

All of my case study volunteers had 'big dreams'. Alana J wanted to be a top dancer; Shafiq a world famous intellectual; Chris, rather covertly, to be an acclaimed artist; David B a pop star; Alison the lover or wife of a top (handsome) doctor. I myself wanted to discover the illusions of thought itself and to go even beyond Kant. Big dreams mean fairly large discrepancies from one's current status and thus induce high drive or high arousal for their attainment. In the risk of failing in big dreams, the door is opened to despair, mourning and perhaps even madness. Simultaneously, with the high arousal induced by these goals all my case study volunteers found themselves trapped and isolated by their own behaviour as if socially underwater. Indeed they all, like myself, had difficulties in communicating. At times they were trapped koan-like in knots by Catch 22 situations and double binds. There was nowhere to go, nowhere to move to. Special people with big dreams, trapped and misunderstood, uncertain and isolated, every move blocked and tangled with no one to whom they could really talk to explicate their situation.

The very brain biases which had gently, over the years, produced this state – perhaps through also encouraging spectacular imaginings (contemplated with higher than usual confidence), high reinforceability (and hence sometimes sexual variation – the latter perhaps also related to a hemisphere imbalance), great sensitivity (and hence protective 'spoiling'), but at the same time a feeling of 'difference' – then operated to help solve the very problem they had helped create.

The delusion, whose actuation remains a mystery, certainly seems to relate closely to the wishes and fears of the psychotic; hence, it is not, I think, generated by completely independent processes as claimed (admittedly as an aside) by Argyle (1988). The delusional episode – with the delusion as a novel, wide, synthesizing gestalt, but with intense unidirectional reasoning character – is a meaning-impregnated crescendo to the psychotic's life, explaining and/or culminating that life in one great clarifying and stupendously arousing and exciting vision.

The alternative but related solution to uncertainty and entrapment is the mystical state. David B did not only suffer delusion but also attained mystical intuitions such as unity experiences and distortions of the time sense; Alana J also had unity experiences and loss of self. (Neither had transsensate experiences or (from their reports) ineffability.) The mystical and delusional states may be related as are the music and the libretto. Perhaps mystical experiences are right-hemisphere mediated (Fenwick 1983), hence their ineffability if focused upon and their slipperiness if not attended to. Delusional experiences could be left-hemisphere attempts to flesh out these intuitions or brief feelings using situationally derived attributions and dynamically organized conceptualizations enriched by external stimuli. Thus, to understand delusion fully we may need to understand the 'language' of the right hemisphere and how it relates, for example, to the left hemisphere in the generation of the vitally important 'meaning feeling'. (Jungians would probably interpret the latter as archetype emergence, as an archetype *is* a form without content.)

The loss of balance between the two hemispheres would account for the diminution or loss of control in psychosis or Borderline experiences. This may also apply to a reduced extent in neurosis, creative 'flows', sexually variant states and the experience of being 'madly in love', all of which may thus exist on a continuum with psychotic states. Creative people, after all, do not have ideas; ideas have them. Neurotic people do not have a complex; the complex has them. Fetishists do not have a fetish; the fetish has them. And deluded psychotics do not have a delusion; it has them.

The mystical and delusional states, rather than being irrational and inexplicable, I thus see as solutions to an intolerable reality. Having been taken gently, year by year, away from a state of enculturation into society, the potential psychotic, like the mystic, discovers a new mode of brain functioning (physiology), a new perception or interpretation of the world through enhanced relational judgement (psychology) and perhaps even at times a new deeper dimension of reality (physics). In this context perhaps the mystical state is not only a Borderline state philosophically and psychologically between sanity and madness, actuality and possibility, but an intermediate form of brain functioning.

Looking down on the brain, with the two cortices enclosing the limbic lobes, the patterns of excitation and inhibition (which would reduce the excitation) in the three states might be as shown in Figure 13.2 – indeed it could be said that all three modes are *special forms* of balance.

In modes 2 and 3 the paranormal is normal and perhaps levels of description and experience denied to a normal brain are attainable. In

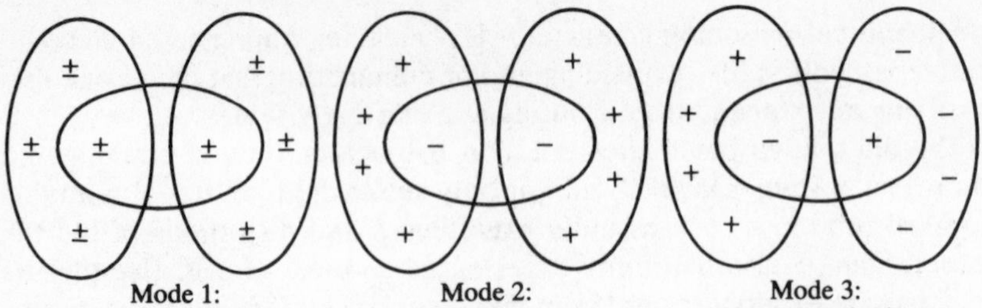

Figure 13.2 Three possible modes of patterning of high (+) and low (−) excitation in cortical and subcortical structures in the left and right hemispheres

these modes spiritual 'forces' may be able to have tangible physical effects (as in the episode of resolution of my taps and clicks) and may be able to produce major psychological effects on the person. These possibilities are obviously only highly tentative; certainty is not an addition *to* knowledge but a mode *of* knowledge. The certainty of the mystic offers no guarantees. Nonetheless, the door is left ajar to such possibilities.

It seems, then, that in delusional, mystico-delusional and mystical states the brain, or local processes in the brain, continually enriched by external stimuli, respond to needs or globally mediated decisions and processes. Psychotics in ego-weakening uncertainty need certainty, in delusion and hallucination the brain compensates and gives them certainty; they may need punishment yet in doubt they fear the worst, just in case. In delusion and hallucination these fears and needs are combined multiplicatively and they are given punishment greater than the severity of their own conscience. They need confirmation of their fears to keep ahead of the action; uncannily they are given confirmation. They need to see patterns and meanings to 'keep up with what is going on'; their right hemisphere responds, they pick up the patterns, they see the meanings. At this stage confirmation bias and similarity perception, having encouraged delusion, now propel its continuation.

Like all masochists psychotics are also sadists; they want control. They are given control: the 'voice people' in their heads are tied to commenting on or echoing their every thought; they exist as if on strings, following them everywhere, observing everything like nosey neighbours at a wall with a listening glass. At the same time they punish the very person who gives them their entire *raison d'être*. The 'thought people' of the pseudocommunity have nothing better to do than devote their entire waking hours to monitoring them and plotting against them, making the psychotic the centre of their whole world. They, like the voice people, live for them. At the same time they punish. The sado-masochistic theme is obvious.

Innocence is not achieved; shame is not eliminated; hostility is not denied; but certainty, centrality, control and punishment *are* achieved.

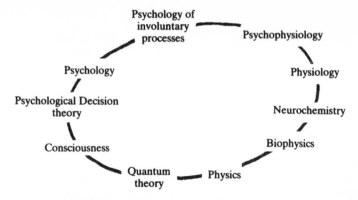

Figure 13.3 Psychology, physiology, chemistry and physics exist not as a hierarchy of 'levels of explanation' but as a 'wheel' of disciplines interacting and grading into one another at their apparent limits

Alas, through their inferences and attributions to the effect that external malign persistent forces are at work against them, the price they pay is one of anguish, torment, anger and fear. If, as problems escalate, there ever is a wish to avoid *depression* by this attribution of responsibility to an external source (see pages 90–1 and also Zigler and Glick 1988) (something which I most strongly suspected with David B), it nonetheless returns eventually by the back door (see Table 9.1, feature 38), accompanied by exarcerbated heartache.

It would be wrong to conclude this work with inferences that seem to imply that psychosis results only from intrapsychic and intracerebral rearrangements in people whose social world is much the same as for everyone else. The social world of the psychotic continues to need intense study; psychosis is not only a medical and perceptual-cognitive problem but a dilemma for social psychology. The implicit rules of working-class life and the characteristics and behaviour of 'psychotogenic' people seem particularly worthy of study. The study of the consequences in social situations of the perceptual sensitivity of paranoids would also form a more fine-grained and perhaps more useful starting point for a psychoanalytic social psychology than the more molar approaches of Horney and Fromm.

Also, I think it would be wrong to argue that in research on psychosis there is some 'most suitable unit for analysis'. Different units are most appropriate for generating predictions in different contexts. A holistic theoretical approach, as eventuated in orchestra theory, seems to be the most appropriate coordinating and guiding framework as psychosis is a phenomenon that touches all the interrelated realms shown in Figure 13.3, and of course, many others. Indeed the study of psychosis may unify them conceptually as they are graphically in Figure 13.3.

SUMMARY

The reader can probably tell from these pages that I have risked madness myself to research productively in this field. I have had to be both IN the world and, like a kind of individuated pantheist, able to observe it as if merely OF the world. Indeed, as Hokusai said: 'If you want to draw a bird, you must become a bird' (Maslow 1967). What *I* was trying to do was to validate the psychotic and mystical experiences. Hence this book had two theoretical levels: one high level, almost transcendental, and one low level and rooted very much in this world as we consensually perceive it. The connection between these levels is that the very processes which distort perception of this world of middle magnitudes may permit and facilitate the perception of the magical and mystical 'purple' realm which could well be nonetheless real. The psychotic is therefore caught between distortional semi-hallucinations, compelling needs, misattributions and false-alarm perceiving on the one hand and occasional genuine extra-dimensional intuitions of real value on the other. One purpose of this research has been to try to disentangle these levels of perception and show how they could be, in real time, confused and mutually reinforced to produce delusional cognitions.

NOTES

2 INTRODUCTION TO THE CASE STUDIES AND THE CASE OF DAVID B: 'ERRATICA AND EROTICA'

1 Hallucinations can be construed as existing on a continuum – as also suggested by Strauss (1969). David's 'incipient hallucinations' were mid-way between very clear hearing (at left of Figure 2.1) determined largely by sensory input and outright hallucinations (at right of Figure 2.1) determined entirely by supplementation or top-down addition. The phonemic restoration effect (Warren 1970), where people actually hear missing phonemes when the gap in input is embedded in the context of a sentence, lies to the left in the spectrum shown in Figure 2.1. A continuum model suggests that the study of hallucinations should be part not only of psychiatry but of the psychology of auditory processing and hence should be researched in cognitive psychology units. Cognitive models of hallucinations, also construing them in this way, have been suggested by Horowitz (1975), Slade and Bentall (1988) and Bentall (1990a) and a scale measuring predisposition to hallucinations in non-psychotic volunteers has been devised by Launay and Slade (1981) and Bentall and Slade (1985). (See also Bentall (1990b) for a more general discussion.)
2 This centrality of the self, so common in deluded psychotics, could be referred to as The Medius Complex, after the Latin *medius* which, of course, means 'centre'.
3 His verbal creativity on the word association tests – both variants of Mednick's Remote Associates Test (Mednick 1962) – was much higher than his vocabulary score would ever have predicted. This led me to question seriously an assumption made early in the investigation that these tests tapped creativity under more 'constrained' conditions than did the fluency and uses tests.

3 SHAFIQ: 'THE GREATEST MAN IN THE WORLD?'

1 Although such a belief sounds 'bizarre and obviously impossible' it would be wrong to infer a schizophrenic delusional condition on hearing it. A friend of mine who was a policeman told me that a scandal sheet has in the past been put out on someone. Apparently a man, who was acquitted of rape, was the victim of one distributed by the raped girl's family. The sheet carried a photograph of the man, with personal details about him, describing him as a rapist.

4 MYSTICISM, DELUSION AND THE PARANORMAL

1 Needless to say, there is indeed an 'I Ching' Chinese restaurant at the north end of Earls Court Road.

2 This use of the term 'Borderline' is of course highly confusing given that the term already has been embedded, with many meanings, in the psychiatric and psychoanalytic literature (Liebowitz 1979; Stone 1980). Clarification has been achieved through the work of Spitzer *et al.* (1979) whose investigations led to the DSM–III (1980) categories of 'schizotypal personality disorder' and 'borderline personality disorder'. Both of these categories do, in a sense, describe people of borderline psychotic type, the latter referring to the unstable, erratic and unpredictable and the former being linked more directly on genetic evidence (Rieder 1979; Spitzer *et al.* 1979) to schizophrenia. The 'schizotypal' diagnosis is indicated by the presence of magical thinking, illusions of 'forces' being present, depersonalization and derealization, odd speech and paranoid ideation, inadequate face-to-face rapport, and high anxiety in social situations.

   It is clear that the crisis to be recounted, viewed from a medical model standpoint, is of 'schizotypal' rather than 'borderline' form in the terms of the categories used in current psychiatric descriptive practice. Had I been seen by a psychiatrist, equipped with DSM–III, early in 1979 I would almost certainly have been diagnosed as suffering from a mild form of schizotypal personality disorder and what happened subsequently would have been seen as an exacerbation of that disorder under 'life change' stress (Holmes and Rahé 1967; Brown and Birley 1968).

3 One theory of interest was that some of the events may have been due to my subliminally perceiving a stimulus in peripheral vision (say a black cat); this may then have activated the appropriate knowledge structures and thus issued forth in congruent thoughts (e.g. 'It would have been nice to have had a black cat'). Then the stimulus might happen to come into clear foveal vision (the cat would cross the road in front of me). Such an event could easily be wrongly perceived as an instance of precognition or synchronicity. This may explain some of the more trivial incidents.

4 Hermann Lenz informs me that several of his patients have experienced such taps and clicks and independently discovered the one tap for 'Yes' and two taps for 'No' code (Personal Communication, 26 October 1987). Lake (1986: 146) also mentions 'rappings' from the walls being experienced in paranoid psychotic crises (but treats the phenomenon dismissively). Such tappings are reminiscent of Jung's famous 'bang in the bookcase' which occurred during the crucial meeting with Freud when the fundamental break between the two was taking place (Jung 1963: 152; McGuire 1974).

5 THE ROUTE TO HELL AND BACK

1 See also the important articles in Kahneman *et al.* (1982).

2 To check whether brain dysfunction was involved in my deteriorating state in 1979 I had EEGs taken, thanks to contacts, at two London hospitals. No abnormalities could be detected.

3 Progoff (1973: 168) seeks to see if creative persons show a particular tendency towards the occurrence of synchronistic events. In this book I am essentially doing the reverse of this: seeking to find if people who have suffered a lot of synchronistic events turn out to be highly creative.

4 Although movement from the material to the transcendent realms always involves an unsatisfactory discontinuity (suggestive of 'escape') when represented in a

verbal-conceptual format (Camus 1988) progression from realism to magic, from the mundane to the sacred, is quite easy and continuous via dance – for example, the candomblé dance of Afro-Brazilians as portrayed by David Byrne (Nugent 1989).

6 ALANA J: 'I'M DANCING AS FAST AS I MUST'

1 I shall define 'kindling' as continual subthreshold activation that does not quite recruit the response which, at higher intensity, would be appropriate. Living with a person, for example, who continually talks in sarcastic innuendo, would be living with 'a kindler'.
2 We shall see further evidence of the Jacksonian idea of psychosis as 'dreaming while awake' in the case of Alison (Chapter 8). See also Dement (1972) on this, and Storr (1989: 24).

8 ALISON: 'I'M WAITING'

1 Nympholepsy is a term given to ecstacy or frenzy caused by desire for the unattainable.
2 Interestingly Poincaré (1914: 56) discusses the dangerous certainty that also accompanies inspiration, especially when ideas come in a semi-somnolent state.
3 Instructions to stop delusional behaviour may have increased its rate through drive increase making the habit more dominant. Hence, an approach invoking hypothetical constructs could accommodate this finding.

9 OVERVIEW AND REFLECTIONS ON THE CASE STUDIES

1 The status of the meaning feeling as an affect is, I admit, rather vulnerable.
2 On this view, Luria's (1987) view of abstract contextualism as 'an overgeneralized nullity' is far too intellectual and pessimistic.

10 THE EXPERIMENTAL STUDY: THE THEORIES AND HOW THEY WERE TESTED

1 I therefore find Perkins's argument (1988) to the effect that the RAT is only a hypothesis testing task, with no involvement of activation spread, untenable.
2 The *systematizing* of the delusion may be an attempt by the individual to control arousal escalation with fragmentation occurring when this is beyond the ego/cognitive capacity of the individual. Systematized delusions may therefore imply a greater measure of control and less severe crisis than those unsystematized.
3 Given four levels of arousal and roughly a 40 per cent spread in creativity scores from lowest to highest values, the predicted pattern that should emerge is shown in Figure 10.1. The location of scores is within cells in a 4×4 matrix. The chances of the predicted pattern emerging is 1 in 4^4, i.e. 1 in 256.

   It can be shown that with a 4×4 matrix the chance of *any* concave U-shaped trend is 1 in 7.11; the chance of a quadratic trend of any form is 1 in 3.55. However, if one makes a specific prediction, the likelihood of that predicted trend is, as shown, much reduced.
4 For criticism of such tests, which must be admitted, see Kogan and Pankove (1974) and Mansfield and Busse (1981).

11 THE EXPERIMENTAL STUDY: RESULTS AND ANALYSES

1 Because the assessment of verbal confirmation bias was subjective, three procedures were used to minimize bias in my scoring:

   a When doubt arose regarding whether or not a response should be scored for confirmation bias, scoring was slanted against the hypothesis. Hence the confirmation bias scores for the psychotics are a minimum and the scores for the non-psychotics are a maximum.

   b All answer sheets for the 2–3 and 3–4 tests were scored twice.

   c When an answer was extremely ambiguous in regard to how it should be scored it was discussed at length with an independent rater.

2 That visual confirmation bias score reflects right-hemisphere functioning is particularly likely as out-of-focus slides present the viewer with low spatial frequency information and these seem to be processed largely by the right hemisphere (Sergent 1982, 1983).

3 *Verbal confirmation bias score* is total number of answers on the 2–3 and 3–4 tests in which confirmation bias was manifest, divided by the total number of answers on both tests, expressed as a percentage. *Visual confirmation bias score* is the total number of focusing position changes through which incorrect hypotheses were maintained, divided by the total number of incorrect hypotheses generated on the Slide Viewing Task as a whole.

4 Sensitivity values for the three groups in Figure 11.2 are:

	P	High N	Low N
d'_e	2.64	2.90	3.10
$\triangle_m$	3.000	3.375	3.915

These values differ slightly in magnitude from the means of the individual volunteers' values due to the difficulty in accurately plotting ROC lines at the individual level.

Sensitivity values for the groups in Figure 11.3 are:

	Paranoid psychotics	*Non-paranoid psychotics*
d'_e	2.80	2.48
$\triangle_m$	3.02	2.69

5 Because, in this task, high confidence signals were rated 5 and low confidence signals 0, a risky criterion, here, has a *high* B value not a low one.

6 This pattern of an overactivated left cortex and an underactivated right cortex in positive symptom patients is clearly confirmatory of Gruzelier's findings (1984). It is unclear whether this is a fixed structural or reversible dynamic pattern; however, it is not eliminated by medication and hence it seems unlikely that it is a neurotransmitter concentration or activity asymmetry. Disruption of an inter-hemispheric activation control mechanism seems a likely candidate.

12 IMPLICATIONS FOR THERAPY

1 See also Brown and Birley (1968).

2 It is interesting but tragic that government policy to have recovering psychotics cared for in the community obtains despite minimal research having been done to date on just how environmental manipulations can prevent relapse. It also obtains despite an absence of funds for such research which, were it to be done,

would make the policy more viable. Incredibly, community care decisions are typically taken *before* evaluative research is done (Leff 1988).

3 Much of what passes for catharsis is, I think, not genuine or truly honest. True and effective catharsis is more difficult to achieve than many people realize – particularly with reference to the most painful memories and feelings. The client may tell a tale or relate an experience a *shade* too light-heartedly, or may relate it just a shade too intellectually. It may be related too quickly or too vaguely yet the dishonesty may be barely perceptible. Most misleading of all is what I call 'overcatharsis'. People may put themselves in *too bad* a light, overexpress the anger involved, overexpress the fear involved. Rather than 'going over the top' they could be said to be 'going under the bottom'. They are not *releasing* pent-up anguish, etc., they are *generating* it partly to fit the theory and/or please the therapist. Overcatharsis *seems* to be very honest yet it is just as dishonest as, say, intellectualization and is not therapeutically effective in the long term, however dramatic it may appear.

4 Pauli himself may have had a glimpse of the negative aspect of the Borderline. He sensed evil and revenge in the irrational should we attempt to proceed only rationally and scientifically. Pauli, however, does not speak, at least not clearly, of the emotive substrate, the quality of the *motive* we have in the search for deeper reality, the importance of care, of love, of empathy for nature and the psyche. The Borderline, I think, can only be safely reached in love but in a love where reason and feeling are fused, not schizophreniacally split. Then perhaps we shall see not only the agony of nature and of the psyche but its genuine ecstacy and radiance, and remain unharmed.

5 In the same way psychotics' transparency or translucency feelings can be eased by 'playing parapsychology' with them: trying, sportively, to read their thoughts – and failing. (Such games are also excellent opportunities for humour.)

6 Although some readers may be rather taken aback by my suggestion of feedback procedures, especially perhaps by the walk game, I personally see no harm in providing a previously psychotic client with information about what *really is* going on around them. This was, after all, what they were trying to discover in their agonizing delusional schemes. Freud long ago recognized that the dividing lines between delusions, phobias and obsessions were very fine. Just as every therapist knows that there comes a time when a phobia must be faced by a client, so, if practicable, should it be with a delusion. As the ancient Chinese proverb says: 'Go straight to the heart of danger, for there you will find safety' (Davison and Neale 1986: 128).

7 Given the generally low scores of paranoid volunteers on the tests of creativity it would seem reasonable to encourage creative endeavour particularly in this group, perhaps even via 'lateral thinking' exercises (e.g. De Bono 1967) to help jolt them out of their singularly linear, narrowly focused thinking style.

BIBLIOGRAPHY

Allport, D.A. (1983a) 'Patterns and actions: Cognitive mechanisms are content specific', in G. Claxton, *Cognitive Psychology: New Directions*, International Library of Psychology, London: Routledge & Kegan Paul, Chapter 2, pp. 26–64.

——(1983b) 'Attention and performance', in G. Claxton, *Cognitive Psychology: New Directions*, International Library of Psychology, London: Routledge & Kegan Paul, Chapter 4, pp. 112–53.

Andreasen, N.J. and Canter, A. (1974) 'The creative writer: Psychiatric symptoms and family history', *Comprehensive Psychiatry* 15: 123–31.

——and Powers, P.S. (1975) 'Creativity and psychosis', *Archives of General Psychiatry* 32: 70–3.

Argyle, M. (1988) 'Social cognition and social interaction', *The Psychologist* 1 (5; May): 177–83.

Arieti, S. (1974) 'Acting out and unusual behaviour in schizophrenia', *American Journal of Psychotherapy* 28: 333–42.

Arthur, A.Z. (1964) 'Theories and explanations of delusions: A review', *American Journal of Psychiatry* 121: 105–15.

Arthur, R. and Schumann, S. (1970) 'Family and peer relationships in children with paranoid delusions', *Child Psychiatry and Human Development* 1 (2; Winter): 83–101.

Bachtold, L.M. (1980) 'Speculation on a theory of creativity: A physiological basis', *Perceptual and Motor Skills* 50: 699–702.

Baddeley, A.D. (1976) *The Psychology of Memory*, New York: Basic Books.

——,Grant, S., Wight, E. and Thompson, N. (1974) 'Imagery and visual working memory', in P.M.A. Rabbitt and S. Dornic (eds) *Attention and Performance*, vol. V, London: Academic Press, pp. 205–17.

——and Hitch, G. (1974) 'Working memory', in G.H. Bower (ed.) *The Psychology of Learning and Motivation*, vol. 8, London: Academic Press.

Bak, R.C. (1953) 'Fetishism', *Journal of the American Psychoanalytic Association* 1: 285–98.

Banquet, J.P. (1973), 'Spectral analysis of EEG in meditation', *EEG and Clinical Neurophysiology* 35: 143–57.

Barron, F. (1953) 'Complexity–simplicity as a personality dimension', *Journal of Abnormal and Social Psychology* 48: 162–72.

——(1962) 'The psychology of imagination', in S.J. Parnes and H.F. Harding, *Source Book for Creative Thinking*, New York: Charles Scribner, Selection 19, pp. 227–37.

——(1972) 'The creative personality. Akin to madness', *Psychology Today* 6 (2; July): 42–4 and 84–5.

Bateson, G., Jackson, D.D., Haley, J. and Weakland, J. (1956) 'Toward a theory of schizophrenia', *Behavioural Science* 1: 251–64.

Beatrice, J. (1985) 'A psychological comparison of heterosexuals, transvestites, preoperative transsexuals and postoperative transsexuals,' *Journal of Nervous and Mental Diseases* 173 (6): 358–65.

Bear, D.M. and Fedio, P. (1977) 'Quantitative analysis of interictal behaviour in temporal lobe epilepsy', *Archives of Neurology* 34: 454–67.

Bebbington, P. and Kuipers, L. (1988) 'Social influences on schizophrenia', in P. Bebbington and P. McGuffin (eds) *Schizophrenia: The Major Issues*, London: Heinemann, pp. 201–25.

Bennett, J. (1964) *Rationality – An Essay Towards Analysis*, London: Routledge & Kegan Paul.

Bentall, R.P. (1990a) 'The illusion of reality: A review and integration of psychological research on hallucinations', *Psychological Bulletin* 107 (1): 32–95.

——(1990b) 'The syndromes and symptoms of psychosis – or why you can't play "twenty questions" with the concept of schizophrenia and hope to win', in R.P. Bentall (ed.) *Reconstructing Schizophrenia*, London: Routledge, pp. 23–59.

—— and Slade, P. (1985) 'Reliability of a scale measuring disposition towards hallucinations: A brief report', *Personality and Individual Differences* 6: 527–9.

Bentler, P.M. and Prince, C. (1970a) 'Personality characteristics of male transvestites', *Journal of Clinical Psychology* 26: 287–91.

——and——(1970b) 'Psychiatric symptomatology in transvestites', *Journal of Clinical Psychology* 26: 434–5.

Blum, G.S. (1961) *A Model of the Mind*, New York: Wiley.

Blythe, R.H. (1976) *Games Zen Masters Play* (ed. by R. Sohl and A. Carr), New York: New American Library.

Bohm, D. (1985) *Wholeness and the Implicate Order*, London: Ark Paperbacks.

Bohr, N. (1958) *Atomic Theory and Human Knowledge*, New York: Wiley.

Bonime, W. (1979a) 'Paranoid psychodynamics', *Contemporary Psychoanalysis* 15 (4; October): 514–27.

——(1979b) 'Reply to Dr. Meissner', *Contemporary Psychoanalysis* 15 (4; October): 539–44.

Bower, G.H. and Cohen, P.R. (1982) 'Emotional influences in memory and thinking: Data and theory', in M.S. Clark and S.T. Fiske (eds) *Affect and Cognition: The 17th Annual Carnegie Symposium on Cognition*, Hillsdale, N.J.: Erlbaum, pp. 291–332

Broadbent, D.E. (1971) *Decision and Stress*, London: Academic Press.

Brody, N. (1972) *Personality*, London: Academic Press.

Brown, G.W., Bone, M., Dalison, B. and Wing, J.K. (1966) *Schizophrenia and Social Care*, London: Oxford University Press.

——and Birley, J.L.T. (1968) 'Crises and life changes and the onset of schizophrenia', *Journal of Health and Social Behaviour* 9: 203–14.

Brown, L.G. (1934) *Social Psychology*, New York and London: McGraw-Hill.

Bruner, J.S. and Potter, M.C. (1966) 'Interference in visual recognition', *Science* 144: 424–5.

Bucke, R.M. (1901) *Cosmic Consciousness*, New York: Dutton.

Busby, D.E. (1967) 'Precognition and a test of sensory perception', *Journal of Parapsychology* 31 (2; June): 135–42.

Cacioppo, J.T., Petty, R.E. and Quintanar, L.R. (1982) 'Individual differences in relative hemispheric alpha abundance and cognitive responses to persuasive communications', *Journal of Personality and Social Psychology* 43: 623–36.

Cameron, N. (1943a) 'The development of paranoic thinking', *Psychological Review* 50: 219–33.

——(1943b) 'The paranoid pseudocommunity', *American Journal of Sociology* 49: 32–8.

——(1944) 'Experimental analysis of schizophrenic thinking', in J. Kasamin (ed.) *Language and Thought in Schizophrenia*, Berkeley, California: University of California Press.

——(1951) 'Perceptual organisation and behaviour pathology', in R.R. Blake and G.V. Ramsey, *Perception – An Approach to Personality*, New York: The Ronald Press, pp. 283–306.

——(1959) 'Paranoid conditions and paranoia', in S. Arieti (ed.) *American Handbook of Psychiatry*, vol. 1, Chapter 25, pp. 508–39.

Camus, A. (1988) *The Myth of Sisyphus*, Harmondsworth: Penguin. (Originally published in France as *Le Mythe de Sisyphe* (1942), Gallimard.)

Cattell, R.B. and Butcher, M.J. (1968) *The Prediction of Achievement and Creativity*, Indianapolis: Bobbs Merrill.

——and Drevdahl, J.G. (1955) 'A comparison of the personality profile of eminent researchers with that of eminent teachers and administrators', *British Journal of Psychology* 46: 248–61.

Chadwick, P.D.J. and Lowe, C.F. (1990) 'Measurement and modification of delusional beliefs', *Journal of Consulting and Clinical Psychology* 58 (2): 225–32.

Chadwick, P.K. (1971) 'Theoretical, experimental and field studies on folds and cleavage,' unpublished Doctorial Dissertation, University of Liverpool (October).

——(1972) *Linkages between Geology and Psychology*, Contribution to Geological Society of London Tectonic Studies Group colloquium, University of Bristol (December).

——(1975a) 'A psychological analysis of observation in geology', *Nature* 256 (5518; 14 August): 570–3.

——(1975b) 'The psychology of geological observations', *New Scientist* 68 (18–25 December): 728–32.

——(1976a) 'Tectonic structures: A classification', *Tectonophysics* 30: T3–T9.

——(1976b) 'Visual illusions in geology', *Nature* 260 (1 April): 397–401.

——(1977a) 'Geological perception and the core curriculum', *Geology Teaching* 2 (2): 95–103.

——(1977b) 'Scientists can have illusions too', *New Scientist* 73 (31 March): 768–71.

——(1977c) 'The perception and interpretation of continuity and discontinuity', *Catastrophist Geology* 1 (3): 35–48.

——(1978a) 'T.N. George on science, philosophy and reflection: a rejoinder', *Geology Teaching* 3 (2; June): 72–6.

——(1978b) 'Some aspects of the development of geological thinking', *Geology Teaching* 3 (4; December): 142–8.

——(1979) 'Half man, half boat, the mind of the Borderline Normal', unpublished manuscript, London (June).

——(1981) 'Optical illusions: Fooling the eye', *Insight* 5 (Part 66): 1813–17.

——(1982) '"Earth boundedness" in geological observation,' *Geology Teaching* 7, (3; March): 16–22.

——(1983) '"Peak preference" and waveform perception', *Perception* 12: 255–67.

——(1988) 'A psychological study of paranoia and delusional thinking', Doctoral Dissertation, University of London (August).

——and Hughes, E.M. (1980) 'Which way-up is upside down?', *Geology Teaching* 5 (3; September): 87–9.

Chambless, D., Foa, E., Graves, G. and Goldstein, A. (1979) 'Flooding with Brevital in the treatment of agorophobia: countereffective', *Behaviour Research and Therapy* 17: 243–51.

Chapman, L.J. and Chapman, J.P. (1980) 'Scales for rating psychotic and psychotic-like experiences as continua', *Schizophrenia Bulletin* 6: 477–89.

——and Miller, E.N. (1982) 'Reliabilities and intercorrelations of eight measures of proneness to psychosis', *Journal of Consulting and Clinical Psychology* 30: 187–95.

——, —— and Raulin, M.L. (1978) 'Body image aberration in schizophrenia', *Journal of Abnormal Psychology* 87: 399–407.

Christensen, P.R., Guilford, J.P., Merrifield, P. and Wilson, R. (1960) *Alternate Uses*, Beverly Hills, California: Sheridan Psychological Service.

Claridge, G.S. (1967) *Personality and Arousal*, Oxford: Pergamon.

——(1978) 'Animal models of schizophrenia: The case for LSD-25', *Schizophrenia Bulletin* 4: 187–209.

——(1981) 'Arousal', in G. Underwood and R. Stevens (eds) *Aspects of Consciousness: Volume 2. Structural Issues*, Chapter 4, London: Academic Press, pp. 119–47.

——(1985) *Origins of Mental Illness*, Oxford: Blackwell.

——(1988) 'Schizotypy and schizophrenia', in P. Bebbington and P. McGuffin (eds) *Schizophrenia: The Major Issues*, London: Heinemann, pp. 187–200.

Colby, K.M. (1975) *Artificial Paranoia: A Computer Simulation of Paranoid Processes*, New York: Pergamon.

——(1976) 'Clinical implications of a simulation model of paranoid processes', *Archives of General Psychiatry* 33: 854–7.

——(1977) 'Appraisal of four psychological theories of paranoid phenomena,' *Journal of Abnormal Psychology* 86: 54–9.

——(1981) 'Modelling a paranoid mind', *Behavioural and Brain Sciences* 4: 515–60.

——, Weber, S. and Hilf, F.D. (1971) 'Artificial paranoia', *Artificial Intelligence* 2: 1–25.

Conrad, K. (1968) *Die beginnende Schizophrenie: Versuch einer Gestaltanalze des Wahns (Commencing Schizophrenia: An Attempt at a Gestalt Analysis of Delusion)*, Stuttgart: Thieme.

Cooper, C. and Kline, P. (1986) 'An evaluation of the Defence Mechanism Test,' *British Journal of Psychology* 77: 19–31.

Cromwell, R., Rosenthal, D., Shakow, D. and Zahn, T. (1961) 'Reaction time, locus of control, choice behaviour and descriptions of parental behaviour in schizophrenic and normal subjects', *Journal of Personality* 29: 363–79.

Cross, P., Cattell, R. and Butcher, H. (1967) 'The personality patterns of creative artists', *British Journal of Educational Psychology* 37: 292–9.

Curran, D., Partridge, M. and Storey, P. (1976) *Psychological Medicine: An Introduction to Psychiatry*, Edinburgh: Churchill Livingstone.

Davis, J.M. (1978) 'Dopamine theory of schizophrenia: A two-factor theory', in L.C. Wynn, R.L. Cromwell and S. Matthysse (eds) *The Nature of Schizophrenia*, New York: Wiley.

Davison, G.C. and Neale, J.M. (1986) *Abnormal Psychology*, New York: Wiley.

De Bono, E. (1967) *The Five-day Course in Thinking*, Harmondsworth: Penguin.

Deikmann, A.J. (1966), 'Deautomatization and the mystic experience,' *Psychiatry* vol. 29, reprinted in R. Ornstein (1986) *The Psychology of Consciousness*, Chapter 7, New York: Penguin, pp. 200–20.

——(1977) 'Comments on the GAP report on mysticism', *The Journal of Nervous and Mental Disease* 165, (3): 213–17.

Dement, W.C. (1972) *Some must watch while some must sleep*, Stanford: Stanford Alumni Association.

Depue, R.A. (1974) 'The specificity of response interference to schizophrenia', *Journal of Abnormal Psychology* 83: 529–32.

——and Fowles, D.C. (1974) 'Conceptual ability, response inteference and arousal in withdrawn and active schizophrenics', *Journal of Consulting and Clinical Psychology* 42: 509–18.

Dornic, S. (1977) 'Mental load, effort, and individual differences', Report, Department of Psychology, University of Stockholm, No. 509.

Douglas, R.J. (1967) 'The hippocampus and behaviour', *Psychological Bulletin* 67 (6): 416–42.

Draguns, J.G. (1963) 'Responses to conceptual and perceptual ambiguity in chronic and acute schizophrenics', *Journal of Abnormal and Social Psychology* 66 (1): 24–30.

Drake, R.A. (1983) 'Towards a synthesis of some behavioural and physiological antecedents of belief perseverance', *Social Behaviour and Personality* 11 (2): 57–60.

——and Bingham, B.R. (1985) 'Induced lateral orientation and persuasibility', *Brain and Cognition* 4: 156–64.

DSM–III (1980) *Diagnostic and Statistical Manual of Mental Disorders* (3rd edn), Washington DC: American Psychiatric Association.

Dykes, M. and McGhie, A. (1976) 'A comparative study of attentional strategies of schizophrenic and highly creative normal subjects', *British Journal of Psychiatry* 128: 50–6.

Easterbrook, J.A. (1959) 'The effect of emotion on cue utilisation and the organisation of behaviour', *Psychological Review* 66: 183–201.

Ehrenwald, J. (1972) 'A neurophysiological model of Psi phenomena', *The Journal of Nervous and Mental Disease* 154 (6): 406–18.

Eckblad, M. and Chapman, L.J. (1983) 'Magical ideation as an indicator of schizotypy', *Journal of Consulting and Clinical Psychology* 51: 215–55.

Eisenbud, J. (1972) 'Some notes on the psychology of the paranormal', *Journal of the American Society of Psychical Research* 66: 27–41.

Ellis, H. (1936) *Studies in the Psychology of Sex*, vol. 1, London: Heinemann.

——(1942) *Studies in the Psychology of Sex*, vol. 2, London: Heinemann.

Epstein, S. and Coleman, L. (1970), 'Drive theories of schizophrenia', *Psychosomatic Medicine* 32: 113–40.

Erikson, E.H. (1950) *Childhood and Society*, Harmondsworth: Pelican.

Estes, W.K. (1972) 'An associative basis for coding and organisation in memory', in A.W. Melton and E. Martin (eds) *Coding Processes in Memory*, Washington DC: Winston.

Eysenck, H.J. (1957) *The Dynamics of Anxiety and Hysteria*, London: Routledge & Kegan Paul.

——(1967) *The Biological Basis of Personality*, Illinois, NJ: Springfield.

——(ed.) (1981) *A Model for Personality*, Berlin, Heidelberg: Springer Verlag.

——and Eysenck, S.B.G. (1975) *Manual of the Eysenck Personality Questionnaire (Junior and Adult)*, Kent: Hodder & Stoughton.

——and——(1976) *Psychoticism as a Dimension of Personality*, London: Hodder & Stoughton.

Eysenck, M.W. (1982) *Attention and Arousal*, Berlin, Heidelberg: Springer Verlag.

——and Folkard, S. (1980) 'Personality, time of day, and caffeine: Some theoretical and conceptual problems', *Journal of Experimental Psychology (General)* 109: 32–41.

Eysenck, S.B.G. and McGurk, B.J. (1980) 'Impulsiveness and venturesomeness in a detention centre population', *Psychological Reports* 47: 1299–306.

Feder, R. (1982) 'Auditory hallucinations treated by radio headphones', *American Journal of Psychiatry* 139 (9; September): 1188–90.

Federn, P. (1977) *Ego Psychology and the Psychoses* (edited and with an introduction by Edoardo Weiss), London: Maresfield Reprints.

Fenwick, P. (1983) 'Some aspects of the physiology of the mystical experience', in B.M. Foss and J. Nicholson (eds) *Psychology Survey Number 4*, Chapter 8, The British Psychological Society, pp. 203–23.

Forrest, D.V. (1976) 'Nonsense and sense in schizophrenic language', *Schizophrenia Bulletin* 2: 286–301.

Frankl, V. (1959) *From Death Camp to Existentialism*, Boston: Beacon Press.

——(1963) *Man's Search for Meaning*, New York: Washington Square Press.

Freedman, A., Kaplan, H. and Sadock, B. (1975) *Comprehensive Text-book of Psychiatry*, Baltimore: Williams & Wilkins.

Freud, S. (1911) 'Psychoanalytic notes on an autobiographical account of a case of paranoia (dementia paranoides)', S.E. vol. 12, London: Hogarth Press, pp. 3–82.

Fromm-Reichmann, F. (1948) 'Notes on the development of treatment of schizophrenics by psychoanalytic psychotherapy', *Psychiatry* 11: 263–73.

Gabb, W.J. (1944) *Beyond the Intellect: Tales of Tokuzan*, Reprinted as *The Goose is Out* (1956), London: The Buddhist Society.

Gardner, H. (1985) *Frames of Mind: The Theory of Multiple Intelligences*, London: Paladin.

Garety, P. (1985) 'Delusions: Problems in definition and measurement', *British Journal of Medical Psychology* 58 (Part 1; March): 25–34.

Gellhorn, E. and Kiely, W.F. (1972) 'Mystical states of consciousness: Neuropsychological and clinical aspects', *Journal of Nervous and Mental Disease* 154 (6): 399–405.

Geschwind, N. (1978) 'Behavioural changes in temporal lobe epilepsy', *Psychological Medicine* 9: 217–21.

Gilkey, L. (1966) *Shantung Compound*, New York: Harper & Row.

Gjerde, P.F. (1983) 'Attentional capacity dysfunction and arousal in schizophrenia', *Psychological Bulletin* 93 (1): 57–72.

Glucksberg, S. (1962) 'The influence of strength of drive on functional fixedness and perceptual recognition', *Journal of Experimental Psychology* 63: 36–41.

——(1964) 'Problem solving: Response competition and the influence of drive,' *Psychological Reports* 15: 939–42.

Goldstein, K. and Scheerer, M. (1941) 'Abstract and concrete behaviour: An experimental study with special tests', *Psychological Monograph*, No. 1.

Goldstein, M. and Rodnick, E. (1975) 'The family's contribution to the etiology of schizophrenia: Current status', *Schizophrenia Bulletin* 14: 48–63.

Gosselin, C. and Wilson, G. (1980) *Sexual Variations: Fetishism, Sado-Masochism and Transvetism*, London: Faber & Faber.

Gray, J.A. (1970) 'The psychophysiological basis of introversion–extraversion', *Behaviour Research and Therapy* 8: 249–66.

——(1972) 'The psychophysiological nature of introversion–extraversion: A modification of Eysenck's theory', in V.D. Nebylitsyn and J.A. Gray (eds) *Biological Basis of Individual Behaviour*, London: Academic Press.

——(1973) 'Causal theories and how to test them', in J.R. Royce (ed.) *Multivariate Analysis of Psychological Theory*, London: Academic Press.

Greyson, B. (1977) 'Telepathy in mental illness: Deluge or delusion?', *The Journal of Nervous and Mental Disease* 165: 184–200.

Grof, S. (1975) *Realms of the Human Unconscious – Observations from LSD Research*, New York: Viking Press.

Group for the Advancement of Psychiatry (1976) *Mysticism: Spiritual Quest or Psychic Disorder?*, New York: Brunner/Mazel.

Gruzelier, J.H. (1978) 'Bimodal states of arousal and lateralised dysfunction in schizophrenia', in L.C. Wynne, R. Cromwell and S. Matthysse (eds) *The Nature of Schizophrenia*, New York: Wiley.

——(1981) 'Hemispheric imbalances masquerading as paranoid and non-paranoid syndromes', *Schizophrenia Bulletin* 7: 662–73.

——(1984) 'Hemispheric imbalances in schizophrenia', *International Journal of Psychophysiology* 1: 227–40.

Gur, R.E. (1978) 'Left hemisphere dysfunction and left hemisphere overactivation in schizophrenia.' *Journal of Abnormal Psychology* 87 (2): 226–38.

Haddon, C. (1982) *The Limits of Sex*, London: Michael Joseph.

Hall, C.S. (1966) *The Meaning of Dreams*, New York: McGraw-Hill.

Hargreaves, D.J. and Bolton, N. (1972) 'Selecting creativity tests for use in research', *British Journal of Psychology* 63: 417–62.

Harré, R., Clarke, D. and de Carlo, N. (1985) *Motives and Mechanisms: An Introduction to the Psychology of Action*, London: Methuen.

Harris, J.P., Phillipson, O.T., Watkins, G.M. and Whelpton, R. (1983) 'Effects of chlorpromazine and promazine on the visual after-effects of tilt and movement', *Psychopharmacology* 79: 49–57.

Hasher, L. and Zacks, R.T. (1979) 'Automatic and effortful processes in memory', *Journal of Experimental Psychology (General)* 108: 356–88.

Hastings, D.W. (1941) 'A paranoid reaction with manifest homosexuality', *Archives of Neurology and Psychiatry* 45: 379–81.

Hausman, C.R. (1976) 'Creativity and rationality', in A. Rothenberg and C.R. Hausman (eds) *The Creativity Question*, Durham, NC: Duke University Press, pp. 343–51.

——(1985) 'Can computers create?', *Interchange*, 16 (1): 27–37.

Heisenberg, W. (1958) *Physics and Philosophy*, New York: Harper & Row.

Heston, L.L. and Denney, D. (1968) 'Interaction between early life experience and biological factors in schizophrenia', in D. Rosenthal and S.S. Kety (eds) *The Transmission of Schizophrenia*, New York: Pergamon, pp. 363–76.

Hirai, T. (1974) *Psychophysiology of Zen*, Tokyo: Igaku Shoin.

Holmes, D.S. (1981) 'Existence of classical projection and the stress-reducing function of attributive projection: A reply to Sherwood', *Psychological Bulletin* 90 (3): 460–6.

Holmes, T.H. and Rahé, R.H. (1967) 'The social readjustment rating scale', *Journal of Psychosomatic Research* 11: 213–18.

Horney, K. (1939) *New Ways in Psychoanalysis*, New York: Norton.

Horowitz, M.J. (1975) 'A cognitive model of hallucinations', *American Journal of Psychiatry* 132: 789–95.

Houston, J.P. and Mednick, S.A. (1963) 'Creativity and the need for novelty', *Journal of Abnormal and Social Psychology* 66: 137–41.

Humphreys, C. (1986) *Zen Buddhism*, London: Allen & Unwin.

James, W. (1936) *The Varieties of Religious Experience*, New York: Longman Green.

Janke, W. and Debus, G. (1972) 'Double-blind psychometric evaluation of pimozide and haloperidol versus placebo in emotionally labile volunteers under two different work load conditions', *Pharmakopsychiatrie Neuropsychopharmakologie* 15: 34–51.

Jarvik, L.F. and Deckard, B.S. (1977) 'The Odyssean personality: A survival advantage for carriers of genes predisposing to schizophrenia', *Neuropsychobiology* 3: 179–91.

Jaspers, K. (1962) *General Psychopathology*, Manchester: Manchester University Press.

Johnson, W.G., Ross, J.M. and Mastria, M.A. (1977) 'Delusional behaviour: An attributional analysis of development and modification', *Journal of Abnormal Psychology* 86: 421–6.

Johnson-Laird, P.N. and Wason, P.C. (1977) 'A theoretical analysis of insight into a rescuing task', in P.N. Johnson-Laird and P.C. Wason (eds) *Thinking*, Cambridge: Cambridge University Press.

Jones, E.E. and Nisbett, R.E. (1971) 'The actor and the observer: Divergent perceptions of the causes of behaviour', in E.E. Jones, D.E. Kanouse, H.H. Kelley *et al.* (eds) *Attribution: Perceiving the Causes of Behaviour*, Morristown, NJ: General Learning Press, pp. 79–94.

Josephson, B.D. (1977) 'Science and God', *New Scientist (Letters)* 74 (1057): 733–4.

——(1987) 'Physics and spirituality: The next grand unification?', *Physics Education* 22: 15–19.

Jung, C.G. (1963) *Memories, Dreams, Reflections*, London: Collins/Routledge & Kegan Paul.

——and Pauli, W. (1955) *The Interpretation of Nature and the Psyche*, New York: Pantheon Books.

Kahneman, D. (1973) *Attention and Effort*, Englewood Cliffs: Prentice Hall.

——Slovic, P. and Tversky, A. (1982) *Judgement under Uncertainty: Heuristics and Biases*, Cambridge: Cambridge University Press.

Kaney, S. and Bentall, R.P. (1989) 'Persecutory delusions and attributional style', *British Journal of Medical Psychology* 62: 191–8.

Kar, B.C. (1967) 'Muller-Lyer illusion in schizophrenics as a function of field distraction and exposure time', Unpublished Masters thesis, George Peabody College of Teaching.

Karlsson, J.L. (1972) 'An Icelandic family study of schizophrenia', in A.R. Kaplan (ed.) *Genetic Factors in Schizophrenia*, Springfield, Ill.: Charles C. Thomas, pp. 246–55.

——(1978) *Inheritance of Creative Intelligence*, Chicago: Nelson Hall.

Keefe, J.A. and Magaro, P.A. (1980) 'Creativity and schizophrenia: An equivalence of cognitive processing', *Journal of Abnormal Psychology* 89 (3): 390–8.

Kendler, K.S., Glazer, W.M. and Morgenstern, H. (1983) 'Dimensions of delusional experience', *American Journal of Psychiatry* 140 (4; April): 466–9.

Kinsbourne, M. (1982) 'Hemispheric specialisation and the growth of human understanding', *American Psychologist* 37: 411–20.

Klein, D.F. and Davis, J.M. (1969) *Diagnosis and Drug Treatment of Psychiatric Disorders*, Baltimore: Williams & Wilkins.

Klein, H.R. and Horowitz, W.A. (1949) 'Psychosexual factors in the paranoid phenomena', *American Journal of Psychiatry* 105: 697–701.

Kline, P. (1981) *Fact and Fantasy in Freudian Theory*, London: Methuen.

Knight, M. (1954) *William James*, London: Pelican.

Knight, R.P. (1940) 'The relationship of latent homosexuality to the mechanism of paranoid delusions', *Bulletin of the Menninger Clinic* 4: 149–59.

Knowles, J.B. and Krasner, L. (1965) 'Extraversion and duration of the Archimedes spiral after-effect', *Perceptual and Motor Skills* 20: 997–1000.

Koegler, R.R. and Kline, L.Y. (1965) 'Psychotherapy research: An approach utilising autonomic response measurements', *American Journal of Psychotherapy* 19: 268–79.

Koffka, K. (1935) *Principles of Gestalt Psychology*, New York: Brace.

Kogan, N. and Pankove, E. (1974) 'Long term predictive validity of divergent thinking tests: Some negative evidence', *Journal of Education Psychology* 66: 802–10.

Kovel, J. (1977) *A Complete Guide to Therapy*, Brighton: The Harvester Press.

Kretschmer, E. (1929) *Geniale Meuschen*, Berlin: Springer.

Kuipers, L. (1979) 'Expressed emotion: A review', *British Journal of Social and Clinical Psychology* 18: 237–43.

Laing, R.D. (1965) *The Divided Self*, Harmondsworth: Penguin.

——(1969) *Phänomenologie der Erfahrung*, Frankfurt a.M.: Suhrkamp.

——and Esterson, A. (1964) *Sanity, Madness and the Family*, London: Tavistock.

Lake, F. (1986) *Clinical Theology*, London: Darton, Longman & Todd.

Lapidus, L.B. and Schmolling, P. (1975) 'Anxiety, arousal and schizophrenia: A theoretical integration', *Psychological Bulletin* 32 (5): 689–710.

Launay, G. and Slade, P. (1981) 'The measurement of hallucinatory predisposition in male and female prisoners', *Personality and Individual Differences* 2: 221–34.

La Russo, L. (1978) 'Sensitivity of paranoid patients to non-verbal cues', *Journal of Abnormal Psychology* 87 (5; October): 463–71.

Laurikainen, K.V. (1988) *Beyond the Atom: The Philosophical Thought of Wolfgang Pauli*, Berlin: Springer Verlag.

Leff, J.P. (1976) 'Schizophrenia and sensitivity to the family environment', *Schizophrenia Bulletin* 2: 566–74.

——(1988) 'Special needs and their assessment', in P. Bebbington and P. McGuffin (eds) *Schizophrenia: The Major Issues*, London: Heinemann, pp. 244–56.

——,Kuipers, L., Berkowitz, R., Eberlein-Fries, R. and Sturgeon, D. (1982) 'A controlled trial of social intervention in schizophrenic families', *British Journal of Psychiatry* 141: 121–34.

——,——,——and Sturgeon, D. (1985) 'A controlled trial of social intervention in schizophrenic families: Two year follow-up', *British Journal of Psychiatry* 146: 594–600.

Lehmann, H.E. and Csank, J. (1957) 'Differential screening of phrenotropic agents in man: Psychophysiologic test data', *Journal of Clinical and Experimental Psychopathology* 18: 222–35.

Lenz, H. (1979) 'The element of the irrational at the beginning and during the course of delusion', *Confinia Psychiatrica* 22: 183–90.

——(1983) 'Belief and delusion: Their common origin but different course of development', *Zygon* 18 (2; June): 117–37.

Lerner, M. (1970) 'The desire for justice and reactions to victims', in J. MacAuley and L. Berkowitz (eds) *Altruism and Helping Behaviour*, New York: Academic Press, pp. 205–29.

——(1974) 'Social psychology of justice and interpersonal attraction', in T.L. Huston (ed.) *Foundations of Interpersonal Attraction*, New York: Academic Press, pp. 331–51.

Levy, P. and Lang, P.J. (1966) 'Activation, control and the spiral aftermovement', *Journal of Personality and Social Psychology* 3: 105–12.

Lewine, R.J. (1978) 'Response complexity and social interaction in the psychophysical testing of chronic and paranoid schizophrenics', *Psychological Bulletin* 85 (2): 284–94.

Lewis, A.J. (1956) 'Discussion of W.H. Gillespie, "Experiences suggestive of paranormal cognition in the psychoanalytic situation"', in G.E. Wolstenholme and E.C.P. Millar (eds) *Extrasensory Perception: A Ciba Foundation Symposium*, Boston: Little, Brown & Co., pp. 215–16.

Lewis, M.D. (1963) 'A case of transvestism associated with multiple body-phallus identifications', *International Journal of Psychoanalysis* 44: 345–51.

Lidz, T., Fleck, S. and Cornelison, A.R. (1965) *Schizophrenia and the Family*, New York: International University Press.

Liebowitz, M.R. (1979) 'Is borderline a distinct entity?', *Schizophrenia Bulletin* 5: 23–38.

Liem, J.H. (1974) 'Effects of verbal communications of parents and children: A comparison of normal and schizophrenic families', *Journal of Consulting and Clinical Psychology* 42: 438–50.

Luria, A.R. (1987) 'Reductionism in psychology', in R.L. Gregory (ed.) *The Oxford Companion to the Mind*, Oxford: Oxford University Press, pp. 675–6.

Lüscher, M. (1971) *The Lüscher Colour Test*, London: Pan Books.

MacCarthy, B., Hemsley, D., Schrank Fernandez, C., Kuipers, L. and Katz, R. (1986) 'Unpredictability as a correlate of expressed emotion in the relatives of schizophrenics', *British Journal of Psychiatry* 148: 727–30.

MacKay, C. (1841) *Memoirs of Extraordinary Popular Delusions*, London: Richard Bentley.

Mackay, C., Cox, T., Burrows, G. and Lazzerini, T. (1978) 'An inventory for the measurement of self-reported stress and arousal', *British Journal of Social and Clinical Psychology* 17: 283–4.

MacKinnon, D.W. (1961) 'The study of creativity and creativity in architects', in *Conference on the Creative Person*, Berkeley, California: University of California Institute of Personality Assessment and Research.

Magaro, P. (1981) 'The paranoid and schizophrenic: The case for distinct cognitive styles', *Schizophrenia Bulletin* 7: 632–61.

——(1984) 'Psychosis and schizophrenia', in W.D. Spaulding and J.K. Cole (eds) *Theories of Schizophrenia and Psychosis*, Nebraska Symposium on Motivation, 1983, University of Nebraska Press, pp. 157–229.

Maher, B.A. (1957) 'Personality, problem solving and the Einstellung effect', *Journal of Abnormal and Social Psychology* 54: 70–4.

——(1974) 'Delusional thinking and perceptual disorder', *Journal of Individual Psychology* 30: 98–113.

——(1988) 'Anomalous experience and delusional thinking: The logic of explanations', in T.F. Oltmanns and B.A. Moher (eds) *Delusions Beliefs*, New York: Wiley, pp. 15–33.

Malmo, R.B. (1957) 'Anxiety and behavioural arousal', *Psychological Review* 64: 276–87.

Mansfield, R.S. and Busse, T.V. (1981) *The Psychology of Creativity and Discovery*, Chicago: Nelson Hall.

Martindale, C. (1972) 'Anxiety, intelligence and access to primitive modes of thought in high and low scorers on the RAT', *Perceptual and Motor Skills* 35 (2): 375–81.

——(1975) 'What makes creative people different?', *Psychology Today* 9 (July): 44–50.

——and Armstrong, J. (1974) 'The relationship of creativity to cortical activation and its operant control', *The Journal of Genetic Psychology* 124: 311–20.

——and Greenough, J. (1973) 'The differential effect of increased arousal on creative and intellectual performance', *The Journal of Genetic Psychology* 123: 329–35.

Maslow, A.H. (1967) 'The creative attitude', in R.L. Mooney and T.A. Razik, *Explorations in Creativity*, New York: Harper & Row, pp. 43–54.

——(1968) *Toward a Psychology of Being*, Princeton, NJ: D. Van Nostrand.

——(1970) *Motivation and Personality*, New York: Harper.

——(1971) *The Farther Reaches of Human Nature*, New York: Viking.

McGhie, A. and Chapman, J.S. (1961) 'Disorders of attention and perception in early schizophrenia', *British Journal of Medical Psychology* 34: 103–16.

McGuire, W. (ed.) (1974) *The Freud–Jung Letters*, London: Hogarth Press.

McNicol, D. (1972) *A Primer of Signal Detection Theory*, London: Allen & Unwin.

Mednick, S.A. (1958) 'A learning theory approach to research in schizophrenia', *Psychological Bulletin* 55: 316–27.

Mednick, S.A. (1962) 'The associative basis of the creative process', *Psychological Review* 69 (3): 220–32.

Melges, F.T. and Freeman, A.M. (1975) 'Persecutory delusions: A cybernetic model', *American Journal of Psychiatry* 132: 1038–44.

Meissner, W.W. (1978) *The Paranoid Process*, New York: Aronson.

Meyer, R.G. and Salmon, P. (1984) *Abnormal Psychology*, Massachusetts: Allyn & Bacon.

Miller, J.G. (1951) 'Unconscious processes in perception', in R.R. Blak and G.V. Ramsey (eds) *Perception: An Approach to Personality*, Chapter 9, New York: Ronald Press, pp. 258–82.

Milner, P. (1957) 'The cell assembly – Mark II', *Psychological Review* 64: 245–52.

Mintz, S. and Alpert, M. (1972) 'Imagery, vividness, reality testing and schizophrenic hallucinations', *Journal of Abnormal Psychology* 79: 310–16.

Mitroff, I. (1974) *The Subjective Side of Science*, Amsterdam: Elsevier.

Moor, J.H. and Tucker, G.J. (1979) 'Delusions: Analysis and criteria', *Comprehensive Psychiatry* 20 (4): 388–93.

Mynatt, C.R., Doherty, H.E. and Tweney, R.D. (1977) 'Consequences of confirmation and disconfirmation in a simulated research environment', *Quarterly Journal of Experimental Psychology* 30: 395–406.

Neisser, U. (1967) *Cognitive Psychology*, New York: Appleton, Century Crofts.

Nisbett, R. and Ross, L. (1980) *Human Inference: Strategies and Shortcomings of Social Judgement*, Englewood Cliffs, NJ: Prentice Hall.

Norton, J.P. (1982) 'Expressed emotion, affective style, voice tone and communication deviance as predictors of offspring schizophrenia spectrum disorders'. Unpublished Doctoral Dissertation, Los Angeles: University of California.

Nowlis, V. (1965) 'Research with the mood adjective check list', in S.S. Tomkins and C.E. Izard (eds) *Affect, Cognition and Personality*, New York: Springer.

Nugent, S. (1989) 'Review of Ilé Aiyé (The Hour of Life), a film by David Byrne', *The Times Higher Education Supplement* (17 March): 16.

Ottmanns, T.E. (1978) 'Selective attention in schizophrenia and manic psychoses', *Journal of Abnormal Psychology* 87: 212–25.

Oppenheim, H. (1890) 'Thätsachliches und Hypothetisches über das Wesen der Hysterie', *Neurologische Beiträge* (*Leipzig*) 1: 20–4.

BIBLIOGRAPHY

Orme-Johnson, D.W. (1973) 'Autonomic stability and transcendental meditation', *Psychosomatic Medicine* 35: 341–9.

Ornstein, R. (1986) *The Psychology of Consciousness*, Harmondsworth: Penguin.

Osgood, C.E. (1960) 'Some effects of motivation on style of encoding', in T.A. Sebrok (ed.) *Style in Language*, New York: Wiley.

Ovesey, L. and Person, E. (1978) 'Transvestism: New perspectives', *Journal of the American Academy of Psychoanalysis* 6: 301–23.

Paykel, E.S. (1979) 'Recent life events in the development of the depressive disorders', in R.A. Depue (ed.) *The Psychobiology of the Depressive Disorders*, New York: Academic Press.

Payne, R.W. (1973) 'Cognitive abnormalities', in H.J. Eysenck, *Handbook of Abnormal Psychology*, London: Pitman.

——and Friedlander, D. (1962) 'A short battery of simple tests for measuring overinclusive thinking', *Journal of Mental Science* 108: 362–7.

Payne, S.M. (1939) 'Some observations on the ego development of the fetishist', *International Journal of Psychoanalysis* 20: 161–70.

Perkins, D.N. (1988) 'Creativity and the quest for mechanism', in R.J. Sternberg and E.E. Smith, *The Psychology of Human Thought*, Chapter 11, Cambridge: Cambridge University Press, pp. 309–36.

Pine, F. (1959) 'Thematic drive content and creativity', *Journal of Personality* 27: 136–51.

——and Holt, R.R. (1960) 'Creativity and primary process – a study of adaptive regression', *Journal of Abnormal and Social Psychology* 61: 370–9.

Poincaré, H. (1914) *Science and Method*, London: Nelson.

Popper, K.R. (1959) *The Logic of Scientific Discovery*, London: Hutchinson.

——(1963) *Conjectures and Refutations*, London: Routledge & Kegan Paul.

Powell, R.R. (1982) 'Technique for differentiating cortical hemispheric activity following exercise', *Perceptual and Motor Skills* 54: 923–32.

Prabhakaran, N. (1970) 'A case of Gilles de la Tourette's Syndrome with some observations on aetiology and treatment', *British Journal of Psychiatry* 116: 539–41.

Prentky, R.A. (1979) 'Creativity and psychopathology: A neurocognitive perspective', in B. Maher (ed.) *Progress in Experimental Personality Research*, vol. 9, New York: Academic Press.

Pribram, K.H. and McGuinness, D. (1975) 'Arousal, attention and effort', *Psychological Review* 82: 116–40.

Progoff, I. (1973) *Jung, Synchronicity and Human Destiny: Non-causal Dimensions of Human Experience*, New York: The Julian Press.

Rausch, R. (1977) 'Cognitive strategies in patients with unilateral temporal lobe excisions', *Neuropsychologia* 15: 385–95.

Raven, J.C. (1976) *Extended Guide to using the Mill Hill Vocabulary Scale*, London: H.K. Lewis.

Reider, R.O. (1979) 'Borderline schizophrenia: Evidence of its validity', *Schizophrenia Bulletin* 5: 39–46.

Rogers, C.R. (1942) *Counselling and Psychotherapy: New Concepts in Practice*, Boston: Houghton Mifflin.

——(1951) *Client-centred Therapy*, Boston: Houghton Mifflin.

——,Gendlin, G.T., Kiesler, D.V. and Truax, C.B. (1967) *The Therapeutic Relationship and its Impact: A Study of Psychotherapy with Schizophrenics*, Madison: University of Wisconsin Press.

Rosenfeld, H. (1949) 'Remarks on the relationship of male homosexuality to paranoia', *International Journal of Psychoanalysis* 30: 36–47.

173

Rosenhan, D.L. and Seligman, M.E. (1984) *Abnormal Psychology*, New York and London: W.W. Norton.

Ross, L. (1977) 'The intuitive psychologist and his shortcomings: Distortions in the attribution process', in L. Berkowitz (ed.) *Advances in Experimental Social Psychology*, New York: Academic Press, pp. 173–220.

Rubin, Z. and Peplau, L. (1975) 'Who believes in a just world?', *Journal of Social Issues* 31: 65–88.

Rudden, M., Gilmore, M. and Frances, A. (1982) 'Delusions: When to confront the facts of life', *American Journal of Psychiatry* 139 (7; July): 929–32.

Sacks, O. (1986) *The Man who Mistook his Wife for a Hat*, London: Picador.

Sagan, C. (1977) *The Dragons of Eden. Speculations on the Evolution of Human Intelligence*, London: Hodder & Stoughton.

Schenk, R.U. (1982) *The Other Side of the Coin: Causes and Consequences of Men's Oppression*, Wisconsin: Bioenergetics Press.

Schneider, K. (1959) *Clinical Psychopathology*, New York: Grune & Stratton.

Schrödinger, E. (1955) *What is Life and Mind and Matter?*, Cambridge: Cambridge University Press.

Sekuler R. and Blake, R. (1985) *Perception*, New York: Knopf.

Selfridge, O.G. (1955) 'Pattern recognition and modern computers', *Proceedings of the West Joint Computer Conference*, Los Angeles, California.

Sergent, J. (1982) 'The critical and methodological consequences of variation in exposure duration in visual laterality studies', *Perception and Psychophysics* 31: 451–61.

——(1983) 'The role of input in the visual hemispheric asymmetry', *Psychological Bulletin* 93: 481–512.

Shapiro, A.K. and Shapiro, E. (1968) 'Treatment of Gilles de la Tourette's Syndrome with haloperidol', *British Journal of Psychiatry* 114: 345–50.

Shepherd, G. (1988) 'The contribution of psychological intervention to the treatment and management of schizophrenia', in P. Bebbington and P. McGuffin (eds) *Schizophrenia: The Major Issues*, London: Heinemann, pp. 226–43.

Sherwood, G.G. (1981) 'Self-serving biases in person perception: A re-examination of projection as a mechanism of defense', *Psychological Bulletin* 90 (3): 445–59.

Shiffrin, R.M. and Schneider, W. (1977) 'Controlled and automatic human information processing: II. Perceptual learning, automatic attending and a general theory', *Psychological Review* 84: 127–90.

Slade, P.D. and Bentall, R.P. (1988) *Sensory Deception: A Scientific Analysis of Hallucinations*, London: Croom Helm.

Snyder, S.H. (1974) *Madness and the Brain*, New York: McGraw-Hill.

——(1981) 'Dopamine receptors, neuroleptics and schizophrenia', *American Journal of Psychiatry* 138: 460–4.

Spitzer, R.L., Endicott, J. and Gibbon, H. (1979) 'Crossing the border into borderline personality and borderline schizophrenia: the development of criteria', *Archives of General Psychiatry* 36: 17–24.

Sprinchorn, E. (1968) Introduction to A. Strindberg, *A Madman's Defence*, London: Cape.

Stone, M.H. (1980) *The Borderline Syndrome*, New York: McGraw-Hill.

Storr, A. (1970) *Human Aggression*, Harmondsworth: Pelican.

——(1972) *The Dynamics of Creation*, London: Secker & Warburg.

——(1989) *Solitude*, London: Flamingo.

Strauss, J.S. (1969) 'Hallucinations and delusions as points on continua: Rating scale evidence', *Archives of General Psychiatry* 21: 581–6.

Sutherland, N.S. (1976) *Breakdown: A Personal Crisis and a Medical Dilemma*, London: Weidenfeld & Nicolson.

Taft, R. (1955) 'The ability to judge people', *Psychological Bulletin* 52: 1–23.

Talbot, M. (1981) *Mysticism and the New Physics*, London: Routledge & Kegan Paul.

Taylor, A.J. and McLachlan, D.G. (1963) 'MMPI profiles of six transvestites', *Journal of Clinical Psychology* 19: 330–2.

Telling, W.H.M. (1928) 'The value of psychical research to the physician', *Journal of Mental Science* 74: 634–48.

Thornton, N. (1948) 'Some mechanisms of paranoia', *Psychoanalytic Review* 35: 290–4.

Thurstone, L.L. and Thurstone, T.G. (1941) *Factorial Studies of Intelligence*, Chicago: University of Chicago Press.

Toulmin, S. (1972) *Human Understanding*, vol. 1, Oxford: Oxford University Press.

Turner, R.J. and Wagonfield, M.O. (1967) 'Occupational mobility and schizophrenia', *American Sociological Review* 32: 104–13.

Tweney, R.D., Doherty, M.E. and Mynatt, C.R. (1981) *On Scientific Thinking*, New York: Columbia University Press.

Ullman, M. (1973) 'Psi and psychiatry: The need for restructuring basic concepts', in W.G. Roll, R.L. Morris and J.D. Morris (eds) *Research in Parapsychology 1972*, Metuchen, NJ: Scarecrow Press, pp. 110–13.

Vaughn, A. (1979) *Incredible Coincidences*, New York: Lippincott.

Vaughn, C.E. and Leff, J.P. (1976) 'The influence of family and social factors on the course of psychiatric illness. A comparison of schizophrenic and depressed neurotic patients', *British Journal of Psychiatry* 129: 125–37.

Von Krafft-Ebbing, R. (1886) *Psychopathia Sexualis*, Stuttgart: Ferdinand Enke.

Wachtel, P.L. (1967) 'Conceptions of broad and narrow attention', *Psychological Bulletin* 68: 417–29.

Wagstaff, G.F. (1982) 'Attitudes to rape: The "Just World" strikes again?', *Bulletin of the British Psychological Society* 35: 277–9.

——(1983) 'Correlates of the Just World in Britain', *The Journal of Social Psychology* 121: 145–6.

——and Quirk, M.A. (1983) 'Attitudes to sex-roles, political conservatism and belief in a Just World', *Psychological Reports* 52: 813–14.

Walters, J.M. and Gardner, H. (1986) 'The theory of multiple intelligences: Some issues and answers', in R.J. Sternberg and R.K. Wagner (eds) *Practical Intelligence: Nature and Origins of Competence in the Everyday World*, Chapter 8, Cambridge: Cambridge University Press, pp. 163–82.

Warren, R.M. (1970) 'Perceptual restoration of missing speech sounds', *Science* 167: 392–3.

Wason, P.C. (1960) 'On the failure to eliminate hypotheses in a conceptual task', *Quarterly Journal of Experimental Psychology* 12: 129–40.

——(1971) 'Problem solving and reasoning', *British Medical Bulletin* 27: 206–10.

——and Johnson-Laird, P.N. (eds) (1968) *Thinking and Reasoning*, Harmondsworth, Penguin.

—— and —— (1972) *Psychology of Reasoning: Structure and Content*, Cambridge, Mass.: Harvard University Press.

Watson, L. (1974) *Supernature: A Natural History of the Supernatural*, London: Coronet.

Watts, F.N., Powell, E.G. and Austin, S.V. (1973) 'The modification of abnormal beliefs', *British Journal of Medical Psychology* 46: 359–63.

Wechsler, D. (1958) *The Measurement and Appraisal of Adult Intelligence*, Baltimore: Williams & Wilkins.

Weiner, B. (1986) *An Attributional Theory of Motivation and Emotion*, Berlin, Heidelberg: Springer Verlag.

Wilson, A. (1983) *Magical Thought in Creative Writing. The Distinctive Roles of Fantasy and Imagination in Fiction*, Strand: The Thimble Press.

Wilson, R.C., Christensen, P.R., Merrifield, P.R. and Guilford, J.P. (1975) *Alternate Uses Test*, Beverly Hills, California: Sheridan Psychological Company.

Wincze, J.P., Leitenberg, H. and Agras, W.S. (1970) 'A sequential analysis of the effects of instructions and token reinforcement in the modification of delusional verbal behaviour in chronic psychotics', *Proceedings of the 78th Annual Convention of the American Psychological Association (Part 2)*, Miami Beach, pp. 737–8.

Winters, K.C. and Neale, J.M. (1983) 'Delusions and delusional thinking in psychotics: A review of the literature', *Clinical Psychology Review* 3 (2): 227–53.

Woody, E. and Claridge, G.S. (1977) 'Psychoticism and thinking', *British Journal of Social and Clinical Psychology* 16: 241–8.

Zaehner, R.C. (1957) *Mysticism: Sacred and Profane*, Oxford: Clarendon Press.

Zigler, E. and Glick, M. (1988) 'Is paranoid schizophrenia really camouflaged depression?', *American Psychologist* 43: 284–90.

NAME INDEX

SUBJECT INDEX

abaissement 52–3
acting out 142–3
actor–observer divergence 129–30
agoraphobia 22, 142
alpha control 104–5
archetype 52–3, 153
arousal 69, 97–107, 122–3,
  150–2, 159
arrogance 15, 17, 26
attentional capacity 98–104,
  112–16, 151
attentional disorder 69, 91, 150
attentional width 99, 135
avoidant personality 68, 87

belief perseverance 101–2
bonding: in love affairs 76
borderline (medical sense) 47, 57,
  87, 158
Borderline (mystical sense) 31–43,
  46, 63–4, 95, 98, 135, 144–5,
  153, 161
Buddhism 32, 50–1, 53

callosal modulation 151, 160
catharsis 133; overcatharsis 161
causal triangle 147–8
cognitive therapy 94, 132–3, 134, 145
coincidences 27–8, 35–40, 46–7,
  91, 94–5
communication deviance 130
compliance with medication 22, 42–3
confirmation bias 1–3, 18, 19,
  25, 28, 77, 88, 97–107, 112–16,
  125–6, 128–40, 145, 150–1,
  160
context 47, 67, 132, 152; in recall 131

contextualism 5–6, 148, 159
continuum 33
controlled and automatic processing
  101, 109, 116, 127
creativity 19, 30, 44, 54–5,
  60, 67–72, 84, 104–9, 120–6,
  137, 147, 149–50, 159, 161; and
  confirmation bias 2, 125–6, 128;
  and synchronicity 158

dance: and mental health 55, 58–64,
  158–9
de Clerambault's Syndrome 73–8
deep truth 95, 98, 129
delusional mood 80, 92
delusional pseudocommunity 91, 100,
  137, 154
delusion removal 79, 141–3, 145
delusional thinking: evoked by
  ambiguity 70; and attitude change
  procedures 143; and attributional
  style 90–1, 155; as cognitive
  hyperorder 92, 97, 107; continuum
  view of 53, 82, 101, 119, 128, 152;
  and conviction 74, 86, 119, 142; as a
  coping device 74, 143; and cortical
  overactivity 116, 149; and depression
  68, 90–1, 142, 155; and dreaming
  74, 138, 159; as an educational
  problem 94; evidence for 27, 82, 142;
  health, step towards 69–70, 72,
  76, 152; and hypnagogic imagery 64;
  and incentive 100; and insight 119,
  143; and invalidating experiences 25,
  63, 145; and love 23, 36, 75–6;
  and magical thinking 46, 83–4;
  and malnutrition 34, 59, 74; and

179